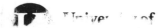

A HISTORY OF BRITISH LABOUR LAW

A History of
British Labour Law
1867–1945

DOUGLAS BRODIE
Reader in Law
The University of Edinburgh

·HART·
PUBLISHING
OXFORD AND PORTLAND, OREGON
2003

Published in North America (US and Canada) by
Hart Publishing
c/o International Specialized Book Services
5804 NE Hassalo Street
Portland, Oregon
97213–3644
USA

Hart Publishing is a specialist legal publisher based in Oxford,
England. To order further copies of this book or to request a list
of other publications please write to:

Hart Publishing, Salters Boatyard, Folly Bridge, Abingdon Rd,
Oxford, OX1 4LB Telephone: +44 (0)1865 245533 Fax: +44
(0)1865 794882
email: mail@hartpub.co.uk
WEBSITE: http//www.hartpub.co.uk

British Library Cataloguing in Publication Data
Data Available
ISBN 1–84113–015-X (hardback)

Typeset by Hope Services (Abingdon) Ltd
Printed and bound in Great Britain by
Biddles Ltd, *www.biddles.co.uk*

Contents

Acknowledgements   ix

INTRODUCTION   xi

1 Labour Law 1867–1880   1
Introduction   1
The Report of the Royal Commission   2
  i) Collective Bargaining   6
The Legislative Settlement   10
The Settlement of 1871—The Aftermath   15
  i) Picketing   15
  ii) Collective Bargaining   17
The Disraeli Government   18
Conclusions   25

2 Labour Law 1880–1900   27
Introduction   27
Litigation   27
The Royal Commission   38
Legal Regulation   49
Conclusions   58
Appendix   61

3 1900–1914   63
Wages Legislation   65
Hours of Work   72
Dispute Resolution   74
Compulsory Arbitration   77
Other Measures   82
Conclusions   83

4 Responding to *Taff Vale*   87
Introduction   87
Pragmatism and Solutions   88

The Royal Commission   95
The Trade Union View   100
The Liberal Government   101
The Judicial Reaction   106
   Responding to the 1906 Act   106
   The Osborne Judgment   109
Rights, Immunities and Non-Intervention   115
Conclusions   117

5 The Impact of War 1914–18   119
Introduction   119
The 1915 Act   121
   Compulsory Arbitration   121
Mobility of Labour   127
Wage Control and Restrictive Practices   133
   Wage Control   133
   Dilution   134
   Further Wage Control   142
Conclusions   146

6 The Aftermath of War 1918–21   149
Introduction   149
Planning for the Future—Promoting Collective Bargaining   151
After the Armistice   156
The End of the Dream   166
Dispute Resolution and Control   166
State Control of Industry   171
Conclusions   180

7 Labour Law Between the Wars   183
Introduction   183
Labour Law in the 1920s   184
The 1927 Act   192
Labour Law in the 1920s—An Overview   196
Labour Law in the 1930s   198
The 1930s Assessed   211
Judicial Attitudes   214
Conclusions   218

8 The Impact of the Second World War 223
  Introduction 223
  Wartime Controls 223
    Movement of Labour 223
    Terms and Conditions of Employment 227
    Wage Control 231
      The Conditions of Employment and National Arbitration
      Order (SR & O 1940/1305) 231
    Consultation 237
  Industrial Relations Beyond the Hostilities 238
    Wartime and Beyond 239
    The Catering Wages Act 241
    Wages Councils 243
  Conclusions 246

9 Concluding Remarks 249

Index 257

Acknowledgements

This is a book which I have wanted to write for a long time and I am extremely grateful to Richard Hart for giving me the opportunity to do so. I encountered Labour Law for the first time when, as an undergraduate, I was taught by Keith Ewing in 1981/2. His teaching, and the works which he introduced me to (most notably Kahn-Freund's *Labour and the Law*), inspired a fascination with the subject which has endured to this day. Subsequently, during the course of working on my doctoral thesis on the law relating to collective agreements, I became increasingly aware that much of the history of Labour Law in the UK remained relatively unexplored. In examining the development of collective Labour Law between 1867 and 1945 I hope to make a modest contribution towards remedying that state of affairs.

Whatever the merits of the work I owe a huge debt to a considerable number of people. For the last twenty years I have had the good fortune to be on the staff of the Law School at Edinburgh University and have been privileged to enjoy the highly supportive and collegiate working environment of Old College. In that regard, and somewhat invidiously, mention should be made of Sandy Eden, Bob Lane, Graeme Laurie, Colin Munro, and Neil Walker. I am also very grateful to Peter Young for encouraging me to persevere. I have also benefited greatly from the wisdom, knowledge and experience of other Labour Lawyers and particular mention should be made of Keith Ewing, Roy Lewis, Kenny Miller and Brian Napier.

This book is dedicated to Lilian Haire with love and affection.

23rd July 2003
Old College, Edinburgh

Introduction

In the UK the received wisdom has tended to be that, historically, British Labour Law was abstentionist or non-interventionist. In the words of Wedderburn '. . . collective bargaining has developed in a system which depends very little on the law, which is covered by very few decisions of the judges, and which is controlled by statute very little, if at all.'[1] Thus, on the whole, the law did not seek to '. . . regulate the structure, methods or outcome of collective bargaining . . .'[2] Equally there was little in the way of individual employment legislation with the exception of matters such as health and safety. An important part of the abstentionist analysis was to categorise much of the legislation that did exist as auxiliary rather than regulatory. The auxiliary function of the law is to 'support the autonomous system of collective bargaining—by providing norms and sanctions to stimulate the bargaining process itself, and to strengthen the operation, that is promoting the observance of concluded agreements.'[3] Regulatory legislation, on the other hand, provides 'a code of substantive rules to govern terms and conditions of employment.'[4] It is not until we reach the Industrial Relations Act 1971 that we discover the first attempt in peace time to move to a legally regulated system. However, the accuracy of the non-interventionist depiction does very much depend on the period which is examined. It is the aim of this work to examine both the role given to law, and that anticipated for it, in the period 1867–1945.

[1] KW Wedderburn, *The Worker and the Law*, p 18 (2nd edn).
[2] *Ibid* at p 16.
[3] O Kahn-Freund, 'Industrial Relations and the Law – Retrospect and Prospect' (1970) *BJIR* 301 at 302.
[4] Kahn-Freund, above n 3, at p 304.

1

Labour Law 1867–1880

INTRODUCTION

IN 1867 A ROYAL Commission on Trade Unions was appointed. This was to prove to be a decisive moment in the development of UK labour law. Without doubt the legislation which followed the ensuing report, in 1869, can be regarded as the foundation of the modern law.[1] The appointment of the Commission followed the so-called 'Sheffield outrages': 'the culmination of a long series of acts of violence directed against non-unionists in the Sheffield cutlery trades.'[2] However, the establishment of the Commission also gave the unions the chance to lobby for reform of the law given that they had a variety of reasons to be less than contented. Examples of dissatisfaction are easy to find; two will suffice for the purposes of illustration. First, there was the impact of the decision in *Hornby v Close*.[3] At common law, because a trade union was an unincorporated body, there were difficulties in recovering union property where it had been misappropriated by a member or an officer. In order to protect union property, a number of unions had registered under the Friendly Society Acts which provided a statutory remedy. However, while most unions carried out the functions of a friendly society they also had objects which were unlawful in the sense of being in restraint of trade. This element of unlawfulness led the court in *Hornby* to deny trade unions the protection of the Friendly Society's legislation. Second, the existence of the Master and Servant legislation hindered the capacity of employees to take industrial action. The legislation had been reformed in 1867 but remained a source of discontent. In theory, it was possible for both employers and employees to incur criminal penalties under the 1867 Act. In practice, it was employees who were prosecuted and who were, in many cases, convicted. The

---

[1] Royal Commission on Trade Unions (Cd 4123, 1869).
[2] P Smith, *Disraelian Conservatism and Social Reform*, (London: Routledge & Kegan Paul, 1967) p 45.
[3] [1867] 2 QB 153.

later Royal Commission of 1875 was to testify to the unsatisfactory administration of the Act:

> From a careful observation of the cases of conviction under this Act which have taken place at petty sessions, it certainly appears that the Act has been misconstrued and misunderstood in many points, and that many of the convictions, if made the subject of appeal, would in all probability have been quashed; for we find cases where imprisonment in the case of non-payment of a fine imposed has been awarded for a longer period than the law allows. Hard labour has been made part of the sentence where the terms of imprisonment, in default of the fine, has been fixed by the court; whereas by the 11th section it is specially provided that no such imprisonment should be with hard labour. Adjudications have been double, that is to say, requiring the defendant to do two or more things legally inconsistent. Defendants have been brought into court without knowing what the complaint required, the amount of compensation, damages, or other remedy being omitted from the summons, contrary to the direction contained in section 4, which expressly requires that these particulars shall be stated in the summons.[4]

The foregoing indictment is particularly cogent given that the Royal Commission of 1875 was not well disposed to the interests of labour.[5] Moreover, the legislation was used to defeat strike action:

> In small strikes it was a common practice to have all the strikers arrested and then to confront them with the stark choice: either return to work at once on the employer's terms or go to prison . . . In bigger strikes, where the arrest of all the strikers was impracticable the law was used to behead the strike by imprisoning the leaders.[6]

THE REPORT OF THE ROYAL COMMISSION

As a result of the deliberations of the Royal Commission both a majority and a minority report was issued. Leaving aside the subsequent legislation, the Royal Commission and the reports thereof were of great significance for the public standing of trade unions. The

---

[4] Royal Commission on Labour Laws (Cd 1157, 1875) at p 13.

[5] D Simon, 'Master and Servant' in J Saville (ed), *Democracy and the Labour Movement* (London: Lawrence & Wishart, 1954), observed at p 160 that 'this law was far from being a dead letter, for in the 18 years (1858–75) for which statistics are available there were on average 10,000 prosecutions of workmen each year in England and Wales alone.'

[6] *Ibid* at p 171.

published evidence and reports presented a very detailed study of the work and activities of trade unions. The picture painted was sufficiently favourable so as to more than dispel the damage done to the image of trade unionism by the Sheffield fiasco. The labour movement and its sympathisers had made the most of the opportunity presented by the appointment of the Commission. It must also be said that the appointment of the positivist, Frederick Harrison, was of great importance. When the Commission came to report it emerged that the Majority Report was 'an inconclusive and somewhat inconsistent document,' which saw little value in trade unions for society in general, or even for the workers themselves, but argued for some legal protection of organisations whose rules were free 'from such restrictive clauses as those limiting the number of apprentices and the use of machinery, or prohibiting piecework and subcontracting.'[7] As will be seen, the Minority Report was much more sympathetic to trade unionism and, in the event, much more influential.

A key difference between the two reports was that the majority favoured incorporation. The majority recommended that:

> facilities should be granted for such registration as will give to the unions capacity for rights and duties resembling in some degree that of corporations.[8]

Such registration would be contingent on the union constitution containing no objects regarded as objectionable (eg the object of preventing workmen from working in common with men not members of the union). The minority, on the other hand, rejected incorporation and believed that the State should accord

> to them bare legal recognition under the condition of ample publicity. They would thus be secured against robbery and enabled to protect their property, but would have no other assistance in enforcing contributions or managing their affairs. In return for this recognition a guarantee of perfect publicity in their laws and in their expenditure would be exacted, but these would be in no way interfered with so long as they were clear from crime.[9]

Why did the minority reject incorporation ? A number of reasons for this stance can be gleaned from their report. They took the view that

---

[7] H. Clegg, A. Fox and A. Thompson, *A History of British Trade Unions* (Oxford: Clarendon Press, 1964), pp 44–45.

[8] Royal Commission, above n 1 at para 80.

[9] *Ibid* at p LX.

there was an absence of consensus in society as to the legitimate role of trade unions:

> the conditions on which alone the public would give the full aid of the law to the unions to recover their contributions would be such as few unions would accept.[10]

A few years later the highly tendentious nature of labour law was noted by one judge who declared:

> By the expression that a thing is 'contrary to public policy" I understand that it is meant that it is opposed to the welfare of the community at large. I can see that the maintenance of strikes may be against the interests of employers, because they may be thereby forced to yield, at their own expense, a larger share of profit or other advantage to the employed; but I have no means of judicially determining that this is contrary to the interests of the whole community; and I think that in deciding that it is, and therefore, that any act done in its furtherance is illegal, we would be basing our judgement, not on recognised legal principles, but on the opinion of one of the contending schools of political economists.[11]

Against this backdrop the minority advocated a minimum of control over the objects, rules and other aspects of the internal affairs of trade unions. A minimalistic approach was adopted of necessity; the absence of consensus meant that a detailed legal regime for trade unions would not be possible. The Minority Report was nevertheless a clear and resounding endorsement of the legitimacy of trade union functions. A further reason for rejecting incorporation was that the minority regarded trade unions as voluntary associations. In the words of their report

> Trade Unions are essentially clubs and not trading companies, and we think that the degree of regulation possible in the case of the latter, is not possible in the case of the former. All questions of crime apart, the objects which they aim, the rights which they claim and the liabilities which they incur, are for the most part, it seems to us, such as courts of law should neither enforce, nor modify nor annul. They should rest entirely on consent.[12]

One suspects that a further reason concerned the right to strike. If a trade union became an incorporated body then actions in tort could be brought against it in its own name. In that event some form of legal

---

[10] Royal Commission, above n 1 at p LX.
[11] *Printing and Numerical Registering Co v Sampson* (1875) LR 19 Eq 462 at p 465.
[12] Royal Commission, above n 1 at p lix.

protection would have been called for. It is worth recalling that, by this time, the Court of Appeal had recognised the existence of the tort of inducing breach of contract.[13]

The majority and minority differed not only over the wisdom of incorporation but also over the appropriate stance to take over the right to strike. The minority were particularly concerned to remove special criminal offences—such legislation was seen as a relic of feudalism. Accordingly, the Combination Act 1825 should be repealed:

> it punishes certain acts in the labouring orders of the community which are not penal in any other class. . .it is not administered and is not likely to be administered impartially . . . it is so vague, that it is readily perverted to an oppressive use.[14]

The minority acknowledged that criminal offences might be committed in the course of a trade dispute but believed that such incidents could and should be dealt with by the general criminal law. In consequence, there was no need for specific legislative provision on picketing. Moreover, any such legislation would be unfair since such weapons of the employer as the blacklist would remain lawful. One slightly surprising omission from the Minority Report is any explicit discussion of the Master and Servant legislation. The signatories to the Minority Report may well have felt that was covered by their call, in general, for the 'removal of special legislation dealing exclusively with the employment of labour.'[15] The minority did not greatly concern themselves with civil liabilities for industrial action. This is perhaps surprising until it is realised that the Commissioners would undoubtedly have assumed that a trade union could not be sued in tort. Legal protection against specific common law liabilities would not, therefore, be necessary. Indeed the minority recommended that a union should not be capable of being sued as a corporate body.

The report of the majority was much less well disposed to the right to strike. Admittedly, the majority recognised the right to combine. However, if that right was to be meaningful, the boundaries of lawful industrial action would have had to be set in a reasonable fashion and the majority appear to have been unwilling to recommend this. Whilst trade unions were to be corporations no immunities against common law liabilities in tort/delict were to be provided. This appears to have

---

[13] *Lumley v Gye* (1853) 2 E & B 216.
[14] Royal Commission, above n 1, at p lvii.
[15] *Ibid* at p xxx.

been recommended despite the assumption that not only was inducing breach of contract a tort, but intentionally interfering in the trade or business of another even in the absence of unlawful means was also tortious. The majority's approach to the right to strike is illustrated by its recommendation that section 3 of the Combination Act 1825 should be retained. Section 3 made it a criminal offence for a person to achieve, or attempt to achieve, certain industrial aims by means of violence to the person or property, or by threats or intimidation, or by molesting or in any way obstructing another. This provision had been used, for example, to restrict the ability of workers to picket. In charging the jury in one section 3 case Bramwell stated that:

> Even if . . . the picket did nothing more than his duty as a picket, and if that duty did not extend to abusive language and gestures such as had been described, still, if that was calculated to have a deterring effect on the minds of ordinary persons, by exposing them to have their motions watched, and to encounter black looks, that would not be permitted by the law of the land.[16]

A highly restrictive interpretation in a case involving picketing may not seem altogether surprising but it must be appreciated that section 3 encompassed activities other than picketing. In the case of *R v Skinner* the threat of strike action unless an employee become a union member was held to be an offence within the section.[17] The majority's acceptance of the right to combine was a grudging one. The right to strike was to exist only to the extent permitted by the individualistic common law. On the one hand, legalisation of trade unions was to be contingent upon incorporation which involved significant restrictions on the legitimate objects of a union. On the other, pursuit of trade union objects would also have been highly problematic.

Collective Bargaining

Both the Majority and Minority Report contain little discussion as to the regulation of collective bargaining. This is scarcely surprising since, during much of the nineteenth century, employers were much more likely to determine terms and conditions of employment unilaterally

---

[16] *R v Druitt* (1867) 10 Cox 592 at pp 601–2.
[17] (1867) 10 Cox 493.

than to bargain collectively.[18] Collective agreements were somewhat thin on the ground; partly it must be said because of unilateral action on the part of employees. For example,

> In the craft industries . . . employers . . . had given the lead towards collective bargaining, and some of the national agreements represented a joint victory for employers and trade union leaders over the hostility of a rank and file which was still wedded to the traditions of unilateral regulation.[19]

In keeping with the libertarian philosophy of the times neither the majority nor the minority sought to inject any legal regulation over the process of collective bargaining, the majority, for example, stating that

> it does not appear to us that any system of compulsory arbitration is practicable, since there are no admitted principles of decision on which the arbitrator may proceed . . .[20]

The Commission did, however, place a good deal of faith in the institutionalisation of conflict through the workings of joint institutions. Even at this point in time, collective bargaining and its product, the collective agreement, were viewed as offering a sound basis from which stable industrial relations might well flow. Thus the minority found that where collectively agreed terms exist,

> no questions appear to arise but those of interpretation and we find the employers on perfectly amicable footing with the union, and both parties often co-operating with each other.[21]

Moreover, the addition of boards or arbitration 'appears to us the nearest solution of the labour and employment questions which has yet shown itself.'[22] This view as to the benefits of joint regulation was evidently shared by the Government. Hughes remarking in the Commons that

> the existence of these unions as legal associations would greatly help the system of arbitration which had done so much to settle disputes between the employer and the employed . . .[23]

---

[18] Hunt, *British Labour History 1815–1914* (London: Weidenfeld and Nicholson, 1981) p 281.
[19] Clegg, above n 5 at p 471.
[20] Royal Commission, above n 1 at para 98.
[21] *Ibid* at p xlix.
[22] *Ibid* at p l.
[23] Parl. Deb., 14.3.1871, HC, vol 204, col 2039. In this light it is surprising that neither the Majority nor the Minority Report discuss the Council of Conciliation Act 1867. The Act enabled employers and employees to jointly apply for a licence to form an

The Government believed that industrial relations would be improved by

> . . . making the law neutral between both parties; by taking care that it should in all respects be just and equal; by promoting in every possible manner a good understanding between them; and by leaving them to arrange so far as that could be done, their disputes among one another rather by force of reason than by force of law . . . [24]

The minority also focused briefly on the subject of legal enforceability of jointly agreed terms, awards, etc. Prior to 1871 the legal status of trade unions would have prevented any legal enforcement of collective agreements. The minority believed that

> it is expedient to declare that whilst all combinations of workmen untainted with a criminal purpose are lawful, certain agreements to be defined, will not be directly enforceable at Law . . . [25]

A particular concern was that litigation between trade union and member should be avoided and this resulted in the enactment of section 4 of the Trade Union Act 1871. External relations were, however, a different matter. Whilst it would be

> inexpedient to give any additional legislative character to courts of conciliation or arbitration; . . . it is expedient to give increased facilities in cases where regulations exist under mutual agreement for the enforcement of the contract against their party who had bona fide accepted it. [26]

Such a recommendation had a certain logic to it. In a society where freedom of contract was a cornerstone of the dominant ideology there must have been a reluctance to do anything other than allow the parties to an agreement to endow it with legal force. Moreover, the implementation of the recommendation would be a legislative endorsement

---

arbitration board. Any board so formed was empowered to adjudicate upon any dispute between employers and employees which was jointly submitted. However 'nothing in this Act . . . shall authorise the said council to establish a Rate of Wages or price of Labour on Workmenship at which the workmen shall in future be paid.' The Act appears to have been a dead letter and though it is not clear why, the rather cumbersome procedure for the setting up of a board may have been a material factor. The powers possessed by the board, such as the right to summons witnesses on pain of criminal penalties, would also have conjured up an image of a very legalistic (if not to say oppressive) body. The fact that disputes over wage demands were not encompassed by the legislation was also highly relevant. Any award made was to be legally enforceable.

[24] Parl. Deb., HC, 14.2.1871, vol 204, Col 269.
[25] Royal Commission, above n 1 at p lxiii.
[26] *Ibid* at p lxiv.

of the value of joint regulation. On the other hand, it was not difficult to foresee potential difficulties. Even if the recommendation was implemented any agreement would only be valid if it satisfied the law on restraint of trade. Again, if it was politically unacceptable to allow a union to resort to law to constrain workmen from going to work, it would be difficult to countenance a union suing an employer for breach of a collective agreement through the employment of non-unionists.

The report is dominated by the ideas and values of the then prevalent laissez-faire philosophy. Trade unions too, at this time, were happy to pay lip-service to the tenets of that philosophy. However, in promoting the interests of their members they took a relaxed view as to what economic orthodoxy would regard as legitimate aims. Thus, by collective action, they sought to reduce the length of the working day with a view to restricting output and hence raising the level of wages. Whilst this may have had the effect of restricting the contractual freedom of individuals it may also be regarded as a legitimate outcome of freedom of association. Such a pragmatic approach was, in any event, sustainable intellectually given the tensions which the philosophy of laissez-faire gave rise to. Dicey drew attention to the fact that

> utilitarians . . . had not given sufficient attention to the difficulty of combining the contractual freedom of each individual when acting alone with that unlimited right of association which, from one point of view is a main element of individual freedom.[27]

To restrict freedom of association is to curtail the contractual power of individuals. On the other hand, the exercise of freedom of association may itself restrict the freedom of individuals contracting and their concerted action may interfere with the freedom of third parties.

The Minority Report (and the subsequent Act) represented a move towards giving greater latitude to freedom of combination:

> we can understand no freedom to trade in which workmen are not free to stipulate with an employer in concert for their own conditions. That their conditions are unreasonable or highly inconvenient to the employer is no coercion.[28]

Two reasons might be suggested by way of explanation. Firstly, there may have been a general tendency at this time to accept what the

---

[27] AV Dicey, *Law and Public Opinion in England During the Nineteenth Century*, 2nd edn (reprinted 1948) (London: Macmillan, 1962) at p 158.
[28] Royal Commission, above n 1 at p lxii.

contracting parties had freely agreed.[29] Heydon, in his work on restraint of trade, quotes an 1875 judgment of Jessel, MR which expressed a concern lest contracts be held void as against public policy and continues 'contracts when entered into freely and voluntarily shall be held sacred and shall be enforced by Courts of Justice.'[30] Secondly, there may have been a realisation that, whatever the theoretical neutrality of laws against combination, their impact was by and large suffered by labour, not capital.[31] Accordingly it was time to concede to the forces of labour the right of combination. Also helping in this direction was a growing intellectual rejection of an important facet of classical economics: the wages fund. It was becoming increasingly accepted that trade unions had a role to play in setting wage levels and even that the existence, and exercise of, collective force was essential if the bargaining power of employees was to increase. To exercise the right of combination was, therefore, carrying with it greater legitimacy.

THE LEGISLATIVE SETTLEMENT

The legislative settlement of 1871 consisted of two Acts of Parliament: The Trade Union Act 1871 and the Criminal Law Amendment Act 1871. The former was more fundamental and I shall deal with it first. The Act sought to give trade unions a legal framework akin to that provided by the Friendly Societies Act. Trade Unions were also freed from the civil and criminal consequences of the restraint of trade doctrine. Section 2 provided that the purposes of any trade union shall not, by reason merely that they are in restraint of trade, be deemed to be unlawful so as to render any member of such trade union liable to criminal prosecution for conspiracy or otherwise. It is not clear to what extent this provision was by this stage merely declaratory of the common law. Section 3 of the Act was similar in design and tackled the civil law aspects: the purposes of any trade union shall not, by reason merely that they are in restraint of trade, be unlawful so as to render void or voidable any agreement on trust. Henceforth, trade unions were to be free to combine unhampered by the doctrine of restraint of trade. The

---

[29] JD Heydon, *The Restraint of Trade Doctrine* (London: Butterworths, 1971), pp 29–30.

[30] *Printing and Numerical Registering Co v Sampson* (1875) LR 19 Eq 462 at p 465.

[31] See, for example, PS Atiyah, *The Rise and Fall of Freedom of Contract*, (Oxford: Clarendon Press, 1979) pp 411–12.

recognition by the law of the right to combine was partly motivated by an awareness of the weakness of the bargaining power of the individual employee and his consequent dependence on association with his fellows to improve his lot. It was pointed out in parliamentary debate that

> Employers of labour were in themselves a great combination, and there ought to be a great countervailing power permitted to the employed to guard their own interests.[32]

As we have seen, the minority had advocated a regime whereby minimal control over trade union internal affairs would be exercised by Parliament or the courts. The legislature agreed and enacted section 4. This section restricted the enforcement of agreements entered into by trade unions by preventing any court from entertaining

> any legal proceedings instituted with the object of directly enforcing or recovering damages for the breach of . . . (a number of specified agreements) . . .

The agreements specified concerned certain agreements between one trade union member and another and also between a trade union and a union member. Section 4, in the main, served to restrict legal involvement in trade union internal affairs. However, in addition, section 4 applied to agreements between one trade union and another. It also applied to agreements to furnish contributions to any employer or workman not a member of the trade union in consideration of such employer or workman acting in conformity with the union rules or resolutions. On the whole section 4 did not affect external relations, the Home Secretary explaining in the Commons that

> . . . one object of this Bill . . . was to remove these disabilities so far as regards contracts entered into by trade unions with third parties.[33]

There was concern over the consequences if the internal affairs of a trade union were made fully subject to the law of contract:

> If such contracts were enforceable our Courts of Equity might be called upon to enjoin masters against opening their works, or workmen from going to work, or discontinuing a strike; whilst our Country Courts would have to make decrees for contributions to strike, or to enforce penalties from workmen who had felt it their duty to resume employment.[34]

[32] Parl. Deb., 14.3.1871, HC, vol 204, col 2039.
[33] Parl. Deb., 14.2.1871, HC, vol 204, col 266.
[34] *Ibid.*

The lack of an underlying consensus as to the development of labour law again played its part. The making and carrying out of the agreements enumerated was not prohibited; instead, trade unions were to be denied access to the courts to enforce such agreements and were confined to the use of social sanctions. Another possible factor was that if trade unions were to be exempt from the general law of restraint of trade the consideration for this should be restricted access to judicial proceedings.

Somewhat curiously, by embracing agreements between trade unions, section 4 applied to agreements between a trade union and an employer's association. Gayler's analysis of this stance is well worth quoting:

> How far the legislative intended this result is difficult to say. Although a definition of the term 'trade union' to include an employers' association is not usual, nevertheless the legislative intention to include that type of association within the definition can hardly be denied. But an examination of the agreements set out in section 4, together with the views of the Royal Commission of 1869, must lead us to the conclusion that, so far as section 4 is concerned, it was merely the intention of the legislature to put union 'domestic' agreements outside the purview of the courts. It was the intention of the legislature that the courts should not interfere with the payment of benefits, imposition of fines and so forth. By the phase 'any agreement between one trade union and another' the draftsman probably meant an agreement between one workers' union and another workers' union as to the membership, terms of apprenticeship, lines of demarcation, amalgamation, etc. It cannot be believed that he had in view a collective agreement between an employers' association and a workers' trade union. This may be first deduced from the fact that multi-party bargaining was not very common in the seventies. If the legislature was trying to stop the slow growth of industry-wide bargaining, it would have been a little more explicit. Secondly, and perhaps alternately, if it had been the intention of the legislature to let collective agreements be merely 'gentlemen's agreements,' provision would have been made for agreements made between a single employer and a worker's trade union.[35]

Thus the failure to give legal effect to collective agreements between trade unions and employers' associations may therefore have been accidental. Certainly, it does not appear to have been the intention of the minority of the Royal Commission to restrict trade unions' capacity to

[35] Gayler, 6th Annual Conference on Labour Law, New York University, p 107 and quoted in N Selwyn, *Legal Aspects of Collective Agreements*, pp 165–66.

contract with third parties. On the other hand, the failure to incorporate meant that there would be considerable procedural difficulties in suits by or against a trade union. In 1871 a representative action could not have been brought in England against a trade union. Prior to *Taff Vale*, the only way to have sued a trade union would have been to sue the trustees. Section 9 of the Act empowered the trustees of any registered trade union to defend any action 'touching or concerning the property, right, or claim to property of the trade union'. It is debateable whether an action for breach of a collective agreement could have been brought under section 9. Ultimately, the extent to which Parliament intended that the external relations of unions were to be regularised is unclear. The remainder of the 1871 Act sought to allow unions, through registration, to attain the legal structure of a friendly society. Ironically it was such 'quasi-corporate' characteristics that were to come to the fore in the *Taff Vale* case. Section 12 provided for the recovery of union funds which had been embezzled by members/officers.

The signatories to the Minority Report wished to allow for the right to strike in order to render the right of combination meaningful. In so far as the civil law was concerned they were successful in this (or at least it appeared so for some years). However, when it came to the role of the criminal law the positivists and the Government were to diverge. The Combination Act of 1825 was repealed but the Government chose to enact the Criminal Law Amendment Act. Section 1(3) made it a criminal offence to molest or obstruct any person in a manner defined by the Act with a view to coercing such a person into performing certain prescribed acts.[36] The significance of the section turned on the definition of molestation and obstruction. It was provided that a person shall be deemed to molest or obstruct another person in any of the following cases: that is to say,

---

[36] The acts prescribed were as follows:

(1) being a master to dismiss or to cease to employ any workman, or being a workman to quit any employment or to return to work before it is finished;
(2) being a master not to offer or being a workman not to accept any employment of work;
(3) being a master or workman to belong or not to belong to any temporary or permanent association or combination;
(4) being a master or workman to pay any fine or penalty imposed by any temporary or permanent association or combination;
(5) being master to alter the mode of carrying on his business, or the number or description of any persons employed by him.

(1) if he persistently follows a person about from place to place;
(2) if he hides any tools, clothes or other property owned or used by such person, or deprives him of or hinders him in the use thereof;
(3) if he watches or besets the house or other place where such person resides or works, or carries on business, or happens to be, or the approach to such house or place, or if with two or more other persons he follows such person in a disorderly manner in or through any street.

Potentially, the most significant form of 'molestation' was watching and besetting. In essence this made picketing, for the objects set out in the section, a criminal offence. However, much more helpfully from a trade union point of view, the Act also restricted the impact of the law of criminal conspiracy. It was provided, by section 1, that no person should be liable to any punishment for doing or conspiring to do any act, on the ground that such act restrained or tended to restrain the free course of trade, unless the act took the form of molestation or obstruction, and was done with the intention of coercing a person into performing one of the prescribed acts.

The positivists can claim much of the credit for the Trade Union Act 1871. Harrison drafted the Minority Report upon which the Act was based. He

> set out in the clearest terms the changes in the law relating to trade unions which seemed to the minority of the commissioners to be appropriate in the light of their interpretation of the evidence.[37]

The passage of the legislation was eased by virtue of the fact that the legal counsel to the Home Office was a positivist, Godfrey Lushington. Unlike some other friends of labour they rejected the notion of incorporation. As Harrison has written,

> it was . . . [their] . . . ingenious suggestion that unions should enjoy the protection of the Friendly Society Acts while acquiring the privilege of being capable of being sued or proceeded against as a corporate entity. The positivists had to work hard to explain to Trade Unionists that mere legalisation would expose them to endless litigation and end in crippling them.[38]

One possible solution which was not adopted was the granting of positive rights to trade unions. Such a possibility was not at all in vogue

---

[37] R Harrison, *The English Positivists and Labour Movements* (Oxford, Unpublished Phd thesis, 1955) p 246.
[38] R Harrison, *Before the Socialists* (London: Routledge & Kegan Paul, 1965), p 277.

in 1871. The positivists played a major part in securing the legislation of 1871. They deserve great credit for devising an imaginative and coherent legal framework for trade unions which afforded them protection by the law but did not constrain them by imposing rigorous legal control over their activities.

Of course, Parliament, through measures in the criminal law, diluted the positivists proposals. In so far as the right to strike was concerned, the Criminal Law Amendment Act had the potential to be very restrictive in its impact. The failure to amend the Master and Servant Act must also be mentioned. Nevertheless, it was to be hoped that a combination of the restriction of the doctrine of criminal conspiracy by section 1 of the Criminal Law Amendment Act and the procedural difficulties involved in bringing a civil suit against a union would provide adequate scope for the right to strike.

THE SETTLEMENT OF 1871—THE AFTERMATH

Picketing

In the wake of the legislation of 1871 a good deal of trade union discontent still existed. At root, this was caused by the very creation of the Criminal Law Amendment Act. First, the Act was open to the very fundamental objection that it perpetuated the existence of class legislation. In the eyes of trade unionists the general criminal law could deal more than adequately with any incidents that might arise in the course of a trade dispute. Second, as a matter of practical concern, there was a fear that the operation of the Act would, in fact, greatly circumscribe the right to strike. The judicial response to the passage of the Act did nothing to dispel the latter concern. In *R v Bunn* gas workers went on strike to secure the reinstatement of a fellow employee who had been dismissed and were charged with conspiracy.[39] The second count of conspiracy was conspiracy to use unlawful means. The unlawful means relied upon being breaches of contract which contravened the Master and Servant legislation. This aspect of the case seems unexceptional and indeed it was on this count that the accused were convicted. Of much greater import was the first count which involved a conspiracy by improper threats to induce the employer to reinstate the former

[39] (1872) 12 Cox 316.

employee. The issue here is to what extent this charge involved the doctrine of restraint of trade. In assessing count one it is necessary, presumably, to disregard the fact that a penal statute had been breached—otherwise there is no difference between count one and count two. If this is accepted, it is difficult to regard count one as involving anything other than a conspiracy in restraint of trade. Brett J suggested that a criminal conspiracy might stem from 'an attempt to interfere with the liberty of the man's will in the conduct of his trade, by menaces and threats.'[40] There are two reasons why the judgment in *R v Bunn* may be viewed as contrary to the legislation of 1871. In the first place section 2 of the Trade Union Act 1871 appeared to protect trade union members from prosecution for a conspiracy in restraint of trade. Even more clearly, the proviso to section 1 of the Criminal Law Amendment 1871 stated that, with the exception of the offences specified in the section, no person shall be liable to any punishment for doing or conspiring to do any act, on the ground that such act restrains or tends to restrain the free course of trade. The immunity provided by the 1871 Act appeared to fall victim to the relabelling of an existing liability. The strikers were treated severely, 12 months' imprisonment with hard labour being imposed.[41]

The subsequent case of *R v Hibbert* served to demonstrate just how difficult it was for a picket to remain within the confines of the law.[42] By virtue of section 1 of the Criminal Law Amendment Act, watching or besetting was unlawful where it was carried out with a view to coerce someone to do certain acts. In his charge to the jury the judge pointed out that coercion might either be effected by physical force or by the operation of fear upon the mind:

> It is possible that there might be such a molestation by watching and besetting premises as might be expected to and would operate upon the mind so as to take away liberty of will, by giving rise to a fear of violence by threats, or to some apprehension of loss or ruin, or to feelings of annoyance.[43]

Picketing, in itself, was said not to be necessarily unlawful. However, in *Hibbert* the necessary element of coercion appears to have been held to exist in the action of the pickets in inviting the employees to quit their employment and promising them money if they did so, and threat-

---

[40] (1872) 12 Cox p 332.
[41] Subsequently the Home Secretary remitted 8 months' imprisonment, and reduced the sentence to four months' imprisonment with hard labour.
[42] (1875) 13 Cox 82.
[43] *Ibid* at p 87.

ening that, if they refused, they would be known as 'black sheep' and would not be able to get employment anywhere.

Whatever the theoretical possibilities of pickets remaining within the law by restricting themselves to peaceful persuasion the evidence suggests that the lower courts were extremely unsympathetic.[44] For example, Howell reports one case where a picket was convicted under section 1 in the following circumstances:

> He was charged with delivering a handbill in the street where he lived, opposite to the employer's premises. The handbill was exceptionally mild; the strongest passages were as follows: After stating the cause of strike, it said, 'We, therefore, appeal to you as fellow-workmen, not to enter into any engagement with our late employers unless on the condition that the nine hours per day commence at once. By so refusing you will forward our cause as well as your own as working men.[45]

The trade union movement oscillated, to some extent, between campaigning for the amendment of the Act and its repeal. The close ties between the trade unions and sections of the Liberal Party appear to have restricted the outlook of some trade union leaders: 'they looked to a negotiated settlement through the support and good offices of advanced liberal and other parliamentaries . . .'[46] In 1872 the Parliamentary Committee of the TUC sponsored a bill which would have amended the Criminal Law Amendment Act, in the main by removing watching and besetting from the list of prescribed acts. This measure was lost at an early stage in the Commons. Thereafter, repeal appears to have become the aim of the labour movement.

Collective Bargaining

The Royal Commission's endorsement of collective bargaining would have been echoed by trade unions. The growth in the extent of joint regulation represented welcome progress from unilateral regulation by the employer. It is interesting to note that members of the Parliamentary Committee of the TUC were instrumental in securing the passage of legislation on arbitration between employers and

---

[44] In England prosecutions under the 1871 Act could be heard by a magistrate or two or more justices of the peace.

[45] G Howell, *Labour Legislation, Labour Movements and Labour Leaders* (London: Fisher Unwin, 1916) p 203.

[46] Harrison, above n 37 at p 309.

employees in 1872. Dissatisfaction with the impact of partisan legislation does not seem to have resulted in a more wide ranging opposition
to further legislation.[47] Any piece of prospective legislation would be
judged purely on its merits. The approach of the Parliamentary
Committee was in line with the view of the Minority Report of the
Royal Commission that it would be

> expedient to give increased facilities in cases where regulations exist under
> mutual agreement for the enforcement of the contract against either party
> who has bona fide accepted it.

It appears, however, that some unions would have favoured some
means of compelling reluctant employers to negotiate. The Act enabled
the parties to a collective agreement to provide that disputes be referred
to arbitration. Awards were enforceable by a range of sanctions which
included imprisonment. However, no use appears to have been made
of the Act. The role for imprisonment is unlikely to have helped given
the operation of legislation such as the Master and Servants Act.

THE DISRAELI GOVERNMENT

The Conservative government elected in 1874 lacked any considered
legislative programme, though many MPs elected in the 1874 election
had been obliged to commit themselves on trade union questions as a
result of pressure from trade unions:

> Conservative candidates in the larger boroughs, especially in the industrial
> north, had frequently little option but to endorse the working men's objec-
> tives.[48]

The newly elected member for Manchester remarked that

> The elections in Lancashire have largely hinged on 2 questions—the 9 hours
> bill and the demands of the Trade Unionists. On both these points—every
> candidate for a borough constituency has had to promise compliance . . .[49]

The Conservatives appointed a Royal Commission to look at the question of labour law reform. This move was viewed with great suspicion
at the time but in hindsight

---

[47] Having said that, trade unions would have been unlikely to advocate regulatory legislation at this time since they still tended to adhere to the philosophy of laissez-faire at
this time.

[48] Smith above n 2 at p 188.

[49] *Ibid.*

The real object of Disraeli's exercises was not, however to divide and conquer; but to divide so that he could gracefully concede. One of his first decisions was to settle the labour laws question and he needed the Commission so as to cover himself against the charge that he had yielded to popular demand. He knew that, once the government's Bills came before the House, nobody would pay the least attention to the fact that they owed next to nothing to the recommendations of the commissioners.[50]

The Royal Commission of 1875 found little to fault in the existing trade union laws and, had reform been based on this report, it would have been very much in the realm of minor repeals and re-drafting of provisions to furnish greater clarification. The right of combination was re-affirmed but the right to strike was viewed with great suspicion. In outlook the report was heavily influenced by the doctrine of restraint of trade and great concern was shown lest the freedom not to combine be fettered. The Criminal Amendment Act was viewed as essential:

> That the conduct which is made penal by the Act is an outrage on the rights of others and ought to be repressed by law, does not seem to be seriously disputed . . .[51]

Complaints from trade unionists in respect of the scope of the right to picket were brushed aside on the basis that picketing which involved no more than peaceful persuasion was lawful, the judgment of Lush J in *R v Shepherd* on the pre-1871 law being cited.[52] However, the scope for lawful action was, in fact, decidedly limited as the later case of *R v Hibbert* was to demonstrate.

One of the issues addressed by the Commissioners was the law of criminal conspiracy, a particularly contentious area being where neither the object of the conspiracy nor the means by which it was furthered were per se, criminal. Thus the tort of inducing breach of contract would not have been a crime when committed by an individual but combining for that purpose might well have been. Clearly, in the trade union context, the transposing of a civil wrong into a criminal action was potentially very important. Given that the Commission was firmly attached to common law doctrines a radical recommendation was not going to be forthcoming. However, it was recommended that provision should be made to the effect that no person shall be liable to be indicted for conspiracy, by reason only of the object of the

---

[50] Harrison, above n 37 at p 303.
[51] Royal Commission, above n 4 at p 22.
[52] (1869) 11 Cox 325.

combination being to force or control the action or will of any master or workman in any matter relating to the mode of carrying on his business or work, unless the means of coercion to be resorted to shall be one of these mentioned in the Criminal Law Amendment Act, or be the wilfully breaking or procuring others to break any contract of hiring or service, and unless the object of such coercion shall be one of the purposes set forth in that Act. This would have had the effect of rendering the first count in *R v Bunn* invalid. On the other hand, the express inclusion of inducing breach of contract meant that the recommendation would not be welcome to the trade union movement. As we have seen, at this time, it would have been unlikely that a union would have been liable for the tort of inducing breach of contract due to the procedural difficulties involved in suing a trade union. However, the approach in criminal cases, such as *R v Bunn*, would serve to undermine this protection by, potentially, criminalising trade union activists. The Commissioners strongly believed in allowing matters to be settled by the free operation of market forces. Nevertheless, their defence of the role of the criminal law was, in part, justified by reference to the public interest: workers should incur criminal liability as a result of their

> combining to break contracts where public mischief or inconvenience must result from a concerted and abrupt breach of their engagements.[53]

One of the main grievances of trade unionists at this time was the existence of the Master and Servant legislation. The Commissioners, though, displayed considerable sympathy for the aims of the legislation. They believed that, in the event of an employee failing to comply with an order under section 9 of the Act, the sanction of imprisonment should be retained:

> the remedy by an action for damages by the employer by reason of any such loss, must be negatory as against the workmen, who, in the great majority of instances, has no resources beyond the wages he earns by his labour, nor has he property by seizure of which the damages awarded could be realized.[54]

The Commissioners were divided as to whether section 14, which provided for imprisonment for an aggravated breach, should be retained.

---

[53] Royal Commission, above n 4 at p 27.
[54] *Ibid* at p 10.

Fortunately, from a trade union perspective, the Conspiracy and Protection of Property Act 1875 bore little resemblance to the report of the Royal Commission. The Act was considerably bolder in its vision. This was to a large extent due to the stance taken by the Home Secretary, Cross. Cross' approach was too radical for a number of his Cabinet colleagues but, with the strong support of Disraeli, he prevailed. Indeed, as the bill passed through the house, Cross introduced amendments which made the measure even more pro-union.[55] The Master and Servant legislation was repealed and, with the removal of its penal provisions, the employment relationship moved into the sphere of normal contractual relations. The fact that the relationship had not been normalised earlier has already been discussed. Penal provisions were introduced though in two particular situations. Section 4 made it a criminal offence for an employee of a gas or water company to wilfully and maliciously break his contract of service. For an offence to have been committed the employee had to know, or have reasonable cause to believe, that the probable consequences of his breach, either alone, or in combination with others, will be to deprive consumers wholly or to a great extent of their supply of gas or water. It seems clear that this provision was aimed at industrial action since the consequence of a breach of contract by any one individual would be unlikely to be significant. The fact that the provision only applied to employees and not, for example, a contractor was the source of much complaint. Section 5 made it a criminal offence for any person to wilfully and maliciously break a contract of employment, knowing or having reasonable cause to believe that the probable consequences of his doing so, either alone, or in combination with others, will be to endanger human life, or cause serious bodily injury or to expose valuable property to destruction or serious injury. Sections 4 and 5 are quite notable in that they seem intended to safeguard the public interest in two specific areas. By way of contrast the labour laws of 1871 set out a general legal framework for trade unions. This served the public interest only in the very general sense that a satisfactory legal structure might help facilitate good industrial relations.

The other notable provisions of the 1875 Act were sections 3 and 7. The former section amended the law of conspiracy, while the latter replaced section 1 of the Criminal Law Amendment Act 1871. Section 3 provided that an agreement or combination by two or more persons

---

[55] Smith, above n 2 at p 216.

to do, or procure to be done, any act in contemplation or furtherance of a trade dispute shall not be indictable as a conspiracy, if such act committed by one person would not be punishable as a crime. This went beyond the recommendation of the Royal Commission which would have allowed for criminal proceedings in respect of a conspiracy to induce a breach of contract. By way of contrast Parliament was determined to ameliorate the impact of the law of criminal conspiracy on trade disputes. In future, the mere fact of combination would not render behaviour criminal. The view was expressed in Parliament that

> The policy of the law, as embodied in the Act of 1871, was to place masters and employed as much as possible on an equality, and if they applied the law of conspiracy stringently to what might be called trade unions, the effect must be to put the employed at a disadvantage as it would happen that certain things would be lawful to the master merely because he was one which would be unlawful to the men because they were many.[56]

If this statement was accurate in its assessment of the policy of the 1871 legislation then the blame for the subsequent difficulties, caused by the law of conspiracy, could not be laid solely at the door of the judiciary. This is because section 1 of the Criminal Law Amendment Act 1871 clearly did not offer immunity against a charge of conspiracy to induce breach of contract.

Finally, and importantly, section 7 of the 1875 Act replaced section 1 of the Criminal Law Amendment Act 1871 and made provision for certain specific offences which might arise in the course of a trade dispute. A person would be guilty of a criminal offence if he, with a view to compelling any other person to abstain from doing or to do any act which such other person has a legal right to do or abstain from doing, wrongfully and without legal authority, committed one of a number of specified acts. It is not clear why the phrase 'wrongfully and without legal authority' was used given that the section provided that the acts specified were to be statutory offences. It may be that the intention was to attach penal consequences to certain civil wrongs. This was the view of the Court of Appeal in *Ward, Lock & Co v Operatives Printers' Assistants Society*:

> The Legislative, by the Act of 1875, gave in respect of some of these nuisances, or to which there was a civil remedy, a summary remedy by summons before a magistrate for acts done for which previously there was only a civil remedy. And it seems to me that the words 'wrongfully and without

---

[56] Parl. Deb., HC, 28.6.1875, vol 225, col 66.

legal authority' were introduced for the very purpose of limiting the remedy by criminal prosecution to cases so tortuous as to give a civil remedy.[57]

One question that might be posed is to what extent section 7 was an improvement on section 1 of the earlier legislation? Paragraph 4 of section 7, in essence, reiterated the element of section 1 which dealt with watching and besetting. However, a proviso to section 7 provided that:

> Attending at or near the house or place where a person resides, or works, or carries on business, or happens to be, or the approach to such house or place, in order merely to obtain or communicate information shall not be deemed a watching or besetting within the meaning of this section.

The capacity of a union to undertake picketing, lawfully, would very much depend upon the manner in which the proviso was interpreted. It is worthy of note just how limited were the ambitions of, at least some sections, of the labour movement. As we have seen, section 7 applied to compelling any other person to abstain from doing or to do any acts which such other person had a legal right to do or abstain from doing. Mundella applauded this on the basis that

> All the working men had demanded was equality in dealing with matters of this kind, and as they had now obtained equality, they could have no grounds for complaint.[58]

At the end of the day, however, offences such as watching and besetting were unlikely to occur other than in the trade disputes context.

The role played by the positivists in the attainment of the 1875 legislation was not as great as it had been in 1871. Nevertheless, they played an important part in persuading trade unionists to demand complete repeal of the Criminal Law Amendment Act and that this aim should be furthered by means, not only of lobbying of sympathetic MPs, but also a broader political campaign. The influence of the positivists was a long term one for they helped stimulate questions

> about the political organisation of Labour and the organisation of a third party, which were to prove to be of the highest importance for the subsequent development of the whole movement.[59]

The positivists themselves sought a Labour party independent of the Liberals.

---

[57] (1906) 22 TLR 327 at p 329 per Vaughan-Williams, LJ.
[58] Parl. Deb., HC, 16.7.1875, vol 225, col 1582.
[59] Harrison, above n 37, p 360.

The 1875 Act is best viewed as a means of consolidating and strengthening the 1871 settlement. Section 7 was intended to allow greater scope for trade unionists to take action to further their aims in the course of trade disputes. Before the right to combine can be regarded as meaningful there must be adequate scope for the right to strike. The Conservatives believed that the reforms would mean that trade unionists would be less inclined to regard the Liberals as their natural ally. Disraeli hoped the Act would 'gain and retain for the Tories the lasting affection of the working classes.'[60] The passing of the Conspiracy and Protection of Property Act was the final element of the 1871 settlement. By virtue of which trade unions would be fully admitted into laissez-faire society; this goal was achieved at the individual level by the repeal of the Master and Servant Legislation.

Factory legislation expanded throughout the course of the nineteenth century. By the second half of the century its existence was seen as an acceptable and established exception to the principles of laissez-faire:

> The conclusions of political economy against interference with liberty of contract, as between as employers, have been allowed full sway whenever they were not overruled by other considerations, founded upon the established rules of hygiene or the more obvious interests of society.[61]

Legislating in this area had reached the stage where, while there was expansion into new areas, much of any new legislation dealt with refinement, and modifications, to the existing Acts. The Act of 1878 was a consolidating Act and was one of the major achievements of the Disraeli administration. It is also the case that, of particular interest, are measures restricting the hours of work of women and children. In the analysis of British labour law the absence of legislation on the hours of work of adult males has always been viewed as a significant factor. However, Parliament was well aware that restricting the hours of work of women and children would in practice, likewise, restrict adult males. Hutchins and Harrison conclude that

> the trade unions have urged shorter hours by law for women and children, not in order to oust them as competitors and work longer themselves, but to secure short hours all round.[62]

---

[60] Smith, above n 2 at p 217.
[61] Royal Commission on the Factory and Workshops Acts (C 1443), para 45.
[62] BL Hutchins and A Harrison, *History of Factory Legislation* (London, 1926) pp 197–98.

Employers too often sought advantages in the state legislating in this area: they want to be bound by something stronger than a moral obligation . . . for fear lest anyone should break faith, and thus be able to take advantage of the rest.[63] It is important also to appreciate that by the second half of the nineteenth century the degree of compliance with the legislation was regarded as satisfactory.[64]

CONCLUSIONS

Let us now try and assess the state of labour law policy after the legislation of 1871–1875. Viewed in the round the premise of the legislation might be thought to be a recognition of the right to combine so that the forces of labour might be able to stand against capital. Consequently, various legal obstacles would have to be removed. On the other hand, no use would be made of the law to redress any imbalance in the power of the opposing social forces: the appropriate stance for the State was 'absolute impartiality.' Similarly, any measures to regulate the operation of the labour market, such as compulsory arbitration, were ruled out. The merits of collective bargaining were already being appreciated. It was hoped that conflict might be reduced through the voluntary use of joint regulation. In a society where freedom of contract was promoted the desire, of the signatories of the Minority Report, for the facilitation of legal enforceability of collective bargains was understandable. With respect to the legal status of trade unions there was to be no incorporation; to lay down positively the terms upon which incorporation would be granted would be too tendentious. Moreover, in a laissez-faire world, to disallow objects of a voluntary association was seen as undesirable:

> it is not the duty of the State . . . punish unsocial conduct, and that such part of the conduct of the unions as is unsocial without being criminal ought not in good policy to be visited by legislative disabilities or penalties.[65]

Again, as discussed, it was felt desirable to restrict access to the courts. The implementation of this restriction in the form of section 4 was rather at odds with the desire to facilitate optional legal enforceability of collective agreements. The Minority Report and the parliamentary

---

[63] Report of Inspectors of Factories, 1870, (C 215) paras 48–49.
[64] Royal Commission, above n 61, paras 248–76.
[65] Royal Commission, above n 1 at p lxiii.

debates both contain references to the value of a policy of State neutrality but, clearly, it would be erroneous to assume that a policy of non-intervention can be equated with neutrality. At any one time the balance of social and economic forces may be heavily in favour of one class in society. Accordingly, to omit to redress the balance by legislative intervention is to favour one class. The legislation of 1871 permitted a relatively free hand to monopoly forces of capital and labour but this was scarcely a policy of neutrality.

The Trade Union Act of 1871 survived until 1971. However, its significance to UK labour law is much more fundamental than that. The Act, based on the Minority Report, sought to allow trade unions to combine in a meaningful way by allowing for the exercise of the right to strike. Protection from the civil law was achieved through a combination of not electing for incorporation and failing to provide an alternative means of suing a trade union. In effect the privilege bestowed by section 4 of the 1906 Act appears for the first time. Protection from the criminal law was less resolute. Trade union internal affairs were also to be kept outwith the gaze of the courts. Trade unions were to remain unincorporated associations with quasi-corporate features—a state of affairs that endures to this day.

2

Labour Law 1880–1900

THE PERIOD FROM 1880 to 1900 was an important one in the development of British industrial relations. By the end of the century there had been a significant increase in the role played by collective bargaining; trade union membership had increased from around 700,000 in 1889 to over 2,000,000 in 1900[1]; employers too had become more organised; politically there was a tendency to move away from Lib-Labour. What of labour law? The 1880s were decidedly quiet. Little in the way of litigation appears to have taken place and a limited amount of legislation was enacted. Further reform of the factories legislation did take place; the Employers Liability Act was passed in 1880 and a number of other measures were enacted. However, both the volume and significance of legislative and judicial activity was much greater in the 1890s. Moreover, and perhaps more importantly, a greater role was envisaged for legal regulation.

LITIGATION

During the 1880s there appears to have been very little in the way of litigation brought against trade unions. The explanation most often given for this is the economic depression which existed during much of this decade and which reduced trade union activity. It is then argued that employers had little need to have recourse to law. This was to change during the 1890s when employers had much more extensive recourse to the courts. It should also be said that the beginning of the decade was notable for the emergence of 'new unionism' and this phenomenon appears to have considerably exacerbated establishment

---

[1] HA Clegg et al, *A History of British Trade Unions Since 1889* vol 1 1889–1910, Appendix (Oxford: Clarendon Press, 1964).

concern over trade union power. Indeed it has been argued that during the 1890s the courts acted in line with public opinion and displayed greater hostility towards trade unions.

One dimension of trade union activity which one might have expected to provoke litigation is picketing—partly because of the importance of this weapon to 'new unionism'. Two of the major cases of the 1890s deal with this: *Connor v Kent*[2] and *Lyon* v *Wilkins*.[3] Given that the former was decided in 1891 it is remarkable for its restrained approach. The case arose out of the threat of strike action over a demarcation dispute and the employment of non-unionists. The decision in *Connor* centred around section 7 of the 1875 Act and the court started from the premise that the underlying policy of the Act was to relax the law in favour of trade unions. Thus the court inclined to the view that paragraph 1 which penalised intimidation required the threat of personal violence. The common law of simple conspiracy was also referred to and the view was expressed that provided trade unionists were acting to further their own interests then liability for simple conspiracy was unlikely—a view which might be said to give the benefit of *Mogul Steamship v McGregor*[4] to trade unions. The court acknowledging that

> where the object is to benefit oneself, it can seldom, perhaps it can never, be effected without some consequent loss or injury to someone else.[5]

A similar approach to the question of intimidation was taken in the Scottish case of *Agnew v Munro* where it was said that

> To prove the statutory charge I think it is sufficient to prove that the intimidation used was such as to induce serious apprehension of violence in the mind of a man of ordinary courage.[6]

Sympathy for the aims of trade unionism was certainly not to the fore in the subsequent Court of Appeal decision in *Lyon* v *Wilkins*. The case arose out of a run of the mill picketing situation. The court held that picketing for the purpose of persuading individuals not to work amounted to the crime of watching and besetting; albeit that communicating information per se was said not to be unlawful. The question of whether the tort of inducing breach of contract would have had to

[2] [1891] 2 QB 545.
[3] [1896] 1 Ch 811.
[4] (1889) 23 QBD 598.
[5] *Connor*, above n 3, at p 563.
[6] (1891) 18 R 22.

be committed does not seem to have been viewed as relevant; consequently the approach would seem to deny any meaning to the words 'wrongfully and without legal authority' in section 7. The decision meant that any successful picketing would almost certainly be a criminal offence: 'You cannot make a strike effective without doing more than is lawful.'[7] A restrictive approach is also evidenced by the case of *Farmer* v *Wilson*.[8] The case involved the picketing of a depot ship which had on board seamen contracted to a shipping federation. However, the federation did not possess a Board of Trade licence to engage or supply seamen and section 111 of the Merchant Shipping Act 1894 made it a criminal offence to engage or supply seamen in the absence of such a licence. It was argued on behalf of the pickets that no offence had been committed under section 7 because that section only operated where a person was compelled to abstain from doing or to do any act which he had a legal right to do or abstain from doing. It was said that the seamen beset were engaged in what they had no legal right to do: 'They were taking their daily wages under an illegal contract.'[9] The argument for the defendant was rejected:

> The contract may have been an improper or illegal contract but there was nothing to prevent these persons going on board the ship and staying there . . . They had a legal right to be there, and the respondents had no right to beset them.[10]

The argument the other way is not without its merits. One might argue that what the pickets objected to was not the fact that the seamen were on board the ship but that they were contracted to the federation. Assuming that the contractual arrangement was tainted by illegality then the pickets were seeking to persuade the seamen to abstain from doing something that they did not have a legal right to do. Nevertheless, in the aftermath of *Lyon,* it is hardly surprising that such a line of defence was unsuccessful.

A restrictive law of picketing would obviously threaten to curtail trade union power. Similarly any expansion, at common law, of the economic torts is likely to pose problems for trade unionists. The main controversy in the case law, during the 1890s, was over whether intentional interference in the economic interests of someone else was

[7] *Lyon,* above at p 820.
[8] 69 LJQB 496.
[9] *Ibid* at p 506.
[10] *Ibid.*

actionable. *Temperton v Russell* dealt with the tort of inducing breach of contract in a non controversial way.[11] More interestingly, it also suggested that liability may exist for persuading someone not to enter into contractual relations. Esher MR denied the validity of any distinction between these two bases of liability:

> I do not think that distinction can prevail. There was the same wrongful intent in both cases, wrongful because malicious. There was the same kind of injury to the plaintiff . . .[12]

However, the basis of liability in the landmark case of *Lumley v Gye* had been much narrower, liability in tort being contingent on the inducee's breach of contract.[13] As Erle J explained:

> the class of cases referred to rests upon the principle that the procurement of the violation of the right is a cause of action . . .[14]

However, the underlying thrust of Esher MR's dictum must be that to intentionally inflict economic harm upon another is prima facie unlawful. This was also the view of Hawkins J in *Trollope v London Building Trades Federation.*[15] As with developments in the law of picketing the judiciary did not speak with one voice over the way forward for the economic torts. Whilst *Temperton* favoured expansion of liability, obiter remarks in *Connor,* as we have seen, had indicated that a less interventionist stance might be employed by the courts. *Jenkinson v Neild* was another decision in the *Connor* mould.[16] *Jenkinson* was decided by the Divisional Court in 1892 and had the unusual feature of being an action brought against an employer. The case centred over the operation of a blacklist and was an action for damages for conspiracy. The plaintiffs lost and it was pointed out that 'no doubt the act complained of was calculated to injure a man to a certain extent, but it was done entirely for trade purposes and to defeat and counteract the purposes of an opposing trade union'. As Mather LJ said: 'this was a case governed by the famous *Mogul Steamship* case.' Whilst the case was brought against the employer it was, nevertheless, a clear declaration that *Mogul* was applicable in the field of industrial relations.

---

[11] [1893] 1 QB 715.
[12] *Ibid* at p 728.
[13] 2 E. & B. 216.
[14] *Ibid* at 231.
[15] (1895) 72 LT 342.
[16] (1892) 8 TLR 549.

By far the most important economic tort decision of the 1890s was *Allen* v *Flood* which established that the intentional infliction of economic harm upon another was not, per se, actionable.[17] A decision to the contrary would have greatly increased the extent to which trade union officials might be harassed by the threat of litigation. The prospect of such an extension in liability was clearly found disturbing by at least one of the majority in the Lords:

> I can imagine no greater danger to the community than that a jury should be at liberty to impose the penalty of paying damages for acts which are otherwise lawful, because they choose, without any legal definition of the term, to say that they are malicious. No one would know what his rights were.[18]

Such an extension would, in any event, have been difficult to contemplate in a market economy society. It is undoubtedly the case that, if the decision in *Allen* had gone the other way, a defence of justification would have had to be developed; what allowance this would have made for the promotion of trade union interests will always remain a moot point. It is interesting to note that in *Allen* the trial judge found no evidence of conspiracy. It is not clear upon reading the judgments of the majority what difference such a finding would have made. However, the fact that this issue was not properly explored would make it easier for the court in *Quinn* to adopt an approach hostile to trade unionism.

Mogul Steamship and *Allen* differ in that the latter did not involve the element of combination. However, they share the same underlying rationale in that they assume that the courts should not seek to say what is unfair economic pressure. Instead, the economic torts should provide a remedy where independently unlawful acts have been committed in order to inflict economic harm. The policy justification for this was to be found in the Court of Appeal judgment of Fry LJ in *Mogul*:

> To draw a line between fair and unfair competition, between what is unreasonable and unreasonable, passes the power of the courts.[19]

Ironically, in view of his stance in the subsequent case of *Quinn*, Halsbury LC in *Mogul* saw great danger in allowing liability on the basis of mere malicious infliction of economic harm:

---

[17] [1898] AC 1.
[18] *Ibid* at p 118, per Lord Herschell.
[19] *Mogul* above n 3 at p 626.

it is impossible to suggest any malicious intention to injure rival traders, except in the sense that in proportion as one withdraws trade that other people might get, you, to that extent, injure a person's trade when you appropriate the trade to yourself. If such an injury, and the motive of its infliction, is examined and tested, upon principle, and can be truly asserted to be a malicious motive within the meaning of the law that prohibits malicious injury to other people, all competition must be malicious and consequently unlawful, or sufficient reductio ad absurdum to dispose of that head of suggested unlawfulness.[20]

The case law of the 1890s paints a picture of considerable judicial uncertainty as to the extent to which common law regulation of economic power is appropriate. One might, however, have thought that the decision in *Allen* would have signified that exponents of minimal intervention had won out. Any such thoughts were soon dispelled. An injunction was granted in the 1899 case of *Walters* v *Green* to restrain the defenders from conspiring to persuade individuals not to work for an employer.[21] The decision in *Quinn* v *Leathem* struck a much bigger blow.[22] The case stemmed from an attempt to persuade an employer to employ union rather than non-union labour. In furtherance of the dispute a customer of the employer was persuaded not to enter into further contracts with him. The House of Lords held for the plaintiffs despite the fact that no act unlawful, per se, had been committed. For the Law Lords the most significant element in the case appeared to be the finding of conspiracy. Later cases would focus strongly on this element.

The decision in *Quinn* was delivered more or less contemporaneously with that in *Taff Vale*.[23] Taken together they threatened to entangle any attempt to take industrial action in a web of litigation. Industrial action would frequently involve the commission of the tort of inducing breach of contract but, after *Quinn*, even where it did not there would still be the possibility of liability for an unlawful conspiracy. In trade disputes a finding that a number of trade unionists had conspired together would generally be easy to arrive at. As I have indicated, it is puzzling that in *Allen* v *Flood* it was held, on the facts, that there was no element of conspiracy. Many points might be made about the decision in *Quinn* but it suffices for present purposes to mention but

---

[20] [1892] AC 25 at p 37.
[21] [1899] 2 Ch 696.
[22] [1901] AC 495.
[23] *Taff Vale Railway Co v Amalgamated Society of Railway Servants* [1901] AC 426.

a few. First, a number of the dicta in the case are simply not reconcilable with the decision in *Allen*; for example,

> if the above reasoning is correct, *Lumley v Gye* was rightly decided, as I am of the opinion it clearly was. Further the principle involved in it cannot be confined to inducements to break . . . contracts. The principle which underlies the decision reaches all wrongful acts done intentionally to damage a particular individual and actually damaging him. *Temperton v Russell* ought to have been decided and may be upheld on this principle.[24]

At the time there must have been considerable concern that the authority of *Allen* would be steadily eroded. Second, assuming that the basis of liability in *Quinn* was simple conspiracy, the issue arises as to the circumstances in which the aims of a combination of trade unionists would be viewed as legitimate. After all, the desire to replace non-union labour with trade unionists would seem to be a standard trade union aim. Moreover, it was undoubtedly the case that the law of conspiracy allowed that the aims of a combination might serve to prevent liability arising. To quote from the judgment of Lord Shand:

> while combination of different persons in pursuit of a trade object was lawful, although resulting in such injury to others as may be caused by legitimate competition in labour, yet that combination for no such object, but in pursuit merely of a malicious purpose to injure another, would be clearly unlawful . . .[25]

Indeed in *Quinn* itself Lord Lindley was prepared to assume that the defendants 'acted as they did in furtherance of what they considered the interests of union men . . .'[26] However, decisions on any defence of justification are likely to be influenced by a judge's view of the merits of a dispute and the results may be capricious. This might be thought to be borne out by comparing *Mogul Steamship* and *Jenkinson* on the one hand and *Quinn* on the other. Indeed in *Allen* Lord Shand had noted that a

> Combination of different persons in pursuit of a legitimate trade object occurred in the case of the *Mogul Steamship Co*, and was there held to be lawful. Combination for no such object but in pursuit really of a malicious

---

[24] *Quinn*, above n 21, at p 535, per Lord Lindley.
[25] *Ibid* at p 512. One may note that the feasibility of such a distinction must be doubted; what appears to be malicious from the point of view of the plaintiff may well be viewed as simple pursuit of self-interest by the defendant.
[26] *Ibid* at p 536.

purpose to ruin or injure another would, I should say, be clearly unlawful: but this case raised no such question.[27]

If such a question had arisen there are passages in Lord Shand's judgment which indicate that he may well have been sympathetic to trade unionists. Thus he says, with reference to *Temperton v Russell,*

> The case was one of competition in labour, which, in my opinion, is in all essentials analogous to competition in trade, and to which the same principles must apply. . .[28]

Can the apparent inconsistency in Lord Shand's approach be explained? It may be that his freedom of manoeuvre was restricted by the finding of the jury in *Quinn* that the aim of the conspirators was to injure the plaintiff rather than to further their own interests. Alternatively, Lord Shand's judgments may simply reflect the volatility of the law in the area of the economic torts.

The extent to which the existence of liabilities in respect of the economic torts would affect trade unions would, in turn, depend upon the remedies available. Prior to *Taff Vale* a union could not be sued in its own name. However, the 1890s were noteworthy for considerable use of interlocutory injunctions against union officials. One might also note that a number of statements, as to the factors to be taken into account in the granting of an injunction, would be heard, many times again, in the years ahead. Thus in *Lyon v Wilkins* North J acknowledged, as an argument in favour of granting the injunction sought, that

> in most of the cases in which trade unions are concerned the persons who are defending are such that a decision that there can be no remedy but damages would be equivalent to a decision that there cannot be any remedy at all.[29]

Kay LJ is also worth quoting:

> it seems to me to be very unlikely that any possible damage can result to them [. . .] from the granting of this injunction; whereas, on the other hand, if it is not granted very grave damage indeed may result to Messrs Lyon & Co.[30]

Without a shadow of doubt, of the cases which deal with a trade union's legal capacity, *Taff Vale* is by far the best known. However, its

---

[27] *Allen,* above n 17, at pp 168–69.
[28] *Ibid* at p 164 and see p 167.
[29] *Lyon,* above n 2, at p 818.
[30] *Ibid* at p 828.

very fame obscures the evolution of the law in this area during the 1890s. During this period the courts grappled with the problems posed by the unincorporated status of trade unions. As a result of procedural changes in the 1870s it might have been thought possible to sue a trade union in a representative action.[31] An attempt to do so was made in the case of *Temperton* v *Russell* in 1893 but was unsuccessful, the court holding that such an action was only competent where the union was asserting or defending a proprietary right. This decision would clearly not assist employers litigating over industrial action. Another possible route was to bring the trustees of a union into the action. Section 9 of the 1871 Act empowered the trustees of any registered trade union to defend any action 'touching or concerning the property, right, or claim to property of the trade union . . .' The ambit of the section is harder to ascertain:

> are the legal proceedings contemplated by the section limited to actions which concern specific property or does any claim which threatens the general assets of the union fall within its scope? . . . Within the narrow construction are claims arising out of particular property, such as a breach of covenant in respect of land vested in the trustees. Within the wide construction fall claims arising out of the activities of the union, but not incidental to the ownership of particular property, as, for example, a claim for damages for wrongful dismissal by an employee.[32]

Dicta in a case prior to the House of Lords decision in *Taff Vale* had lent support to the wider construction. In *Linaker* v *Pilcher* Mr Justice Mathers had stated that

> an action for breach of contract entered into on behalf of the society would be an action touching their property: and likewise an action for damages for tort would be an action touching the property of the society.[33]

That the case of *Linaker* was the cause of some concern to the supporters of labour is evident from the parliamentary debates on the 1906 Act. The view being expressed was that a wide construction of section

---

[31] The procedural obstacles which existed in England as to the suing of voluntary associations by means of a representative action do not appear to have posed a problem in Scotland. Cases from 1862 onwards allow an unincorporated body to be used in its own name 'provided its responsible officers and managers are also called in their representative capacity.'

[32] H Vester and AH Gardner, *Trade Union Law and Practice* (London: Sweet and Maxwell, 1958), p 162.

[33] 1901 17 TLR 256 at p 258.

9 could nullify the effect of section 4.[34] While the Government described such fears as being 'purely imaginary' they led to the modification of section 4(2). As a result, it was expressly provided that the trustees could not be sued in respect of any tortuous act committed by or on behalf of the union in contemplation or in furtherance of a trade dispute. Subsequent to the 1906 Act there were dicta going either way as to the proper construction of section 9.

At first instance in *Taff Vale* Farwell J treated a registered trade union as a quasi-corporation. This was established by deducing the intention of the legislature in enacting the 1871 Act. In the words of Farwell J (whose judgment was adopted by the Lord Chancellor and Lord Brampton in the House of Lords):

> The proper rule of construction of statutes such as these is that in the absence of express contrary intention the Legislature intends that the creature of the statute shall have the same duties and that its funds shall be subject to the same liabilities as the general law would impose on a private individual doing the same thing. It would require very clear and express words of enactment to induce me to hold that the Legislature had in fact legalised the existence of such irresponsible bodies with such wide capacity for evil.[35]

Farwell J acknowledged that the registration of a trade union did not amount to incorporation. On the other hand, he found it significant that registration resulted in the granting of two of the essential attributes of a corporation—the capacity to own property and the capacity to act by agents.

The decision of Farwell J received short shrift in the Court of Appeal. The Master of the Rolls gave the only judgment which was a mere four sides long. The view was taken that a matter of statutory interpretation was at stake and a straightforward one at that. It was assumed that if Parliament had intended that a trade union could be sued in its own name then this would have been expressly provided for or provision would have been made for the incorporation of trade unions. This argument was supported by reference to companies, building societies and industrial and provident societies legislation. It was further pointed out that

> by section 9 of the Act of 1871 it is expressly enacted that the trustees of a trade union registered under the Act . . . may bring or defend any action in

---

[34] See ch. 4.
[35] *Taff Vale*, above n 22, at pp 430–31.

any Court of Law touching the property of the trade union—a most remarkable section if as is argued for the plaintiffs and held by the learned judge,
the purview of the Act is that a trade union can be sued in its registered
name. If this were so, what is the good of this section expressly enabling
the trustees or other officer of the union to sue or be sued in respect of
property ?'[36]

I would submit that the reasoning of the Court of Appeal is highly
persuasive.

Two lines of thought can be found in the judgments in the House of
Lords. The majority did little more than endorse the reasoning of
Farwell J and treated a union as a quasi-corporation. The minority
view, which is to be found in the judgments of Lords MacNaughten
and Lindley, is that, while one can sue a union in its registered name,
the action is a representative one. It must be said that discerning the
ratio of the two minority judgments is somewhat problematic. In the
main this is because no explanation is given of how, if by suing a union
in its registered name one is essentially bringing a representative action,
the numerous and significant technical difficulties of bringing a representative action are overcome. Nevertheless, Lord MacNaughten does
remark that 'The registered name is nothing more than a collective
name for all the members'[37] and Lord Lindley states that

> The Act appears to me to indicate with sufficient clearness that the regis-
> tered name is one which may be used to denote the union as a unincorpo-
> rated society in legal proceedings as well as for business and other purposes
> . . . it is only a more convenient mode of proceeding than that which have to
> be adopted if the name could not be used.[38]

Several years later Lord Lindley was to remark, in similar vein, that 'A
trade union is, and its name is only a convenient designation for, an
unincorporated society of individuals . . .'[39] Whether one looks to the
judgments of the minority or majority the reasoning is far from impres-
sive. As good a critique as any is furnished by the judgments of the
Court of Appeal.

Had an assessment of judicial attitudes been arrived at, on the stance
of the courts, in the decade prior to the decisions in *Taff Vale* and
Quinn it would have been rather mixed. From a trade union point of

[36] [1901] 1 QB 170 at p 176, per AL Smith MR.
[37] *Taff Vale*, above n 22, at pp 439–40.
[38] *Ibid* at p 445.
[39] *Yorkshire Miners' Association v Howden* [1905] AC 256 at p 280.

view, the case law on the economic torts, picketing and the legal capacity of a union were worrying but probably not overly so. Certainly, in all three areas one finds evidence of divergent approaches to the issues raised. With regard to picketing one finds that the less favourable decisions are more concentrated towards the end of the decade. To the extent that judges were indeed responding to changes in public opinion then that transformation must have been a gradual process. The area which perhaps demonstrates the greatest volatility is the common law of economic torts. The judges were caught in a dilemma between achieving consistency in all areas of economic pressure and adopting a special approach for labour relations. However, once *Taff Vale* and *Quinn* were decided matters took on a very different perspective; those decisions cast a very long shadow. To some extent, though with no great conviction, *Quinn* may be explained by the troubled and uncertain development of the economic torts; no such excuse can be offered for *Taff Vale*.

THE ROYAL COMMISSION

A Royal Commission on Labour was set up in 1891 'to enquire into the relations between capital and labour with a view to their improvement.'[40] It followed concern over the unrest associated with the rise of 'New Unions'. However,

> that unrest subsided before the Commission reported and the majority report declared relations to be at their best when both sides were well organised and negotiation was facilitated by voluntary collective bargaining procedures.[41]

More far-reaching reports have been known to emanate from Royal Commissions; the report was decidedly cautious in making recommendations. Nevertheless, it is suggested that the report provides useful evidence of contemporary establishment attitudes towards industrial relations and the role of law. The premise of the report, based on the views of both sides of industry, was that the route to industrial peace lay through collective bargaining:

---

[40] Fifth (final) Report of the Royal Commission on Labour (Cd 7421, 1892)
[41] EH Hunt, *British Labour History 1815–1914*, pp 325–26 (London: Weidenfeld & Nicolson, 1981).

where a skilled trade is well organised, good relations tend to prevail and countless minor quarrels are obviated or nipped in the bud.[42]

It was not imagined that industrial conflict could be eliminated, merely that joint regulation would produce greater stability. Despite the fact that the Commission believed that

> when both sides in a trade are strongly organised and in possession of considerable financial resources, a trade conflict, when it does occur, may be on a very large scale, very protracted and very costly.[43]

It is interesting to note that the Commissioners believed that strong organisation on both sides and a 'fairly equal' balance of power were pre-requisites of successful joint regulation. Whilst in 1867 there had been some understanding of the need for strong organisation there was little understanding of the need for a balance of power. Two reasons might be offered. First, joint regulation was very much in its infancy in 1867 and the role of the balance of power in producing stable industrial relations would have been unlikely to have been perceived. Second, any notion of balance, in a matter to be settled by market forces, would have been difficult to reconcile with the tenets of economic liberalism.

Given that joint regulation was a worthy aspiration it is not surprising that the Commission turned to look at ways in which collective bargaining might be developed and improved, particular attention being paid to modes of conciliation and arbitration. Of the specific matters dealt with in the report one of the more interesting, given subsequent debates about the amenability of collective bargaining in the UK to the legal process, is the treatment of the distinction between conflicts of rights and conflicts of interest. The majority viewed conflicts of rights as adjudicable matters; such issues

> being for the most part connected with the application of rules already recognised, can usually be dealt with and settled, upon the ascertainment of facts, without much difficulty by simple methods or institutions of a judicial kind.[44]

Where a wages board existed a standing committee might be established to deal with such questions; in the absence of a wages board a joint committee of employers and employees might be set up to deal solely with rights issues. Similarly, for the Webbs 'rights' issues were

---

[42] Royal Commission on Labour, above n 40, para 90.
[43] *Ibid* at para 92.
[44] *Ibid* at para 130.

highly adjudicable. They believed that when the application of an agreement was the question at issue

> the settlement should be automatic, rapid and inexpensive. The ideal machinery for this class of cases would, in fact, be a peripatetic calculating machine.[45]

When it came to conflicts of interest the Royal Commission noted that

> the method of judicial arbitration has, as experience shows, not yet been successfully applied to this class of questions, except under special circumstances and in a few industries . . .[46]

The majority believed that the reason for this was because

> such questions are in fact not suitable for judicial decision. They are questions of practical politics, in which the relative strength of the opposite parties is an element that can hardly be left out of account.[47]

The minority believed the explanation to be even more fundamental and one that lay in the realm of disputes over questions of political economy:

> The points at issue are not such as admit of decision upon any principles which both sides admit. In the recent colossal dispute in the coal trade . . . the prior question must first have been settled of whether wages ought to follow prices, or prices wages, a point of social or industrial policy on which there is no agreement.[48]

In any event, arbitration over conflicts of interest would present a number of difficulties: there may be

> a difficulty in finding suitable arbitrators. Either the arbitrator is quite unconnected with industrial work, and then the process of informing his mind upon the matter is too long and costly, or he is in some way connected with the industrial world, and then one party or the other is apt to suspect him of bias and partiality.[49]

Moreover, the respective bargaining power of the parties would often mean that one side would have considerably more interest than the other in making use of an independent arbitrator. In the words of the Commission,

---

[45] S & B Webb, *Industrial Democracy* (London: Longmans, Green, 1920), p 184.
[46] Royal Commission on Labour, above n 38, para 130.
[47] *Ibid* at para 137.
[48] *Ibid* at p 145.
[49] *Ibid* at para 136.

in cases where very strong organisation enables the workmen fully to hold their own, and even gives them advantages in bargaining, they are the more apt to be averse to arbitration by individuals regarding these general questions, while employers are more disposed to resort to it. Certainly the desire for arbitration on general questions, and especially, for some form of State arbitration, seems usually to be stronger among workmen of poorly organised trades.[50]

The Commission devoted a considerable amount of time to canvassing the merits of possible legal reforms. One issue discussed was the legal status of collective agreements, the Commission believing that a combination of a lack of legal personality on the part of trade unions and the effect of section 4(4) of the 1871 Act prevented collective agreements from being legally enforceable. The Commissioners considered proposals which would have allowed trade unions and employer's associations to

> be able by registration to acquire legal personality and to enter into industrial agreements for specific terms, enforceable by monetary penalties of a limited amount upon the organisations parties to it, and upon other persons at any time during the terms of the agreement members of such organisations.[51]

In the eyes of the Commissioners the value of such a reform would be determined by whether greater adhesion to collectively agreed terms was secured. More particularly, would the respective organisations who were party to collective agreements be able to control their memberships? For example, the question was posed as to whether an organisation 'would continue to be liable for any breach of agreement by those who had ceased to be members.'[52] The report continues:

> This is an important point; for though it would certainly seem a strong measure to make an association legally responsible for the conduct of persons who were no longer its members, on the other hand if this was not done the scheme hardly appears to dispose of the old difficulty of enforcing legal penalties against a mass of working men.[53]

However, a paradox arose in that in the strongly organised trades

> agreements are, as matters stand now, best observed, even without any right to sue for compensation, while on the other hand a weak and poor union,

[50] *Ibid* at para 137.
[51] *Ibid* at para 150.
[52] *Ibid.*
[53] *Ibid.*

even if endowed with legal personality, and made legally responsible for any breach of agreement by the persons who have ceased to be members of it, would constitute but a feeble guarantee to employers that the terms of the agreement would be loyally observed.[54]

Ultimately, therefore, the report did not recommend facilitating legal enforcement; it was most needed where organisation was weak but equally that was where it was least likely to be effective.

A grouping within the majority were more inclined to facilitate legal enforcement—as is clear from their observations appended to the report—and it is interesting to assess their position.[55] They believed

that the extension of liberty to bodies of workmen or employers to acquire fuller legal personality than that which they at present possess is desirable in order to afford, when both parties wish it, the means of securing the observance, at least for fixed periods, of . . . collective agreements . . .[56]

It was suggested that this would

result in the better observance for definitive periods of agreements . . . (and) . . . would also afford a better basis for arbitration in industrial disputes than any which has yet been suggested.[57]

More interestingly, the view was expressed that

further legislation is desirable in order to bring the law into harmony with the present state of facts and public opinion.[58]

Since 1871 there had been an increasing acceptance of collective bargaining and trade unionism: collective agreements are 'on the whole, in accordance with the public interest and with the circumstances of modern industry.'[59] One could certainly have argued that to have moved towards treating such agreements in the same fashion as other contracts would have been a recognition of the value placed by society on conducting industrial relations by joint regulation. Wholly consistently, this section of the majority also believed that collective agreements

---

[54] Royal Commission on Labour, above n 38, at para 151.
[55] See observations appended to the report, pp 115 et seq.
[56] *Ibid* at p 116.
[57] *Ibid.*
[58] *Ibid.*
[59] *Ibid.*

would be subject, like agreements between individuals, to the restrictions flowing from the common law doctrine in discountenancing restraint of trade.[60]

Nevertheless, their final conclusion was distinctly tepid in that

> The evidence does not show that public opinion is as yet ripe for the changes in the legal status of Trade Associations which we have suggested; but we have thought it to be desirable to indicate what may . . . ultimately prove to be the most natural and reasonable solution of some at least of the difficulties which have been brought to our notice.[61]

The Commission also considered whether special tribunals should be set up to deal with cases involving employment contracts. In rejecting such proposals the same pragmatism was demonstrated that was evidenced in the discussion of the legal enforceability of collective agreements. Thus the establishment of such tribunals would be of limited value since

> in this country, the only disputes which lead to serious actual conflict are those relating to the terms, not of existing, but of future agreements.[62]

In addition, there appears to have been a prejudice against any form of legislative intervention. Here, for example, all that was at stake was ease of access to the courts; there was no question of seeking to regulate collective bargaining by law. Nevertheless, the report was quite content to rely on the power of social forces to safeguard the interests of employees, it being noted that

> in large and well organised trades the workmen employees have already quite sufficient means of obtaining remedy for grievances connected with existing or implied agreements or trade customs.[63]

Quite consistently social power would not be legally reinforced, even where it was manifestly unable to protect workers. So

> in unorganised occupations, especially in the case of unskilled labour, a dispute on questions of this kind is more likely to be terminated by cessation of the engagement between an employer and an employee than by a resort to any tribunal however constituted.[64]

---

[60] *Ibid* at p 117.
[61] *Ibid* at p 119.
[62] *Ibid* at para 296.
[63] *Ibid*.
[64] *Ibid*.

Various suggestions as to compulsory arbitration were aired and the Commission considered proposals such that strikes and lock-outs should be unlawful unless arbitration had first been resorted to. They did not favour this given the practical obstacle of finding a method to enforce a law prohibiting strikes and lock-outs against large bodies of employees and employers. This early and frank recognition of the unworkable nature of such proposals is striking. Building upon their view concerning facilitating legal enforceability of collective agreements the same grouping within the majority appended observations with the aim of encouraging arbitration backed by legal sanctions. However, it seemed to them (despite their greater inclination towards the legal process)

> to be obvious (1) that the State cannot compel either individuals or bodies of men to enter into agreements; and (2) that the State cannot compel employers to give employment or workmen to do work upon terms which they do not respectively accept. In as much as lock-outs and strikes are, in practice, the assertation of these essential liberties on the part of employers and workmen, it is clear that the State cannot prohibit acts of this kind and compel the parties to resort to tribunals of any sort instead.[65]

It was felt that if trade unions could secure legal personality they could, voluntarily, enter into legally binding contracts to submit, present or future, questions to arbitration, the hope being expressed that if

> a more concrete guarantee was given to arbitration, it would be more frequently restored to by those who have a bona fide preference for it over more violent modes of settling differences.[66]

Finally, it falls to be considered what the Commission actually did recommend (it may be noted that four of the seven trade unionists on the Commission signed a minority report). The Commission commended the work done by the Labour Department of the Board of Trade and wished to see its expansion. Their main recommendation was that legislation should endow the Board of Trade with discretionary powers with regard to conciliation and arbitration in trade disputes. This recommendation was implemented by the Conciliation Act, 1896. It is important to note that, under the Act, an arbitrator could only be appointed on the application of both parties.[67] Moreover, the Act contained no mechanism to require the parties to

---

[65] See observations appended to the report, p 117.
[66] *Ibid* at p 119.
[67] S 2(1).

accept the outcome of any arbitration. It also deserves to be pointed out that the recommended role in respect of conciliation and arbitration recommended by the Commission was, in practice, already undertaken by the Board of Trade. It was felt, though, that legislation would give the Board greater authority:

> This Bill would enable them to say to the parties: 'This legislature thinks it our duty to place the matter fairly before you.'[68]

The envisaged legislation can be seen as an avowal of State policy that joint regulation, assisted where necessary by conciliation or arbitration, was the way forward. The Commission did not favour the legal regulation of collective bargaining. All it was prepared to offer the two sides of industry was certain facilities which they could utilise if they wished. This approach had both a pragmatic and ideological basis. The pragmatic base stemmed from the fact that the conduct of industrial relations by voluntary collective bargaining was, in fact, conducive to industrial peace. The Commissioners placed their faith firmly in the institutions of voluntary collective bargaining, the view being expressed that

> the custom . . . (of collective bargaining) . . . may become so strong, even without assistance from law, as to afford in such trades an almost certain and practically sufficient guarantee for the carrying out of industrial agreements and awards.[69]

The ideological basis, on the other hand, was rooted in an aversion to State intervention (this aversion not being confined to the sphere of industrial relations). Whilst Dicey believed that this period bore witness to a decline in the popular authority of the doctrine of laissez-faire the report is still very much in keeping with it. An indication of the continued influence of laissez-faire is revealed through the comments of the Commission as to the dangers of employer and trade unions 'combining together to control an industry injuriously to the public interest.'[70] The report simply states that

> it may be hoped that such combinations would in the end either fall from within or be defeated by competition arising from unexpected quarters, or be destroyed by changes in methods of production.[71]

[68] Parl. Deb., 30.6.1896, vol 42, HC, col 425.
[69] Royal Commission on Labour, above n 40, p 53.
[70] *Ibid* at p 112.
[71] *Ibid*.

Nevertheless, the influence of laissez-faire was definitely on the wane. In the House of Commons in 1895 Mundella justified the need for a conciliation bill on the basis of the damage to the public interest, arising from the economic harm caused by trade disputes. Interestingly enough, many people at this time seem to have viewed 'public opinion' as a neutral force but, at the same time, as a potent weapon that could be deployed to help resolve disputes. Thus one MP stated

> Neither side to a great industrial dispute could carry on the conflict long if the force of public opinion was against them; but there was the difficulty of forming an intelligent and well instructed public opinion. If there could be an authoritative body—a body whom the public could trust—to make a report as to what ought to be done in the future, much would be done to bring a conflict to a termination.[72]

The Commission were not sympathetic to suggestions that the law should step in to regulate terms and conditions of employment. In relation to restricting hours of work the Commission would countenance setting limits by law only where the length of the working week presented a risk to the health and safety of the employees concerned. Thus

> It has been pointed out . . . that, under section 8 of the Factory and Workshops Act, 1891, the Secretary of State has power to establish special rules for the conduct of manufacturing processes which he may certify to be, in his opinion, dangerous or injurious to health. It seems to be the fact that physical exhaustion increases the risk of accident or the susceptibility to disease in some occupations, and we think that the powers of the Secretary of State under this section should be expressly extended so as to include the regulation of hours in the certified industries.[73]

Even where there was such a risk it was preferable that the matter be dealt with by collective bargaining. For example,

> the miners are, moreover, in almost every district a very powerful and highly organised body of workmen, and we do not think that it has yet been proved that they are unable to obtain by voluntary agreement with employers the hours which are best suited to the circumstances and interest of the industry in each district.[74]

Dicey saw the Commission's report as having important consequences in the longer term:

---

[72] Vol 34, col 834.
[73] Royal Commission on Labour, above n 40, p 105.
[74] *Ibid.*

We have reached a merely transitory stage in the effort of the State to act as arbitrator. The attempt, if not given up, must be carried out to its logical conclusion, and assume the shape of compulsory arbitration which is a mere euphemism for the regulation of labour by the State, acting probably through the courts.[75]

Certainly, it is clear, from the observations appended to the report, that a significant section of the majority would have regarded greater legalisation of industrial relations as a natural development. Again, some trade unions were in favour of compulsory arbitration at this time. The unions concerned belonged to areas where labour organisation was weak and what, in fact, was probably desired was legal regulation of wages. Where trade unionism was stronger compulsory arbitration was unlikely to be in demand. Employers too were unlikely to be in favour, viewing it both as an infringement of their 'right to manage' and 'on its economic side, as indefensible an interference with industrial freedom as a legal fixing of wage rates'.[76]

It was also the case that the signatories to the Minority Report (all trade unionists) wished to see much greater State intervention in society to better the working and living conditions of the working class:

The social and economic progress of the workers depends . . . mainly upon the systematic development of democratic public activity in its three principal forms—the national or municipal administration of such industries as can conveniently be managed socially, the regulation of private enterprise in industries not yet taken over by the community, and the public provision, through the taxation of rent and similarly unearned incomes, of educational and other facilities necessary for the mental and moral development of all classes of the community.[77]

Greater legal regulation of employment matters was desired such as the shortening of the working day—a demand which was TUC policy by 1890.[78] In the case of government departments, the minority advocated that an order in council should prescribe eight hours as the normal maximum working day. In the case of private enterprise some industries might be regulated by special Acts. More generally,

what is required is some continuous process of regulations, flexible enough to be adapted to the varied details of different industries, but not dependent

---

[75] AV Dicey, *Law and Public Opinion in England* 2nd edn (London: Macmillan, 1962) p 275.
[76] S & B Webb, above n 45 , at p 227.
[77] *Ibid* at p 129.
[78] BC Roberts *The Trades Union Congress* (London: Allen & Unwin, 1958), p 136.

upon incessant application to Parliament. Such a process is . . . to be found in a development of the system of Administrative or Provisional Orders by which so large a part of modern legislation is effected . . . an Eight Hours' Act should be passed, laying down the principle of a maximum working day, and authorising its application to particular industries, after due inquiry, by orders similar either to those made under the Factory and Workshop Acts, or to the Provisional Orders laid before Parliament on other subjects.[79]

Indeed a number of adherents of 'New Unionism' wished a minimum wage to be established by legislative fiat. This desire for greater state intervention was not shared by trade unionists of the older school. Thus we find Howell adamantly stating that 'an interference with the hours of adult male labour, . . . is outside the domain of law.'[80] Cole, in his discussion of the labour movement in the 1880s, noted that

Trade Unionism, under the control of the older leaders, had surrendered completely to laissez-faire ideas, just at the time when these ideas were wearing out in the face of the changing conditions of trade and industry. The leaders, with few exceptions, were as vehement as the employers against state interference, and believed in settling all issues by conciliation based on the assumption that the real interests of capital and labour were the same.[81]

The minority were opposed to incorporation (though, as we have seen, some unions would have welcomed compulsory arbitration at this time):

To expose the large amalgamated societies of the country with their accumulated funds, sometimes reaching a quarter of a million sterling, to be sued for damages by any employer in any part of the country, or by any discontented member or non-unionist, for the action of some branch secretary or delegate, would be a great injustice.[82]

The minority envisaged greater state intervention of a kind which was not in conflict with the 1871 settlement. They wished trade unions to be free to pursue their interests without fear of litigation while, at the same time, seeking greater legal protection for employees. They also took the view that the State should use its influence as a major contractor to promote better employment conditions. The first Fair Wages Resolution had already been passed and the minority declared that

---

[79] BC Roberts *The Trades Union Congress* (London: Allen & Unwin, 1958), p 133.
[80] G Howell, *Trade Unionism Old and New*, p 171.
[81] GDH Cole, *A Short History of the British Working Class Movement*, vol II, p 156 (London: G Allen and Unwin & Labour Publishing Co., 1926)
[82] Royal Commission on Labour, above n 40, p 146.

It should be regarded as one of the most important functions of public administration so to use its power and influence so as to mitigate seasonal irregularity of employment as far as possible . . . every public authority should take into consideration the state of the labour market in arranging at what season of the year it will have its work executed.[83]

Such recommendations were made in the belief that certain labour questions could only be solved by state and municipal ownership. Between 1900 and 1914 matters were to develop much more in line with the outlook of the minority than they might have anticipated.[84]

LEGAL REGULATION

The conclusions expressed by the majority, in the Royal Commission report, did not point towards a more legally regulated system of industrial relations. However, the serious consideration which was, in fact, given to ideas of that nature tended to suggest that proposals for legal intervention in industrial relations would be likely to receive serious consideration. Indeed, during the 1890s, it was the case that an increase in the actual extent of the legal regulation of employment conditions took place. Two of the most significant measures were the Railway Regulation Act 1893 and the Workmen's Compensation Act 1897. Against this backdrop, it must have seemed to contemporary observers that the terms and conditions which applied to workers would, in future, increasingly be regulated by law. It is significant that one finds that opposition to such legislation was more likely to be based on pragmatic considerations, such as perceived economic disadvantages, rather than a principled objection to the use of law. At this time, it may well have appeared inevitable that more such legislation would be enacted and that this might even extend to wages.[85] During the

---

[83] *Ibid* at p 141.

[84] See ch. 3.

[85] In the period with which this chapter is concerned no legislation was enacted regulating the level of wages. Nevertheless a number of measures were enacted to help combat abuse by employers over payment of wages: Truck Amendment Act 1887, Coal Mines Regulation Act 1887, Truck Act 1896. Also of note are s 24 of the Factories and Workshop Act 1891 and s 40 of the Factories and Workshop Act 1895. With a view to protecting piece workers in certain textile trades s 24 provided that an employer provide sufficient particulars 'to enable [an employee] to ascertain the rate of wages at which he is entitled to be paid for the work . . .' The section provided for a fine in the event of breach. The 1895 Act extended the provision to other textile trade and allowed the Secretary of State to extend it, by regulation, to other non-textile trades.

parliamentary debates on the 1892 Mines (Eight Hours) Bill one MP remarked:

> You cannot possibly limit and interfere with the hours of labour without, at the same time, limiting and interfering with the rate of wages.[86]

Such a view gained validity from the fact that the first Fair Wages Resolution had already been passed in 1891. Considerable support existed amongst many trade unionists for greater legal regulation—a stance which is clearly reflected in the minority report of the Royal Commission.

Before turning to examine the legal measures which were introduced it is worth examining the inception of the first Fair Wages Resolution. Such an administrative measure offered the State an alternative means of regulating terms and conditions of employment. The Fair Wages Resolution of 1891 provided

> That in the opinion of this House it is the duty of the Government in all Government contracts to make provision against the evils which have recently been disclosed before the House of Lords' sweating committee, and to insert such conditions as may prevent the abuses arising from subletting, and make every effort to serve the payment of the rate of wages generally accepted as current for a competent workman in his trade.

Such measures would later be viewed as auxiliary legislation. At the time, however, any commentator would have concluded that a trend towards greater use of regulatory legislation existed. A number of motives lay behind the passing of the resolution, almost certainly the strongest of which was simply to provide a minimum wage. Allied to this was a desire to restrict unfair competition. Was there any intention of lending support to collective bargaining by providing some restraint on under-cutting? Some supporters of the resolution undoubtedly had such aims. Nevertheless, the actual wording of the resolution made no specific mention of collective bargaining. It may well have been the case that those who supported such a link believed that its absence increased the chances of the resolution being passed by the Commons. The administration of the resolution left a great deal to be desired. The 1897 select committee noted that

> in certain quarters, there exists a great lack of confidence in the ability or in the desire of some of the departments to enforce the spirit and letter of the Resolution.[87]

[86] Parl. Deb., 23.3.1892, vol 2, HC, col 1579.
[87] Select Committee on Government Contracts (Fair Wages Resolutions), 1897.

The administration of the resolution in the 1890s paid little regard to collectively agreed terms and an employer might well be found to be in compliance with the resolution even though the wage paid was not the collectively agreed one. Given the vague wording of the resolution this is not too surprising. The unfortunate effect of this is described by Bercusson in his authoritative study:

> With the mass of differing rates that existed in the same industry, trade or district, the determination of a 'current rate' which could be applied as the standard stipulated by the Fair Wages Resolution was almost impossible. The only element of uniformity was to be found in the efforts of trade unions to regularize wages. At this stage in the development of industrial relations, however, the ruling classes in government were not prepared to accept collective bargaining as the standard of a Fair Wages policy. The alternative being no standard at all—no standard at all was chosen.[88]

Most serious of all was the ineffectual stance over enforcement; it appears that a number of government departments paid little, if any, regard to the resolution. Other departments were content to do nothing unless individuals or unions made a complaint; such complaints were likely to be the subject of perfunctory investigation. Even where a complaint was held to be well-founded there was still a great reluctance to penalise contractors. Suggestions to tighten up the administration of the resolution tended to fall upon stony ground. One suggestion had been to involve the Board of Trade; other suggestions involved reliance on trade unions.

One of the most significant indicators of a trend towards greater legal regulation of the employment relationship was the enactment of the Workmen's Compensation Act 1897. Henceforth, irrespective of fault, employers were to be obliged to pay accident compensation to their employees. This was a much more radical step than the 1893 Bill of the then Liberal government which had sought to abolish the doctrine of common employment. The latter doctrine had always been regarded as anomalous and proposed abolition could be presented as a refinement of the common law and thus more in keeping with the tenets of laissez-faire. The 1897 Act, however, compelled the employer to pay compensation in respect of some of life's vicissitudes and opened up the possibility of either the employer or the State becoming responsible for the well-being of others. Indeed at the 1898 TUC Congress one delegate stated that

---

[88] B Bercusson, *Fair Wages Resolutions*, p 41 (London: Mansell Information Publishing, 1978).

> If . . . the national prosperity depends on the well-being of the workers, the
> necessary corollary is that the state should care for him in sickness . . .

The period prior to the passage of the Workmen's Compensation Act
of 1897 witnessed the enactment of the Employers' Liability Act 1880
and subsequently the publication of a number of bills aimed at
modifying the notorious doctrine of common employment. The latter
doctrine prevented an employee suing his employer on the basis of the
employer's vicarious liability for the negligence of a fellow employee.
The 1880 Act prevented the operation of the doctrine in a number of
prescribed situations; for example, where the injury resulted from the
employee following the directions of a foreman which were negligent.[89] The Act went on to place a limit on the amount of compensation recoverable.[90] The courts also held that it was legitimate to
contract-out of the Act.[91] Dealing with this question was to weigh
heavily with the drafters of subsequent bills.[92] For instance, the
Conservative government of 1886–1892 acknowledged the difficulties
inherent in contracting-out given the inequality of bargaining-power.[93]
During this period proposals were made to prohibit completely contracting-out. These were doomed to failure, partly because they would
have involved a complete departure from notions of freedom of contract. In addition, it was assumed that friendly societies would be

[89] S 1(3).
[90] S 3.
[91] *Griffiths v Earl of Dudley* 9 QBD 357.
[92] For instance, the 1888 Bill provided that contracting-out was not permissible unless
the consideration was satisfactory. This would only be the case where the employer made
an adequate contribution to an insurance fund which provided compensation for every
accident occurring in the course of the employment. The fund had also to provide benefits equivalent to those paid under the Act. Where a fund was unable to discharge its
obligation the liabilities reverted to the employer. It was the responsibility of the
Secretary of State (and in some industries the Board of Trade) to determine whether these
conditions had been fulfilled. It should be noted that the fund would have to pay compensation in respect of every industrial injury; the employer's liability at common law
was not relevant. The 1890 bill imposed rather different requirements:

> No contract made after the commencement of this Act, whereby a workman deprives
> himself of any right under this Act, shall constitute a defence to an action brought for
> the recovery of compensation under this Act, unless it is made in pursuance of a sub-
> stantial consideration which is, in the opinion of the Court before which such action is
> tried, a reasonable consideration for the workman so depriving himself of rights under
> this Act, and is other than the consideration of entering upon . . . the employment.

The clauses on contracting-out are interesting and show that the drafters of such bills
believed that the State should police the content of such agreements.
[93] Parl. Deb., 17.5.1888, vol 326, HC, col 636.

adversely affected if it was not possible to contract-out. The interests of organisations operating in accordance with Victorian notions of self-help were bound to be viewed sympathetically.

The Workmen's Compensation Act 1897 was an extremely important piece of legislation. It provided for compensation for industrial injuries where the injury was caused by an 'accident arising out of and in the course of employment.'[94] The compensation was to be paid by the employer but there was a complete defence where the injury was attributable to the serious and wilful misconduct of the injured employee.[95] Where the employer was liable at common law the rights of employees were preserved but an employer was not liable to pay compensation both independently of and also under the Act.[96] Any question as to liability to pay compensation under the Act, or as to the amount or duration of compensation, if not settled by agreement, was to be determined by arbitration in accordance with the schedule to the Act. In the first place the schedule provided that

> If any committee, representative of an employer and his workmen, exists with power to settle matters under this Act in the case of the employer and workmen, the matter shall, unless either party objects, . . . be settled by the arbitration of such committee, or be referred by them in their discretion to arbitration as herein-after provided.

However,

> If either party so objects, or there is no such committee, or the committee so refers the matter or fails to settle the matter within three months from the date of the claim, the matter shall be settled by a single arbitrator agreed on by the parties, or in the absence of agreement by the county court judge . . .

Contracting-out of the scheme was permissible provided that an approved alternative was provided. Approval had to come from the Registrar of Friendly Societies after he had taken steps to ascertain the views of the employer and employees. The Registrar had to be able to certify that any scheme of compensation, benefit, or insurance for the employees was on the whole not less favourable, to the general body of employees and their dependents, than the provisions of the Act. The Act did not apply to all employments but only to railway, factory, mine, quarry or engineering work and some forms of construction

---

[94] S 1(1).
[95] S 1(2)(c).
[96] S 1(2)(b).

work.[97] The underlying rationale for the selection being that priority for inclusion should be given to the more hazardous enterprises.

The Act was a remarkable piece of social legislation and imposed a form of strict liability on employers. Compensation for industrial injuries was now seen as the responsibility of the enterprise:

> Where a person, on his own responsibility and for his own profit, sets in motion agencies which create risks for others, he ought to be civilly responsible for the consequences of what he does.[98]

Uncertainty was expressed as to who would ultimately bear the cost of the scheme:

> whether in the ultimate allocation of that burden the larger share will fall upon profits or upon wages, or whether it will be possible to transfer under existing economic conditions any appreciable portion of that burden upon the consumer in the shape of an added price of goods, are question upon which opinions may very well differ.[99]

Concern was also expressed that such social legislation would make industry uncompetitive but reference was made to the fact that similar schemes already existed in most of Britain's major competitors. A further justification for the legislation was the difficulty for injured employees in proving that their employer had been negligent. It was assumed that a well drafted scheme would lead to much less litigation than that which arose by virtue of matters being regulated at common law. The aim of producing a less legalistic regime was not achieved:

> The present system rests in the last resort upon the threat or the practice of litigation: a misfortune which is often not in any sense the fault of the employer and which he would not have prevented, is treated by methods applicable to fault. This method imports the risk of contention between employer and employee and of legal expenses on a scale exceeding that of the other forms of social security in this country or of compensation for industrial accident or disease in other countries.[100]

It is worthy of note that primacy in dispute solving under the Act was accorded to arbitration and that the preferred mode should be by means of a joint committee representative of the employer and the employees. This accords with the Royal Commission's endorsement of the virtues of joint regulation. However, while,

[97] S 7(1).
[98] Parl. Deb., 3.5.1897, vol 48, HC, col 1427.
[99] Parl. Deb., 3.5.1897, vol 48, HC, col 1441.
[100] Social Insurance and Allied Services (Cmd 6404), para 79.

The authors of the original Act contemplated that disputes would be settled by the friendly and informal arbitration, this hope has not been realised and disputes are now generally settled by formal proceedings in the Courts. In a few mining areas joint committees of employers and employees have been established for settlement of claims, but even these do not always prevent formal legal proceedings in cases where agreement is not reached.[101]

The scheme of dispute resolution adopted also serves to illustrate that the Act did not necessitate any more than minimal administration by a government department.

A further important development in the 1890s was the emergence, in 1893, of the Railway Regulation Act dealing with working hours in the railway industry. One justification for this piece of legislation was that

> the State has a right to interfere with the hours of labour of railway servants for the purpose of protecting the travelling public against the risk of accidents.[102]

Further justification could be found by virtue of the fact that the employees were public servants. In enacting the measure the government was anxious to preserve the notion that the hours of adult male labour should not be dealt with by legislation. Accordingly, the legislative aim was said to be the protection of the travelling public rather than employees. A logical consequence of this stance was the exclusion from the Act of those wholly employed either in clerical work or in the company's workshops.[103] The Act provided that where it was represented to the Board of Trade, by or on behalf of the employees, that the hours of work were excessive then the Board was obliged to make inquiries.[104] One difficulty was that the word 'excessive' was not defined. The failure to state a specific figure was partly the result of laissez-faire sentiments: 'Parliament should rather lay down broad rules and interfere as little as possible between employers and their workmen.'[105] It was also suggested that the variety of railway employments rendered a set figure impractical. Once an inquiry had been concluded, provided that the Board believed that the ground of complaint was reasonable, the Board was under a duty to order the company to submit to them a time schedule for the employees which would, in the opinion of

---

[101] *Ibid.*
[102] Parl. Deb., 24.4.1893, vol 11, HC, col 1090–1.
[103] S 1(7).
[104] S 1(1).
[105] Parl. Deb., 24.4.1893, vol 11, HC, col 1095.

the Board, bring the actual hours of work within reasonable limits.[106] A company might fail to comply either by not submitting a schedule or by not adhering to a schedule submitted and approved. The position then was rather curious. The matter was to be referred to the Railway and Canal Commission who were empowered to make an order requiring the company to submit to the Commission such a schedule as would, in the opinion of the Commission, bring the actual hours of work within reasonable limits.[107] The possibility of a second schedule being required seems difficult to explain. A power to uphold, vary etc a schedule approved by the Board would have seemed much more obvious. Sanctions only existed where a company either failed to return a schedule or failed to adhere to one submitted and approved by the Commissioners. (In relation to an order of the Board the only sanction was the indirect one of a reference to the Commission). In such a case the company was liable to a fine not exceeding £100 for every day during which the default continued.[108]

The Board of Trade seemed happy with the operation of the Act. The following extract from the Board's report for 1898 is typical of these in that period:

> During the five years in which the Act has been in force the railway companies have made large reductions in the hours of labour of railway servants, both at the instance of the Board of Trade and largely on their own initiative.[109]

On the other hand, the number of complaints made was not particularly high and the editor of the Railway Review was to comment that

> For some years past every effort has been made to exploit the Act of 1893 to its full advantage, and yet it cannot be denied that if not a disastrous failure, the success which has been obtained is comparatively slight . . .[110]

The response of the union was 'to fluctuate between the policy of statutory limitation of hours and their limitation by industrial pressure.'[111]

[106] S 1(2).
[107] S 1(3).
[108] S 1(4).
[109] Report by the Board of Trade on Railway Servants (1898) vol 77. A statement which is supported by C.E.R Sherrington, *The Economics of Rail Transport in Great Britain* vol 1 (London: Edward Arnold, 1928) p 241.
[110] The Railway Review, 15.2.1907, quoted in PS Bagwell, *The History of the National Union of Railwaymen* (London: Allen & Unwin, 1963) at p 172.
[111] *Ibid* at p 173.

A number of attempts were made to secure legislation on hours of work for miners. Such attempts aimed to build upon the Coal Mines Act of 1872 which had reduced the daily hours of boys underground to a maximum of 10. The 1872 Act also indirectly had an impact on the hours of adult males. One might have thought that the miners would have a stronger case than the railwaymen since the mines had a higher fatality rate and the work involved was extremely arduous. A strong case could most certainly have been made on the basis of health and safety. Nevertheless, despite considerable parliamentary support for a number of bills, it was not until 1908 that legislation was secured. Unlike the railways, however, the safety of the public was not jeopardised by conditions in the mines. Nevertheless, Chamberlain had advanced the view in the 1890s that attaining the 8 hour day through legislation was in the public interest because it would help avoid recourse to industrial action.

Pollard has pointed out that union demands for legislation on working hours were inspired by a number of aims:

> One, which inspired Tom Mann and also several groups of miners, saw in it a means to limit output and thus keep up prices and wage rates. The second was to confirm the gains made over a longer period by strong unions and within large firms and spread them to weaker sections and smaller firms by means of compulsion through legislation. The third placed it within the long-term movement, begun with the early factory legislation and continued with the nine-hour fight of the 1870s, of converting some of the additional incomes into more leisure.[112]

There were, indeed, a number of good reasons why trade unions should seek legislation on industrial matters. As the second of the reasons stated by Pollard suggests, legislation was potentially universal in that it might be applied to all employees or, at least, all employees of a particular type. Again legislation was potentially more stable than a collective agreement in that, once passed, an Act will govern until Parliament amends or repeals it. A collective bargain

> however stable, is always liable to be changed, in accordance with the relative strength of employers and employed, at each of the successive inflations and depressions which characterise modern industry.[113]

---

[112] S Pollard, in WJ Mommsen and H-G Husung (eds) *The Development of Trade Unionism in Great Britain and Germany 1880-1914* (London: [for] the German Historical Institute [by] Allen & Unwin, 1985) p 47.
[113] S & B Webb, above n 45, at p 256.

It must be said that this potential benefit of legislation may turn out to be a weakness where legislation is not amended in the face of changed economic circumstances. The Webbs were aware of such difficulties:

> An Act of Parliament is hard to obtain, and hard to alter. It is therefore probable that an industry has to go on for some years without the regulation which would be economically advantageous to it, or to endure for some time an obsolete regulation which could advantageously be amended. This want of elasticity to meet changing circumstances is specially noticeable in our legislative machinery of the present day, when the one central legislature is patently incapable of coping with the incessant new applications of law required by a complicated society. It would be interesting to ask whether this defect is inherent in the Method of Legal Enactment. If the principle of regulating the conditions of employment were definitely adopted by parliament, there does not seem any impossibility in the rules themselves being made and amended by the fiat—carrying with it the force of law—of an executive department, a local authority, or a compulsory arbitration court for the particular industry.[114]

CONCLUSIONS

The period between 1880 and 1900 might be felt to be notable for a number of developments: a greater acceptance of the benefits to be gained by conducting industrial relations through the institution of collective bargaining, an increase in the legal regulation of employment conditions and, in the 1890s, greater recourse to the courts. In addition, the State had seemed to begin to accept that it would have to intervene, on occasion, to resolve trade disputes. During the latter part of the nineteenth century industrial relations were increasingly likely to be conducted through collective bargaining, a state of affairs that was given official endorsement by the Royal Commission of 1894. State support for collective bargaining was also evidenced by the operation of the Labour Department of the Board of Trade. The conduct of collective bargaining was not, however, made subject to legal regulation. Nevertheless, more regulatory legislation affecting employment relations was introduced and in 1893, for the first time, the Government directly intervened to try and secure a settlement of a trade dispute.[115]

---

[114] S & B Webb, above n 45, at p 799.
[115] E. Wigham, *Strikes and the Government 1893–1974*, ch 1 (London: Macmillan, 1976).

The economic impact of a national dispute in a major industry such as mining moved the Government to act. Government had also begun to become concerned with being seen to be a 'good' employer.[116] In its role as contractor the Government recognised, through passing the first Fair Wages Resolution 1891, that as an indirect employer, it should pay a rate of wages which would be both reasonable and an example to private employers. Employers looked to law as a possible device to give control in both individual and collective relations. In contrast to the 1880s the 1890s was a litigious period. The prospect of the option of legally enforcing collective agreements may well have had some appeal.[117] After all, use of the law was made by employers in the 1890s to restrict trade union power. Again, in the coal industry some use was made of civil actions for damages of breach of contract against miners arising out of losses caused by industrial action.

By the 1890s there was a greater perception of the significance of the balance of power between the collective parties in producing stable industrial relations but, nevertheless, there was no question of the law intervening to redress any serious disparities. Whilst the first Fair Wages Resolution had been passed in 1891 and Wages Boards were established by statute in 1909 one could not rationalise their role in the way that was subsequently done. They were not established to support collective bargaining but were designed to regulate employment conditions in certain sectors of industry. It was not until 1918 that the Trades Boards legislation might be categorised as auxiliary legislation when it became possible to establish a new Board without showing that wages were 'exceptionally low' in that industry. Whilst free play to the collective forces in society was now permitted the law would not intervene to promote a more equitable equilibrium in the balance of power. The

[116] Government departments were being criticised in the early 1890s not only for failure to implement the Fair Wages Resolution but also for their behaviour as direct employers. There had been much talk by the Liberals in the 1892 election about setting an example to private industry and the subsequent Liberal government were not allowed by the Conservative opposition to forget this. In March 1893 (Parl. Deb., 24.3.1893 vol 9 HC, col 310). Gorst moved in the House of Commons that

no person should be engaged in the naval establishments, at wages insufficient for a proper maintenance, and that the conditions of labour as regards hours, wages, insurance against accident, provision for old age etc should be such as to afford an example to private employers throughout the country.

The Liberals could hardly quarrel with this and Henry Campbell-Bannerman, then Secretary for War, agreed that the Government 'should show themselves to be amongst the best employers.'

[117] And see the appendix to this chapter.

State did not seek to regulate collective bargaining by law. Moreover, in general, terms and conditions of employment were to be settled by the combined forces of capital and labour meeting in the market place.

Whilst in later years many commentators came to regard the absence of law as a virtue the position was different in 1900; there was genuine interest in changing the law to allow the parties to enforce legally collective agreements if they wished, industrial relations being seen as no different to commercial relations. Whilst collective laissez-faire might go hand in hand with legal abstention, economic liberalism and the use of the law were not incompatible. Recommendations as to legal reform were, however, heavily influenced by pragmatic considerations. Hence the reason that any scheme of compulsory arbitration was ultimately rejected was both because voluntary arrangements were felt to be working and enforcing compulsory arbitration was not practicable. On the other hand, had the Government intervened to regulate industrial relations by law in the nineteenth century

> unions might have become sufficiently accustomed to legal constraints, and sufficiently convinced of their long-term benefits, to resist the temptation to cast them aside when they became strong enough to do so.[118]

A further instance of pragmatism is furnished by the majority in 1894 who felt that legally enforcing collective agreements would not achieve much since it would be unlikely to work where it was most needed (ie in weakly organised trades). State policy in the realm of industrial relations become increasingly flexible as allegiance to the laissez-faire doctrines faded. Similarly, purely pragmatic lessons often influenced unions in trying to decide whether to seek legislation:

> By the Method of Collective Bargaining, on the other hand, Trade Unions have not infrequently gained from employers, at times of strategic advantage, not only the whole of their demands, but also conditions so exceptional that they would never have ventured to embody them in a legislative proposal. We shall hereafter see how this consideration deters strong Trade Unions, like the United Society of Boilermakers and Iron Shipbuilders, from going to Parliament about such unsettled problems as Demarcation of Work or the Limitation of Apprentices, on which they feel that they can exact better terms than would be conceded to them by the community as a whole.[119]

---

[118] EH Hunt, above n 41, p 326.
[119] S & B Webb, above n 45, p 255.

Appendix

During the period dealt with by this chapter those involved in industrial relations were very much interested in new approaches (including legal ones). A useful endnote is provided by events in the boot and shoe trade. The early years of the 1890s witnessed considerable dissatisfaction among sections of both sides with regard to the operation of the dispute settlement machinery in the industry. To the employers two factors were proving particularly disquieting: the apparent inability of the union leadership to secure the adhesion of its membership to agreed procedure and the, quite legitimate, use of procedure to challenge the extent of managerial prerogative. Events were to culminate in the lock-out of 1895. This lasted for nearly six weeks and resulted in a settlement favourable to the employers whereby they 'secured important limitations in the scope of collective bargaining.'[120] What of worker discipline? The employers looked to the union to control their membership but in addition to the standard institutions of joint regulation they imposed a trust fund. The following elements of the settlement are of great interest:

> Should any provision of the Settlement, or any award, agreement, or decision be broken 'by any manufacturer or body of workmen belonging to the Federation or the National Union; and the Federation or the National Union fail within ten days either to induce such members to comply with the agreement, decision, or award, or to expel them from their organization, the Federation or the National Union shall be deemed to have broken the agreement, award or decision.[121]

Fox comments that

> The penalty for breaking an agreement, award, or decision was to be a financial one. A Guarantee Fund was set up; each side contributing £1,000. Either side could claim before the Umpire that the other side had defaulted, and should the Umpire agree, he could 'determine that all or any part' of the Guarantee Fund be forfeited to the side 'in whose favour the Award shall be

---

[120] A. Fox, *A History of the National Union of Boot and Shoe Operatives*, (Oxford: Blackwell, 1958) p 232.
[121] *Ibid* at p 233.

made'. The side thus penalised would then have to make good the diminu-
tion of the Fund by bringing it up to its original level.[122]

The use of the Guarantee Fund is fascinating: the agreement corresponds to a legally enforceable collective agreement with a liquidate
damages clause. The greater interest might well be thought to arise
from the fact that this particular agreement was adopted without
prompting from any State body and, given the time of its introduction,
represented a highly innovatory move in a quasi-legal direction. On the
other hand, the extent to which employers regarded the trust fund as a
guarantor of industrial peace must be questioned. Fox has argued that

> the Guarantee Fund had much less significance than has often been thought.
> Certainly, it was guaranteed to drive Union leaders into great efforts to pre-
> vent or settle unofficial strikes of which they disapproved. But the sums
> involved were relatively so small that the prospect of paying even the full
> penalty would be hardly likely to induce Union leaders to submit on any
> issue which they felt to be of more than trivial importance. It could never, by
> itself, have secured industrial peace.[123]

Perhaps the real threat to the power of employees in the industry
was posed by the demonstration of employer power provided by the
lock-out.

Subsequently, the Industrial Council commented on the scheme in
the course of their enquiry into industrial agreements:

> If the fund is intended to be one out of which a penalty is payable equivalent
> to the amount of damage suffered, it is clear that, in order to provide for a
> case involving a large number of persons, the sum of money which it would
> be necessary to deposit would be such that many of the smaller organisa-
> tions would be unable to set aside so large a proportion of their funds, or to
> obtain money for such a purpose. If, on the other hand, the penalty to be
> paid is merely in the nature of a fine, it does not appear that the adoption of
> the principle adds much to the restraining influence which is already exer-
> cised by the moral obligation to observe agreements.[124]

Having said that, the agreement was not a dead letter; the ILO were to
report that up to 1920 there had been 13 instances in which fines had
been imposed.[125]

---

[122] A. Fox, *A History of the National Union of Boot and Shoe Operatives*, (Oxford:
Blackwell, 1958) p 234.
[123] *Ibid* at p 235.
[124] Industrial Council Report on Inquiry Into Industrial Agreements (Cd 6952), para
38.
[125] ILO Conciliation and Arbitration in Industrial Disputes p 156 (Geneva, 1933).

3

1900–1914

INTRODUCTION

THE ROYAL COMMISSION of 1894 had positively endorsed the virtues of collective bargaining; it was a salutary way to conduct industrial relations. It might have been feared that the period after *Taff Vale* would witness a decline in its role. In fact, this was not to be the case and the years following that highly tendentious decision saw collective bargaining continue to increase in significance. Indeed, whilst its value was accepted by Government, its expansion owed more to the attitude of employers:

> This transformation of industrial relations was the consequence not only of trade union growth but also of a rapid increase in organisation among employers. In the craft industries, indeed, they had given the lead towards collective bargaining, and some of the national agreements represented a joint victory for employers and trade union leaders over the hostility of a rank and file which was still wedded to the traditions of unilateral regulation.[1]

The disinclination of employers to take advantage of *Taff Vale* is highly significant:

> Had British employers wished to get rid of trade unions, the depression years of 1902–5, with the *Taff Vale* precedent valid in every court, were as favourable an opportunity as ever presented itself. There are, however, relatively few instances of organised employers taking advantage of it to attempt to weaken or destroy the unions. . . . Moreover, in some industries the employers were willing to take the initiative, and where they did so, as in building and printing, it was to strengthen and extend systems of collective bargaining and to enlarge the scope of joint regulation.[2]

Importantly, it was not simply collective bargaining which continued to develop; the State's role grew very significantly as well. In the period

---

[1] H Clegg, *A History of British Trade Unions Since 1889* (Oxford: Clarendon Press, 1964) vol 1, p 471.
[2] *Ibid* at p 363.

preceding the First World War there was a considerable increase in the extent of state intervention in industrial relations. However, in general, such intervention did not seek to promote collective bargaining; joint regulation was accepted but not overly encouraged.

In examining the State's role in industrial relations the importance of the Trade Disputes Act 1906 cannot be underestimated. In essence, it ring-fenced industrial action from the reaches of the law; the State chose not to intervene to regulate except at the margins. One might argue that, in some sense, this offered indirect encouragement to collective bargaining by allowing the parties to resort to the use of social sanctions. Nevertheless, the extent to which the policy of non-intervention which underpinned the Act is reflected, more generally, in the State's approach to industrial relations in the years immediately following the turn of the century is highly debatable. Even if one disregards, for the moment, legislative measures in the labour law field, the greater extent of government involvement in industrial relations in the early years of the twentieth century is remarkable. This is well illustrated by the way in which Government became involved in attempts to settle a number of major industrial disputes:

> The Liberal government intervened in most of the major industrial disputes between 1907 and 1912. This was a more remarkable development than might appear, since formal government involvement had begun only with the miners' lock-out in 1893.[3]

An industry wide dispute in a major industry was likely to prompt government intervention. For instance, 10 days before the 1912 miners' strike was due to begin the Prime Minister (Asquith) offered mediation. The Government believed that the way forward was by means of district agreements between the parties. However, should this prove unsuccessful, the Government suggested that their representatives should decide any outstanding points.[4] Ultimately the Government was forced to legislate on minimum wages to end the strike.[5] Even without resorting to law, the State was able to achieve the end it desired in other ways. For instance, in 1907, the Government acted to end a

---

[3] J Lovell, 'Trade Unions and the Development of Independent Labour Politics 1889–1906', in B Pimlott and C Cook (eds) *Trade Unions in British Politics* (London: Longman, 1982) p 57.

[4] R Page Arnott, *History of the Scottish Miners* (London: Allen & Unwin, 1955) pp 122–23.

[5] See below at p 69 for discussion of the 1912 Act.

national dispute which had broken out on the railways.[6] A settlement was achieved by the Government suggesting to the employers that rejection of the mooted compromise (a conciliation scheme) might well result in the introduction of a statute making arbitration in railway disputes compulsory.[7] Notably even *The Economist* had advocated compulsory arbitration if Board of Trade intervention did not bear fruit.[8] Administrative reforms made by government also reflected the change in the State's role. For instance, in 1911, the Board of Trade established a separate industrial relations department staffed by full time negotiators.[9]

During the period from 1900–1914 the willingness of the State to intervene in industrial relations increased considerably. The motivation was not always the same. On occasion, the desire to avoid the wider adverse economic and social consequences of industrial action led to intervention. At other times, as with the Trade Boards legislation, the desire for greater social justice predominated. However, what is perhaps almost as worthy of note as the greater extent of state intervention is the utter pragmatism as to the form it might take. Having said that, legislation was often viewed as appropriate and during this period the volume of labour law on the statute book increased considerably.[10] More significantly, the subject matter of the measures enacted might well concern core aspects of employment relations—minimum wage and maximum hours legislation coming into being.

WAGES LEGISLATION

In 1909 the Trade Boards Act was passed which provided minimum wage legislation for the 'sweated' trades. The Act applied to trades where the rate of wages prevailing in any branch of the trade is exceptionally low, as compared with that in other employments, and that the other circumstances of the trade are such as to render the application of this act to the trade expedient.[11] The Act provided for

[6] See P Bagwell, *The Railwaymen* (London: Allen & Unwin, 1963), ch 10.

[7] C Wrigley, 'The Government and Industrial Relations', in C. Wrigley (ed) *A History of British Industrial Relations 1875–1914* (Brighton: Harvester, 1982) pp 143–44.

[8] 19 October 1907, pp 1754–55 quoted in C Wrigley *ibid* at p 143.

[9] R. Davidson 'Government Administration ' in C Wrigley (ed), above n 7, at p 173.

[10] For instance, the Factories Act 1901 was enacted and there were significant amendments to the Workmen's Compensation legislation.

[11] S 1(2).

the establishment of trade boards which were empowered to fix mini-mum rates of wages for timework and piecework. Trade boards were to be comprised of equal numbers of representatives of both sides of industry and a number of independent members appointed by the Board of Trade. Failure to pay the prescribed rates of wages could lead to both a civil action for debt and criminal penalties.[12] Interestingly enough the onus of proof was reversed in the event of any prosecution:

> It shall lie on the employer to prove by the production of proper wage sheets or record of wages or otherwise that he has not paid, or agreed to pay, wages at less than the minimum rate.[13]

Trade boards were empowered to take any proceedings under the Act on behalf of a worker.[14]

The trade boards legislation was subsequently to be regarded as a prop to collective bargaining but one must consider how it would have been viewed at the time of enactment. It can be far from easy to iden-tify the motives which lead to the enactment of a statute. However, perusal of the relevant reports, bills and Parliament debates suggest mixed motives in the case of the 1909 Act. Having said that, I would submit that the predominant motive was simply to set a basic standard:

> it is quite as legitimate to establish by legislation a minimum standard of remuneration as it is to establish such as a standard of sanitation . . . and hours of work . . .[15]

It is not surprising that, particularly in the early years of the twentieth century, proposals for legislation of this sort came up against the argu-ment that they would be economically damaging. Such arguments received a surprisingly robust rejoinder from the select committee on homework:

> if it be said that there may be industries which cannot be carried on if such a standard of payment be enforced, it may be replied that this was said when the enactment of many of the provisions of the factory and other similar acts were proposed, and public opinion supported Parliament in deciding that, if the prognostication were an accurate one, it would be better any trade which could not exist if such a minimum of decent and humane conditions were insisted upon should cease.[16]

---

[12] S 6.
[13] S 6(4).
[14] S 10(1).
[15] Select Committee on Home Work, para 38.
[16] *Ibid.*

The strength of that rejoinder may be an indication that regulatory legislation in this area was seen as being increasingly acceptable and, perhaps even, as the way forward. A secondary motive in the enactment of the legislation stemmed from the view it would promote the growth of collective bargaining. It is important to appreciate that not all supporters of the legislation espoused this belief. The 1908 committee on homework seemed to have believed that workers in the sweated trades would have to look to the law and not to the development of trade union organisation for protection. Aves in his 1908 report on the Wages Boards and Industrial Conciliation and Arbitration Acts of Australia and New Zealand obviously found the issue a difficult one:

> in general the ultimate affect upon trade unionism of the assumption of official responsibility for matters which under a voluntary system would in organised trades be left to the trade union itself, must be to weaken these bodies, since it weakens the motives for their formation and development. At the moment, however, the effect of the special boards, stimulated by a sense of what is regarded as their defects and limitations, appears to be tending to strengthen the trade union movement in Victoria.[17]

On the other hand, Winston Churchill, then the President of the Board of Trade, believed the legislation would foster collective organisation. In what way or ways might the legislation be expected to foster collective bargaining ? In the sweated trades competition was severe and this meant that there was little value in employees seeking to collectively bargain with employers as the latter would not enter into collective agreements for fear of undercutting. Trade boards might be conducive to greater stability and the development of trade union organisation. On the other hand, it might be felt that employees would become dependent on such legislation to the detriment of any expansion of trades unionism and voluntary collective bargaining. Secondly, the composition of the trade boards was possibly seen as a basis for voluntary organisation. Moreover, some anticipated

> that they may possibly by means of these trade boards and trade committees, be able to educate the weak and organised trades and encourage them after a while to combine for their own protection just as better organised and more advanced trades have combined.

---

[17] Report on the Wages Boards and Industrial Conciliation and Arbitration Acts of Australia and New Zealand (Cd 4167), para 58.

Quite clearly one could have set up a statutory scheme for the regulation of wages which did not require the establishment of trade boards. For instance, it would have been possible for the Board of Trade to have fixed the rate of wages directly. Admittedly, it would still have been necessary to have acquired evidence of rates of wages in the relevant industries. Bayliss has suggested that one reason for the creation of trade boards was to disguise the fact of state interference in the fixing of wages:

> The legitimacy of state interference was acknowledged but suspicion of such interference was so strong that the State itself could not be given the power to settle the actual amount of the wage.[18]

There may be something in this, though the form the British legislation took was perhaps mainly the product of Australian/New Zealand experience. At the time of enactment one could not depict the legislation as anything other than regulatory; in 1909 it would most likely have been regarded as a natural extension of the factories legislation. This would have been reinforced by the fact that enforcement of the Act lay through not only the private law mechanism of contract but also Board of Trade inspectorate. The Act could be seen as paving the way for an increasing amount of state interference in the fixing of wages. After all, the question of whether the rate of remuneration was so poor as to justify intervention could be viewed as one of degree:

> The principle of State interference with wages being admitted on the ground that it is desirable in the interests of the community that the workers should be secured a Living Standard, and as that Living Standard must be progressive, the interference of the State to secure an adequate wage must be progressive also.[19]

Initially the Act only applied to four trades. Moreover, the process of determining a wages order was protracted. A trades board was obliged to give notice of the rate which they proposed to fix[20] and consider any objections within three months. After the period during which objections might be made had lapsed the trade board had to give notice of the rate they had determined upon. However, that rate had then to be approved by the Board of Trade before it had full effect. In the interim period it was possible to contract out of the proposed rate.[21] Approval

---

[18] FJ Bayliss, *British Wages Councils* (Oxford: Blackwell, 1962) p 8.
[19] P Snowden, *The Living Wage* (London: Hodder and Stoughton, 1912) p 23.
[20] S 4(2).
[21] S 7(1)(a).

could not be forthcoming until six months had passed from the date of the notice of the rate determined 'by the trade board.'[22] Moreover, the Board of Trade's approval was discretionary. In 1913 five more trades were brought within the scheme. It is thought that this involved an additional 150,000 to 200,000 employees and would thereby increase by about 50 per cent the number of employees benefiting from the legislation.[23]

Further evidence of the State's willingness to regulate wages through statute was furnished by the passing of the Coal Mines (Minimum Wage) Act 1912. However, whilst the 1909 Act had been passed to protect the weakest sections of labour,[24] the 1912 Act served to protect a group of workers who, by this stage, were amongst the strongest. Crucially, neither Act resulted in the State setting rates of wages directly. There was an absence of desire on the part of Government to determine what the appropriate rate of wages should be. Again the drafters of the 1912 Act were anxious not to undermine collective bargaining. It was provided that nothing in the Act was to prejudice the operation of any agreement entered into, or custom existing, before the passing of the Act, for the payment of wages at a higher rate.[25] The Act stipulated that it was to be an implied term of every miner's contract of employment that he be paid a minimum wage fixed under its auspices. Minimum wage rates were to be determined by joint boards for each district. An independent chair was to be appointed by agreement between the two sides; in the absence of agreement the Board of Trade was to appoint. In the event, a limited number of boards were constituted for the purposes of the Act since, in general, existing joint machinery took on board the new statutory function.[26] The wage fixed could be varied at any time by agreement between employee and employer representatives on the board. Alternatively, either side could apply for a variation after one year; provided three months' notice had been given after the expiration of the year. Should a board fail to reach agreement the chairman had powers to settle the rate. As discussed, the background to the passing of the Act was a national miners strike. The Government had intervened to try and resolve the dispute but this

[22] S 5(2).

[23] Bayliss, above n 18, pp 10–11.

[24] The sweated trades also contained a high proportion of female workers.

[25] S 2(1).

[26] H Jevons, *The British Coal Trade* (London: Kegan Paul Trench, Trubner & Co., 1915) p 578.

proved unsuccessful and the strike began in March 1912. The operation of the Act appears to have had a positive impact on the earnings of the miners involved. Writing two years after enactment Jevons noted that in terms of increasing wages the Act was a success:

> it has been found by experience that this act, which is nominally only temporary, does secure to the hewers a substantial minimum of day wages, however unremunerative their conditions of work; and the fixing of rates by the joint boards has, on the whole, considerably increased the wages of the various grades of the less skilled workers.[27]

In the longer term the Act did not have a damaging impact on collective bargaining:

> the machinery set up under the coal mines (minimum wage) act is still in existence and is still used, but the resulting minimum rates have been effective only to a limited extent owing to their having been fixed generally at a lower level than the operative rates arranged from time to time as the result of collective bargaining.[28]

The Act, therefore, seems to have not attracted the sort of criticism that the trades board legislation would subsequently come under.

The State had, since 1891, sought to regulate the level of wages indirectly through the medium of the Fair Wages Resolution. A Fair Wages Committee was established in 1907 to

> report whether any changes are desirable in the administration of the Fair Wages resolution in order to enable its objects to be more effectively attained. It is not intended to amend the terms of the resolution or enlarge its scope.[29]

The Committee were less than fully imbibed with the underlying philosophy of the Fair Wages Resolution:

> if the government is to have its work executed at the ordinary market price it cannot require the contractor to pay more than the market rate of wages.[30]

Nevertheless, the extent to which Government involvement in the fixing of wages was becoming accepted can be seen in the following quotation which indicates the views of employers:

[27] H Jevons, *The British Coal Trade* (London: Kegan Paul Trench, Trubner & Co., 1915) p 599.
[28] BW Bercusson, *Fair Wages Resolutions* (London: Mansell Information Publishing, 1978) p 120.
[29] Report of the Fair Wages Committee (Cd 4422).
[30] *Ibid* at para 22.

it is thought that many employers in these trades [ie unorganised ones] would welcome a scheme under which the government fixed the rate of wages to be paid on contract work. All would be put on an equality in tendering (as is already the case in those trades where a current rate exists) and the better class of employers would feel that they had not to meet the competition of those who cut their prices by sweating their workpeople.[31]

The Committee made a number of recommendations for reform but believed that the wording of the resolution should not be changed. The TUC had been unhappy with the drafting and administration of the resolution. They believed that the extent of evasion was much greater than conceded by Government. In addition, they found the wording of the resolution unsatisfactory given the reference to 'current' rates and the absence of any explicit reference to collective bargaining. As a consequence, they believed that the resolution allowed far too much latitude to government departments by way of interpretation. Bercusson comments that there were

differences of opinion . . . as to whether it meant the wages demanded by trade unions, the average wages of the district, or the wages which individual contractors has been accustomed to paying for similar work.[32]

The recommendations of the Fair Wages Committee notwithstanding, a revised version of the resolution was passed by the House of Commons in 1909. This meant that the following clause would subsequently be found in contracts with government:

The contractor shall, under the penalty of a fine or otherwise, pay rates of wages and observe hours of labour not less favourable than those most commonly recognised by employers and trade societies (or, in absence of such recognised wages and hours, those which in practice prevail amongst good employers) in the trade in the district where the work is carried out. Where there are no such wages and hours recognised or prevailing in the district, those recognised or prevailing in the nearest district in which the general industrial circumstances are similar shall be adopted.

The amended resolution took account of the hours of labour and, much more significantly, appeared to equate a fair rate with a collectively negotiated rate. Nevertheless, it is probably reasonable to conclude that the predominant purpose of the resolution remained the setting of minimum standards rather than the promotion of collective

---

[31] *Ibid* at para 36.
[32] Bercusson, above n 27, p 48.

bargaining. Like the trade board legislation it could not be viewed as auxiliary legislation. During parliamentary discussion of the resolution an unsuccessful attempt was made to extend it so that it would apply to everyone in the employment of a government contractor.

By 1914 regulation of wages had moved clearly into the territory of permissible function for government. Apart from the measures discussed, various other proposals were mooted which, in the event, did not lead to legislation. For instance, in 1914 a Wages Bill was introduced to the Commons which sought to lay down a minimum wage which would apply to all types of employment. Employers would not have been obliged to pay the minimum rate, which was to have been fixed by the local authority, but any employer paying below that rate had to register all employments concerned with the local authority. The Bill, which did not progress beyond the stage of first reading, was aimed at encouraging payment of wages above the recommended minimum. Its sponsors saw it as a step on the road towards a compulsory regime.[33] Again the Industrial Agreements Bill, 1912 sought to give effect to the 'common rule.' The Bill applied to agreements between employers and employees in or about the Port of London concerning wages, hours, or other conditions of labour. Either side of industry could apply to the Board of Trade to have such an agreement registered. The effect of registration would be that the terms of the agreement would become implied terms of the contract of employment and any attempt to contract-out would be void. The main motivation behind the Bill was the desire to prevent under-cutting and the problems arising as a result.

HOURS OF WORK

Regulatory legislation enacted during this period did not concern simply rates of wages but also hours of work. The Coal Mines Regulation Act 1908 was a further example of what, at the time, must have been seen as one of a number of moves towards more extensive regulatory legislation. The Act quite unashamedly restricted the hours of adult male labour:

> I am not going to argue on the abstract ground that is an interference with adult labour. Honourable members have passed that stage.[34]

[33] Parl. Deb., HC, 13.5.1914, vol 62, col 1134.
[34] Parl. Deb., HC, 22.6.1908, vol 190, col 1354.

Whereas the 1893 railways legislation had been justified on the basis of health and safety arguments the Government acknowledged that the 1908 Act would not materially affect the accident rate in the mines. The Government appeared more concerned with such pragmatic issues as the economic impact of legislation:

> The question really is whether this bill now being discussed would have the effect of limiting the output, and, if it limited the output, what would be the effect of the limitation on the price of coal?[35]

Indeed a departmental committee had been set up in 1907 to examine this very question. Having departed from rationales based on health and safety the question arose as to why industries other than coal mining should not benefit from such legislation. The Government had two answers to such questions. In the first place 'for twenty years this proposal has been made by the miners.'[36] Of more interest is the second reason put forward:

> if you take into account the severity of the labour which is performed by the miners, if you take into account the extreme danger of their occupation, and the great discomfort of working day after day and year after year for one's whole working life below ground, out of the sunlight . . . there is no trade in the whole country which for a moment stands in a similar position or can make a claim in an equal degree for a fuller measure of leisure for the men engaged in it.[37]

Whilst one can accept that no other occupation was as unpleasant as coal mining, nevertheless one could surely argue that a number of other trades were sufficiently arduous to warrant legal restraint on the number of hours worked.

During the passage of the 1908 Act the Home Secretary remarked:

> Well, if this bill is not to be passed, and if the miners are to be left to their own devices and to the strength of their own organisation, it means a coal strike and nothing else.[38]

It is noteworthy that the Government was willing to acknowledge explicitly that they might be compelled to enact labour law measures to avert industrial action. Thus, while there might, in any event, be a tendency towards greater legal regulation the possibility of industrial

[35] Parl. Deb. HC, 22.6.1908, vol 190, col 1345.
[36] Parl. Deb., HC, 6.7.1908, vol 191, col 1277.
[37] *Ibid.*
[38] Parl. Deb., HC, 6.7.1908, vol 191, col 1279.

action could be a vital stimulus. This also suggests that the real concern of workers was the achievement of adequate terms and conditions of employment. They were not unduly concerned with the particular means by which this was achieved. It is worth recalling that the 1912 Coal Mines Act was also passed to end a strike. A further restriction on working hours came with the Shops Act 1912 which provided that, on at least one weekday in each week, a shop assistant shall not be employed about the business of a shop after 1.30 in the afternoon. During the period between 1900 and 1914 a succession of bills were brought forward to regulate the hours of work on the railways and in bakeries and factories. Virtually none of these bills reached the dizzy heights of a second reading. A further bill introduced in both 1907 and 1908 sought to restrict the hours of labour in all employments.

DISPUTE RESOLUTION

Against a background of increasing state intervention (often through legal mechanisms) and interest in compulsory arbitration, the Industrial Council Report of Enquiry into Industrial Agreements was produced.[39] The Council was comprised of employer and trade union representatives and was chaired by Askwith. The views of the Council on matters regarding the regulation of industrial relations are of interest. The Council were impressed by the level of adhesion to collectively agreed obligations and went on to consider the circumstances that were conducive to this. Like the Royal Commission on Labour of 1894 they stressed the importance of strong organisation to successful voluntary collective bargaining, problems arising

> in trades which are unorganised or in which one side or the other the organisation is incomplete or is of recent origin.[40]

This corresponds with the fact that the outbreak of industrial militancy in the period 1906 to 1914 was largely confined to low paid and unskilled workers. The question was posed as to whether the law could promote greater adhesion to collective agreements but great caution was displayed when it came to recommending legal intervention. This

---

[39] Report from the Industrial Council on the methods of securing the due fulfilment of industrial agreements, and of enforcing agreements throughout particular trades or districts (Cd 6952).
[40] *Ibid* at p 4.

stemmed not from an aversion to state interference in principle but from a concern lest the sound conduct of industrial relations be impeded. For example,

> the ultimate result of the institution of a system of legal money penalties for breaches of agreements or the legal prohibition of assistance to members in breach might be that the trade union leaders would find themselves precluded from entering into agreements at all, or, if agreements were entered into, that they would be compelled to insist upon the insertion of a clause which enabled them to terminate the agreements upon exceedingly short notice. An alternative to this might be defiance of the law, when there would at once arise all the difficulties inherent in any attempt to enforce the law against a large number of individual workmen—with no ultimate source of pressure short of imprisonment.[41]

The Council believing that agreements were being complied with as far as could reasonably be expected, if law were to demand more the consequences might well be unfortunate. Again there was the belief that the surest guarantee that an agreement would be kept was that it be voluntarily entered into.

The Council did favour some legal reform. They wished to see a process whereby the terms of a collective agreement could be extended and made obligatory on employers who were not party to the agreement but who were engaged in the same trade or district:

> where an agreement has been so declared to be extended, it shall be an implied term of any contract of service in the particular trade or district that the terms of the agreement shall be an essential part of such contract.[42]

This proposal was motivated by a concern that the stability of collective bargaining arrangements might be undermined by undercutting. Extension was to be conditional upon the agreement containing two specific clauses. First, that there should be an agreed term that there should be no stoppage of work or alterations of the conditions of employment until the dispute has been investigated by some agreed tribunal, and a pronouncement made upon it. This was consistent with a general exhortation that all agreements should contain such a clause. Secondly, it was to be a pre-requisite of extension that [a minimum period of] notice be given by either party of an intended change affecting conditions as to wage or hours. In addition, it was recommended that consideration should be given to whether the collective agreement,

---

[41] *Ibid* at para 33.
[42] *Ibid* at para 58.

or the rules of the employer's association or trade union party to the agreement, should contain a rule forbidding financial assistance to any member taking action in breach of the 'peace obligation.' The insistence on such conditions before the 'common rule' would be made obligatory was an indirect method of promoting model collective agreements.

Any discussion of greater legalisation of the machinery of collective bargaining may lead to questions as to the amenability of collective agreements to the legal process. The report took such considerations on board. It was felt by the Industrial Council that

> Industrial agreements cannot fairly be compared with the ordinary commercial contracts made between individuals or corporate bodies . . . in the case of industrial agreements circumstances may arise subsequent to the date of the agreement which might be held to justify a right of relief from the whole or some part of the terms of the agreement.[43]

More interestingly, the difficulties involved in the interpretation of collective agreements were discussed. The Council found that

> The form of words adopted is frequently only an approximation of the real intentions of the parties, the stress of the moment rendering it impracticable (and sometimes even undesirable) to enter into a strict analysis of possible literal meanings of a form of words which has been suggested by one side or other . . . so it sometimes happens that when the agreement comes to be put into practice different interpretations may be put upon some part of the document.[44]

It is open to question whether one implication of the foregoing position was that it would have been inappropriate to leave the interpretation of such an agreement to traditional judicial proceedings. On the other hand, the Council appeared to feel that it was possible to make the distinction between conflict of rights and conflicts of interest.

It can be seen that, as the Royal Commission had in 1894, the Council placed its faith in joint regulation by way of voluntary collective bargaining:

> The desirability of maintaining the principle of collective bargaining— which has become so important a constituent in the industrial life of the country—cannot be called into question, and we regard it as axiomatic that nothing should be done that would lead to the abandonment of a method of

---

[43] Report from the Industrial Council at para 32.
[44] *Ibid* at para 9.

adjusting the relationships between employers and workpeople which has proved so mutually advantageous throughout most of the trades of the country.[45]

Strong organisation and more sophisticated agreements (eg ones with improved disputes procedures) were expected to lead to collective bargaining becoming even more effective as a means of regulation. No theory of non-intervention in the labour law field existed to restrain the Council but, nevertheless, no practical benefits were envisaged from direct legal enforcement of collective agreements.

COMPULSORY ARBITRATION

Between 1900 and 1914 the issue of compulsory arbitration was raised in a variety of forums. It found support in a number of quarters which included weaker trade unions and a number of socialists, including Sidney Webb.[46] It was, however, always unlikely that any such scheme would end up on the statute book. The issue was one on which trade unions were very much divided. However, ultimately, the question of sanctions would always limit the amount of support available for compulsory arbitration. This was the fundamental difficulty which such variants as compelling suspension of hostile action pending arbitration did not, and could not, solve. Discussion on the issue was informed by comparative experience. In the search for greater peace in industrial relations the Government, by this time, was more than willing to take account of experience elsewhere. Askwith, who was then Chief Industrial Commissioner, reported to the Board of Trade on the enactment and operation of the Canadian Industrial Disputes Investigations Act 1907 (the 'Lemieux' Act).[47] The background to this measure was that in 1900 Canada had introduced a Conciliation Act which was a 'purely voluntary conciliation measure' and which was very similar to

---

[45] *Ibid* at para 29.

[46] And see the Report of the Royal Commission on Trade Disputes and Trade Combinations (Cd 2825). The report contains an additional report by Sidney Webb at p 18 which is worthy of attention. He did not regard industrial action as a good way of resolving trade disputes. He was very much drawn to recent developments in Australia and New Zealand:

> Such a system appears to offer, to the general satisfaction of employers and employed, both a guarantee against conditions of employment that are demonstrably injurious to the community as a whole, and an effective remedy for industrial war.

[47] Industrial Disputes Investigation Act of Canada 1907, Cd 6603 1912–13.

the 1896 UK legislation. Several years later the Railway Labour Disputes Act of 1903 was enacted and bestowed various powers on the government, including the ability to set up, what was in essence, a board of inquiry to inquire into the causes of the dispute. Whilst the board might publish its findings and make recommendations, any recommendation made was

> not in the nature of an award, enforceable in court, but rather an adjudication designed to carry with it the sanction of public opinion.

The 1907 Act was an attempt to extend the philosophy of the 1903 Act to a wider range of public utilities and to introduce an element of compulsion. The provisions of the Act were mandatory in certain public utilities[48] and had the effect of suspending the right to strike during a period where a Board of Conciliation investigated and reported on the merits of the trade dispute. Askwith took the view that reference to a board was mandatory in any industry to which the Act applied.[49] However, section 5 would appear to suggest that reference had to be made by one of the parties to the trade dispute. Certainly, once reference had taken place no lawful strike or lock-out could occur before the board had reported. The findings, however, of the board were not binding on the parties. The Act contained criminal penalties which sought to penalise anyone involved in industrial action during the 'cooling-off period.' Thus section 58 provided that any employer declaring or causing a lock-out, contrary to the provisions of the Act, shall be liable to a fine of not less than 100 dollars, nor more than 1,000 dollars, for each day or part of a day that such lock-out exists. Section 59 provided that any employee who went on strike contrary to the provisions of the Act shall be liable for a fine of not less than 10 dollars, nor more than 50 dollars, for each day or part of a day that he was on strike. Section 60 dealt with individuals who incited or encouraged others to take part in industrial action. Askwith found that

> the simple purpose of the act is to ensure the recognition of the interests of the public, as a third party, in trade disputes.[50]

It is interesting to note that the Act also contained a status quo clause (as did, the model clause mooted by the Industrial Council). It was

---

[48] By virtue of s 63 they might also be applied in other industries with the consent of both parties to a dispute.
[49] Industrial Disputes Investigation Act, above n 47, at p 6.
[50] *Ibid* at p 4.

stipulated that at least 30 days notice of an intended change affecting
conditions of employment with respect to wages or hours shall be given
and that, pending the proceedings before the board, in the event of such
intended change resulting in a dispute, the relations to each other of the
parties to the dispute shall remain unchanged, and neither party shall
do anything in the nature of a lock-out or strike.[51]

It must have been striking to contemporary observers just how
quickly the Canadians had moved from an approach involving purely
voluntary conciliation to one involving compulsion and penal sanctions. However, for Askwith, the most significant element of the 1907
Canadian legislation seems to have been the notion of public opinion
as arbitrator. He observed that

> while the public might often have much difficulty in bringing opinion to bear
> in favour of acceptance or rejection of technical decisions, which in many
> trades it would be impossible for persons who had not examined the ques-
> tion to understand, their support to the principle that the ordeal of battle
> should give place to reasonable judgment would probably be emphatic and
> frequently effective.[52]

However, whilst the role of the public was seen in a positive light
Askwith was troubled by the role of criminal penalties. This objection
appears to have been a practical one and not one of principle:

> In . . . cases where, by the imposition of penalties, efforts have been made to
> enforce the Act the results have not been satisfactory.[53]

At one level he observed that the

> government have often taken the line that the infliction of penalties should
> be left to the parties . . . and that it would be difficult for the government to
> treat a lock-out or a strike as if it were a crime.[54]

For the parties, however, the difficulties that the infliction of criminal
penalties might pose for future industrial relations was appreciated:

> the penalties can seldom be exacted by the parties with any advantage, as, if
> the proposals are accepted, a settlement is reached, and it is undesirable to
> raise bad feeling after a settlement. In addition, it is almost useless for
> employers to demand money from their own men, who may have been
> asking for higher wages on the ground that they have not enough money, or

---

[51] S 57.
[52] Industrial Disputes Investigation Act, above n 47, at p 16.
[53] *Ibid* at p 15.
[54] *Ibid* at p 11.

who have to be employed by the very persons who would be endeavouring to exact penalties from them. Attempts to penalise union officials would be likely to have, and in fact have had the effect of causing unnecessary labour resentment against the Act, and of adding to the popularity of the officials upon whom punishment is proposed to be inflicted, without acting in any sense as a deterrent for the future.[55]

Askwith considered whether such legislation might, with profit, be enacted in the UK. Certainly he viewed such a measure as being compatible with voluntary collective bargaining:

it presupposes that industrial differences are adjustable, and that the best method of securing adjustment is by discussion and negotiation.[56]

Given the difficulties perceived with the penal elements he saw 'the spirit and intent of conciliation [as] the more valuable portion of the Canadian Act . . .'[57] Accordingly

even if the restrictive features which aim at delaying stoppage . . . were omitted it would be suitable and practicable in this country.[58]

One might well ask, if such features were omitted, in what way would further legislation have enhanced the existing statutory framework. The answer to that question was probably to be found in the notion of the 'public as arbitrator.' Legislation of this type permits

the parties and the public to obtain full knowledge of the real cause of the dispute, and in causing suggestions to be made as impartially as possible on the basis of such knowledge for dealing with the existing difficulties . . . This action on behalf of the public allows an element of calm judgment to be introduced into the dispute which at the time the parties themselves may be unable to exercise.[59]

Within the UK, for a number of years, there was a motion at every TUC conference on compulsory arbitration. None of these motions were passed though they often attracted a respectable degree of support. The 1905 motion sought to instruct the Parliamentary Committee to draft a bill for presentation to Parliament which would have allowed the parties to a trade dispute to opt for resolution by compulsory arbi-

---

[55] Industrial Disputes Investigation Act, above n 47, at p 14.
[56] *Ibid* at p 7.
[57] Lord Askwith, *Industrial Problems and Disputes*, p 246.
[58] *Ibid*.
[59] Industrial Disputes Investigation Act, above n 47, at p 15.

tration. Arbitration would be undertaken by a Board of Conciliation and Arbitration comprised of an equal number of workers' and employer's representatives. It was envisaged that, in the absence of a mutual agreement, a chair would be appointed by the Labour Department of the Board of Trade. Interestingly enough a number of previous proposals that had come before the TUC had envisaged a judicial chair. This occurred even after the decision in *Taff Vale* and cannot have increased the chances of the TUC supporting compulsory arbitration. The 1905 Bill made no reference to the question of sanctions and, in the absence of any explicit scheme, one assumes that it was intended that contractual remedies would apply. The schemes proposed passed through a series of refinements and the 1906 scheme, highly surprisingly, included a clause allowing for criminal sanctions. This may help explain why the majority of congress against compulsory arbitration increased sizeably compared to 1905.

Compulsory arbitration was favoured by weaker unions, such as those who suffered recruitment and recognition difficulties. More powerful unions had a number of objections to it, one of the strongest (and more obvious) being that such schemes would restrict the right to resort to industrial action. Many trade unionists did not relish relinquishing any of what little control they possessed over their working lives. It may be objected that unions who did not wish to have constraints imposed on their capacity to take industrial action could simply have chosen not to opt for compulsory arbitration. On the other hand, the fear may have been that any actual legislation would have been more all-embracing. Stronger unions also feared that they would achieve less through arbitration than they would through collective bargaining. Those in favour of compulsory arbitration saw no difference in principle between legal regulation of this sort and existing laws such as the Factories Acts. Interestingly enough some opponents of compulsory arbitration already saw the solution to industrial relations difficulties as lying in the direction of nationalisation.

A Trades Disputes Bill was introduced in 1907, 1908 and 1909. It provided for arbitration by a Court of Arbitration, under the auspices of the Board of Trade, at the request of either party to a trade dispute. Binding awards could be issued and clause 10 provided:

> In the case of any breach of any of the terms of the award by the parties thereto or either of them or by any person for whom the court consider either party or parties responsible, the court may from time to time make a further award directing the party or parties in default to pay the other party

or parties such penalty as they think fit not exceeding 10 pounds for every day on which such breach occurs.

None of these bills progressed beyond the stage of a first reading. The Labour Disputes Bill of 1911 sought to compel a suspension of industrial action whilst conciliation was taking place. Supporters of this measure included Arthur Henderson. Clause 32 provided that it was unlawful for any employer to declare or cause a lock-out or for any employee to go on strike, on account of any dispute, prior to or during a reference of such dispute to a board of conciliation and investigation. The Bill went on to provide for financial penalties in the event of breach. It did not get beyond the stage of first reading, but is of note, in part, on account of the composition of its supporters.

OTHER MEASURES

During this period important instances of social legislation, in the wider sense, appeared on the statute book. Parliament introduced legislation dealing with matters such as old age pensions and unemployment and sickness insurance. This served to confirm the State's greater willingness to intervene in society and to regulate through law. It was also the case that the value of labour exchanges began to be extolled to an ever-increasing extent with German experience being a common reference point. Both the majority and minority reports of the Poor Law Commission recommended the establishment of such bodies.[60] The majority regarded this particular recommendation as vital and believed that two objects might be furthered as a result. First, that an increase in the mobility of labour would come about. Second, that information about the unemployed would be collected and distributed.[61] There was, however, to be no compulsion to use the exchanges. In an influential work Beveridge took the view that the deliberate organisation of the labour market was the first step in the permanent solution of the problem of unemployment.[62] In the event, the Labour Exchanges Act 1909 empowered the Board of Trade to establish and maintain labour exchanges. The Board were also empowered, by such means as they thought fit, to collect and furnish

[60] Report of the Royal Commission on the Poor Laws (Cd 4491).
[61] *Ibid* at para 487.
[62] WH Beveridge, *Unemployment: A Problem of Industry* (London: Longmans, Green & Co., 1909).

information as to employers requiring workpeople and workpeople seeking employment. It was believed that the Act would improve the mobility of labour and secure more regular continuity and distribution of employment. The advent of labour exchanges may not be thought to be of great significance in assessing the evolution of labour law. However, arriving at such a judgment would perhaps result from focusing on the permissive nature of the provisions; workers were not required to register nor were employers obliged to notify vacancies. Nevertheless, the Act had the potential to pave the way for much more in the way of State regulation of the labour market. Once such a measure had been enacted it was not difficult to envisage that elements of compulsion might be added. The majority, for instance, had noted that

> another method of compulsion which has been proposed is that the employers should be bound to employ all their casual labour through the labour exchanges.[63]

Indeed the minority had wished to see an element of compulsion in the scheme with the aim of promoting decasualisation in the labour market.

CONCLUSIONS

By the outbreak of the First World War, if one judged matters crudely by volume, there was a considerable amount of labour law on the statute book. A significant amount of this had emerged since 1900. We should not be surprised by this. Social legislation in a wider sense was making its way onto the statute book as the inequities in society (at least at the extremes) were starting to be seen as unacceptable:

> It is doubtful whether there is any more important condition of individual and general well-being than the possibilities of obtaining income sufficient to enable those who earn it to secure, at any rate, the necessaries of life. If a trade will not yield such an income to average industrious workers engaged in it, it is a parasite industry, and it is contrary to the general well being that it should continue.[64]

It is also important to note that employers' attitudes were becoming more flexible:

---

[63] Royal Commission, above n 60, para 565.
[64] Select Committee on Home Work, para 38.

From the late nineteenth century traditional capitalist hostility to government interference in the labour market began to fracture. Progressive employers were affected by the growing recognition of the 'problem of labour': unemployment and poverty, the deteriorating quality of labour power, declining competitiveness and class antagonism all took their toll.[65]

However, no widely subscribed philosophy had yet emerged as to the appropriate role for the law in industrial relations. As Wedderburn has put it 'the doctrine of "non-intervention" was not yet established'.[66] Indeed, if anything, matters appeared to be becoming even more fluid with traditional assumptions over the use of law being set aside. A good example of this is the regulation of the working hours of adult male labour in the form of the 1908 Act. In 1914 could one say that there were any conventions over the use of law? Measures such as the Acts of 1908 and 1912 might be thought to suggest that the scope for legal intervention was enormous. It was not surprising that, at the time, some chose to depict such measures as extensions of the protective philosophy underpinning the factories legislation. It is noteworthy that trade unions might well look to Parliament to regulate conditions of work. For instance, the 1908 Act represented the fulfilment of a long-standing goal of the miners. Similarly the railwaymen looked to Parliament to furnish a right of recognition.[67] Again

> Institutions within the trade union movement, such as the TUC itself, the United Textile Factory Workers' Association, and in its early days perhaps even the Miners' Federation, existed primarily for the purpose of promoting legislation favourable to labour.[68]

It is little wonder that some contemporary commentators saw the trade boards legislation as leading inevitably to much more extensive legislative control over wages. Expansion of the scope of legal regulation did not stand to be restricted by philosophical constraints. Where industrial relations matters were concerned the prevailing ideology was pragmatism.

---

[65] M Langan and W Schwarz (eds), *Crises in the British State 1880–1930* (London: Hutchinson, 1985) p 114.

[66] KW Wedderburn, 'Introduction: A 1912 Overture' in KW Wedderburn and WT Murphy (eds) *Labour Law and the Community—Perspectives for the 1980s* (London: Institute of Advanced Legal Studies, 1982) p 1.

[67] H Clegg, *A History of British Trade Unions Since 1889* vol II (Oxford: Clarendon Press, 1985) pp 11–12.

[68] J. Lovell, above n 3, p 45.

The foregoing notwithstanding, a highly significant factor existed which suggested that there might well be limits to the extent that the scope of legal regulation might expand; that factor was the continued reliance on collective bargaining as a means of rule-making in industry. Moreover, recourse to the social sanction of industrial action was left unimpeded by the Trade Disputes Act 1906. Reliance on collective bargaining was also an increasing one in that it expanded and prospered at this time: 'The development of collective bargaining was the outstanding feature of this period [1889–1910].'[69] In an age still highly ambivalent about the wisdom of state interference (whether in matters of labour or otherwise) it was likely that the existence, or even potential emergence, of collective bargaining machinery would, at least on occasion, be invoked to justify the absence of intervention by government. Such a stance was justifiable not only in terms of political philosophy but also, at least for some of the time, in terms of results:

> Between 1899 and 1907 it might well have been argued that the conclusions of the Royal Commission on Labour were being proved correct. Strong organisation on both sides, together with provision for discussion, bargaining, and, if need be, outside conciliation or voluntary arbitration, seemed to be ushering in an era of industrial peace.[70]

The Government displayed support for collective bargaining in a variety of ways. For instance, the philosophy of the Labour Department of the Board of Trade was that

> industrial relations issues should be handled jointly by employers and workers. To deal with them effectively, the parties needed to be organised into trade unions and employers' associations, and to set up joint machinery . . .[71]

Given this philosophy the department had two fundamental objectives in intervening in a dispute:

> to settle the issues currently in dispute; and to establish or improve permanent arrangements for the conduct of industrial relations.[72]

The department proved to be very active in its encouragement of the establishment of joint machinery. Having said that, Government

[69] Clegg, above n 1, at p 471.
[70] *Ibid.*
[71] Clegg, above n 67, at p 98.
[72] *Ibid.*

did little beyond the work of the Board of Trade to promote collective bargaining. It was enough that self regulation in industry avoided the need for more extensive regulation by government.

4

Responding to Taff Vale[1]

INTRODUCTION

P RESENT DAY COMMENTARY on the law relating to trade disputes has often made much of the form that the British legislation has taken. The system of immunities being regarded as

the curious British method of affording to workers in a modern democratic society what in many other countries are positive rights.[2]

The question of why this form was adopted is undoubtedly an interesting one. However, it might be argued that is has obscured a more fundamental, and much more significant, issue; that being why in the UK legal regulation of trade disputes was traditionally to be seen only at the margins. There is, after all, no automatic link between the existence of a scheme of immunities and a policy of non-intervention. Nevertheless, for most of the twentieth century the law did not seek to regulate the conduct of industrial action to any significant extent. Prior to 1984, and the introduction of strike ballots, statute did not impose any procedural restraints on the taking of industrial action. The means by which industrial action might be furthered were similarly unfettered. Finally, until 1982, the range of purposes for which industrial action could lawfully be taken was very wide. As Kahn-Freund put it the State held the ring in trade disputes.[3] Until the 1980s the statutory law on trade disputes, with the exception of the period 1971–74, had changed little since the Trade Disputes Act of 1906, the latter being

---

[1] For discussion see R Kidner 'Lessons in Trade Union Law Reform: the origins and passage of the Trade Disputes Act 1906' (1982) 2 *Legal Studies* 34, J Saville, 'The Trade Disputes Act of 1906' (1996) 1 HSIR 11.

[2] Lord Wedderburn of Charlton, 'Industrial Relations and the Courts', (1980) 9 ILJ 65 at 70. See also, by the same author, 'The New Structure of Labour Law in Britain' (1978) 13 IR LR 435.

[3] 'Labour Law' in M Ginsberg (ed) *Law and Opinion in England in the 20th Century* (London: Stevens, 1959).

introduced to solve the problem caused by the decision in *Taff Vale*.[4] The Act is very short; comprising only five sections. As has been discussed in chapter three the surprise caused by *Taff Vale* was immense. It would be easy to testify to this by reference to contemporary trade union reaction. However, there might be felt to be a degree of predictability in hostility from the trade union camp. Nevertheless, at least equally cogent evidence is contained in an article published in 1901, very much restrained in tone and content, by Frederic Harrison who had done so much to bring about the 1871 settlement.[5] He wrote that

> It is not too much to say that these judgments have practically made new law; law which might prevent trade unions from doing things that for twenty five years, they have believed they had a right to do; and which exposes the whole of their funds to legal liabilities to which till now they have been thought to be exempt.[6]

PRAGMATICISM AND SOLUTIONS

The Trade Disputes Act 1906, along with the Act of 1871, were to be the key components of British trade union law until, in 1971, the enactment of the Industrial Relations Act. Nevertheless, 1906 did not bear witness to a comprehensive review of the law relating to industrial relations. Both the 1906 Act, and the Royal Commission report which preceded it, were exercises in problem-solving in the wake of *Taff Vale*. The Commission's terms of reference were 'To inquire into the subject of trade disputes and trade combinations and as to law affecting them . . .' The Commission interpreted this as meaning that they should not 'go into such general topics as were covered by the report of the royal commission on Labour, 1894 . . .' This narrow approach was reflected in the content of their report which never really rose above the level of a somewhat dry and technical legal discussion. The subsequent Liberal government did not initiate any further investigation before moving to legislate. In a sense the only, fully elaborated, model schemes available remained those produced by the Royal Commission in 1869. All that said, in looking at the response to *Taff Vale*, two key questions must be

---

[4]   The judgment in *Taff Vale* was handed down on 22 July 1901. Early in 1903 the case was settled for £23,000.

[5]   See ch. 1.

[6]   F Harrison, *Positivist Review* (1901) 9 177 at 177.

posed. First, why was a relatively non-interventionist scheme decided upon? Second, why did that scheme take the form of immunities from common law liabilities? It is particularly important to separate out those matters given the contemporary emphasis on the distinctive nature of the scheme of immunities.

Understanding why the 1906 Act emerged in the form that it did necessitates trying to establish both what contemporary observers would have regarded as the key problems to be confronted and the realistic possibilities available in terms of legislative reform. Clearly the exposure of union funds to tortious liabilities was the most compelling problem to be addressed. The difficulty of picketing within the terms of the law, after *Lyon v Wilkins*, also demanded attention. For some trade unions, at this time, picketing was a crucial means in furthering a strike. Questions were also posed by the developments which had taken place in the law of the economic torts. Turning to possible solutions, it should be made clear that a scheme of positive rights was simply not on the agenda.[7] Instead one finds that the genuine options fell broadly into three categories. First, the position prior to *Taff Vale* might have been restored. Second, a more modest measure might have been introduced to ameliorate the impact of *Taff Vale*; for instance, by amending the law of agency. Third, the route of incorporation (rejected in 1871) could have been followed; this might have been accompanied by other changes such as a refinement of the law of agency in its application to trade unions. A priori, other options might have been possible but, since they were not mooted at the beginning of the twentieth century, need command less attention. By the time the 1906 Liberal government had come to power the trade union movement was adamant that the pre-*Taff Vale* position be restored. However, trade union reaction to *Taff Vale* had been mixed and had legislation arrived earlier things might have turned out differently.[8] Initially, some union leaders appear to have accepted the increase in legal involvement in union activities; others may have been prepared to resign themselves to it.

Of the options under consideration at the time, incorporation would have involved the most radical change. The Act of 1871 had a number of distinctive features. A key one being section 4, which restricted legal

    [7] See below at p 115.
    [8] F Bealey and H Pelling, *Labour and Politics 1900–1906* (London: Macmillan, 1958) p 81, HA Clegg et al, *A History of British Trade Unions Since 1889* (Oxford: Clarendon Press, 1964) p 319.

enforcement of certain agreements entered into by trade unions.[9] Discussion of incorporation tended to assume that, should it take place, section 4 would be repealed in the process. Logically, however, repeal need not have been the corollary of incorporation. Incorporation would have brought trade unions and the law into a much closer relationship. Moreover, it might have had a number of benefits for trade unionists (the actual worth of those potential benefits was, however, a matter for debate). It should be said that, in so far as benefits were involved, they could have been realised, by and large, by the simple repeal of section 4.[10] One such suggested benefit being the ability to enforce by law the contract of membership. This would have allowed, for instance, a union to go to court to recover arrears of subscriptions. The conferring of the capacity of enforcement could have been combined with a legislative scheme of the sort contained in the Friendly Societies Act 1896. Such schemes sought to confer more extensive legal rights without unduly interfering with self-regulation. Thus section 68(1) of the 1896 Act provided that all disputes [of a prescribed nature] should be determined in a manner directed by the rules of the society, and the decision so given shall be binding and conclusive on all parties without appeal. Moreover, the section went on to stipulate that all such disputes were not removable to any court of law or restrainable by injunction. However, in marked contrast to section 4 of the 1871 Act, once a dispute had been so resolved, application might be made for the enforcement thereof to the county court.[11] Turning to actions in tort, incorporation would have made clear that a union was equally capable of suing an employer as being sued by one. One instance, at least in theory, where unions might have wished to found on such capacity would have been to allow them to sue an employer for inducing breach of the contract of membership.[12] The possibility of such an action might have offered a measure of protection against 'union-busting' tactics of an employer. For instance, an employer might have sought to allow only strikers who resigned from the union to return to employment. However, probably the greatest interest posed by the prospect of incorporation would be the change to a trade union's

---

[9] See above at p 11.
[10] Leaving aside questions such as those concerning the capacity of unregistered unions to enter into contracts etc.
[11] C Edwards, (1902) 51 *Nineteenth Century* 233 at p 247.
[12] *Ibid* at p 248.

capacity to enter into contracts with third parties.[13] What might this
have meant on the industrial relations front? If section 4 had also been
repealed a trade union would have been able to enter into fully legally
enforceable collective agreements with both individual employers and
employers associations.[14] Brown has commented that

> it also followed that if unions could be sued as corporate entities then they
> could also enter into legally binding contracts, especially with employers;
> and to some union leaders this was quite an attractive proposition.[15]

Why might this have had appeal for trade unions? It is important to
bear in mind that, at the beginning of the twentieth century, a considerable proportion of workers still lacked recognition for collective bargaining purposes. Accordingly, union leaders would have given serious
consideration to potential ways to entice employers to recognise them.
At least some of them would have considered entering into legally
enforceable collective agreements since their existence might mean that

> there would be even greater tendency than at present to seek a solution of
> labour difficulties in collective agreements between the opposing associa-
> tions of employers and employed. The suspicious employer would the more
> readily acquiesce in such agreements if he felt he could make the workmen's
> union pay for it in case of breach by individual workmen . . . This power
> might, therefore, have a certain steadying effect upon industrial relations,
> without, probably, diminishing the fighting effectiveness of either side.[16]

Legally enforceable collective agreements aside, there was also the
question of compulsory arbitration. Clearly, the Government could
have introduced a scheme of compulsory arbitration irrespective of
whether trade unions were to be incorporated (whether that would
have been sensible is quite another matter). However, for the minority
in the labour movement who would have welcomed the introduction of

[13] One might raise the question as to why post *Taff Vale* a trade union, if it could be
sued in its own name in tort, could not enter into contracts? It might be argued that, in
the light of the majority view, a registered union could sue and be sued in respect of contracts entered into by it. Whilst none of the judgments specifically deal with this issue
their wording is so wide as to suggest that this must be so. In the words of Lord Shand

> the power of suing and liability to be sued in the society's name is clearly and neces-
> sarily implied by the provisions of the statutes.

Nevertheless, the issue remained unclear for a good number of years.
[14] This would have been subject to the proviso that the terms of the agreement did not
offend the law of restraint of trade.
[15] KD Brown, *The English Labour Movement 1700–1951* (Dublin: Gill and
Macmillan, 1982) p 199.
[16] Edwards, above n 11, at p 249.

compulsory arbitration the question seems to have become, to some extent, linked with incorporation. This is perhaps because it was supposed that the basis for arbitration would have been contractual. Clegg writes that Bell of the Railway Servants believed that *Taff Vale* had conferred upon trade unions

> the power of concluding legally enforceable agreements, thus furthering the cause of compulsory arbitration, which he had very much at heart as a means of overcoming the railway companies' resistance to recognition.[17]

The impact of *Taff Vale* on a trade union's contractual capacity had yet to be clarified by Parliament or the courts; incorporation would have achieved this. Viewed from the perspective of a trade union leader at this time incorporation, along with compulsory arbitration, may have seemed an acceptable price to pay for recognition. Finally, 'Some unionists saw in legal liability a way of encouraging responsible behaviour or limiting rank and file militancy.'[18] Presumably this was on the basis that, in the future, union executives would have to be much more discriminating when authorising industrial action. They would also be able to justify decisions not to intervene by reference to the cost of potential actions for damages.

It might be argued, therefore, that incorporation would have brought a number of benefits to trade unions. Whether these benefits would have been regarded as outweighing those conferred by the settlement of 1871 is an entirely different matter. For instance, the fact that incorporation might have lead to legally enforceable collective agreements would, of itself, have prompted union leaders to be cautious over such a reform. There may have been a fear that employers would seek to restrict trade union power by means of collective agreements with stringent 'peace obligations':

> The suspicious employer would the more readily acquiesce in such agreements if he felt he could make the workmen's union pay for it in case of breach by individual workmen.'

Trade unions would not have been attracted at the prospect of being responsible, in law, in the event of a breach of an agreement by their members. Much more fundamentally, whatever its intrinsic merits, incorporation, without more, would not solve the problem caused by

---

[17] Clegg, above n 8, at p 319. Edwards, above n 11, noted that under the Compulsory Arbitration Act in New Zealand trade unions were incorporated.

[18] KD Brown, *The English Labour Movement 1700–1951* above n 15, p 199.

Taff Vale. Nonetheless, it could have been introduced along with protection against the key economic torts such as simple conspiracy and inducing breach of contract. The foregoing is not an outlandish suggestion when it is recalled that incorporation under the companies legislation brings with it the privilege of limited liability. If picketing had been legalised as well trade unions would not have needed any further protection and the privilege of section 4 of the 1906 Act would have been superfluous. The political climate in the aftermath of *Taff Vale* was not overly sympathetic to trade unions and the labour movement might well have been prepared to accept any reasonable settlement. In 1903 a bill to tackle the *Taff Vale* problem, which was backed by the TUC, was introduced to the Commons by Shackleton and was a modest measure. It consisted of only two substantive clauses. It had originally contained a third clause which would have offered protection against liability in tort except where the action had been authorised by the union and was intra vires the rule book. This clause was drafted on the narrow assumption that the problem, that *Taff Vale* had created, for trade unions was potential liability for unofficial action.[19] With respect to the bill that was introduced the first clause aimed to improve the position on picketing and, in fact, closely resembled the section which was actually enacted in 1906. The second clause provided immunity from the tort of simple conspiracy when committed in the context of a trade dispute. The conservatism of this position is reinforced by the fact that Dilke had brought forward a bill in the previous year which provided for an immunity for union funds. Clause 3 of that bill provided that an action shall not be brought against a trade union, or against any person or persons representing the members of a trade union in his or their representative capacity, for any act done in contemplation or furtherance of a trade dispute. Dilke was not content to confine reform to modifications to the law of agency. However, as time went on attitudes hardened and the labour movement became unwilling to settle for anything less than a complete reversal of *Taff Vale*:

> If the government had desired to obtain a moderate bill with the consent of the unions, they could almost certainly have had it in 1903. Since the government chose to reject the overtures of the union leaders, however, the latter had very little incentive to oppose the clamour of their followers for complete immunity, the 'permanent remedy.'[20]

[19] The clause was dropped following an objection by the speaker that it was inconsistent with the title of the bill. See Clegg, above n 8, at p 322.
[20] Clegg, above n 8 at p 324.

If the Conservative government had decided to be pro-active, and had sought to ameliorate the consequences of *Taff Vale* in tandem with a regime which regulated industrial action more closely, they might well have been successful in this. In terms of a legislative model they need have looked no further than that of incorporation which, after all, had been flagged up for use in the trade union context by the majority in 1871. If such a model had formed the basis for reform, law and industrial relations would have moved into much closer proximity. Workers and trade unions might well have become used to a greater degree of legal regulation.

Given that the subsequent return to the position existing prior to *Taff Vale* was at odds with the desires of the Conservatives why did the Government not decide to take the initiative? One explanation for this is that, for a number of Conservatives, the decision in *Taff Vale* did not present a difficulty. The Prime Minister (Balfour) seems to have viewed the decision as representing sound policy: the case

> simply puts the trade unions in the same position as every other company or corporate body, such as a railway or a bank, and makes them subject to the ordinary law of the land.[21]

Moreover, the Prime Minister

> has no doubt that this is in substance right, and that the singular freedom of the country from unnecessary trade disputes is largely owing to it. Nevertheless, from a purely electoral point of view, it will no doubt put those members of the Unionist party who have a large trades union element in their constituencies . . . in a considerable difficulty, and may lose them many votes. The Cabinet were very clearly of opinion that, in spite of electoral considerations, it was our duty in the interests of the country at large to resist any demands which we conceive to be contrary to justice and sound policy.[22]

It was also the case that, to the extent that the solution of incorporation was linked to compulsory arbitration, it would not have appealed to a Conservative government disinclined to state intervention.[23] For some contemporary commentators of a right-wing persuasion the

---

[21] RF MacKay, *Balfour* (London: J Murray, 1891) p 218 quoting from a letter from Balfour to the King dated 12.11.1904.

[22] *Ibid*

[23] A Briggs 'Unions and Free Labour: Background to Taff Vale Decision at p 321 in A Briggs and J Saville (eds) *Essays in Labour History* (London: Macmillan, 1971) notes that 'Intervention and socialism were for many indistinguishable terms . . .'

labour law developments which had recently occurred in Australia were anathema.[24] Leaving aside the 'correctness' of the decision, Balfour did not see the need on tactical political grounds to introduce a limited measure to 'spike' something along the lines of the 1906 Act. This was because there was not the slightest indication, at this stage, that a future Liberal government would seek to restore the position prior to *Taff Vale*. Whatever the reasons, by delaying taking action, the chances of a more legally regulated scheme being introduced were much diminished. The fact that a more interventionist scheme was neither established, nor sought, was to prove highly significant. A state of affairs whereby trade disputes were conducted free of legal interference was being allowed to both continue and develop further. It can be argued that it was the failure to legislate at this time, more than any other factor, which meant that the State would find it difficult to do anything other than 'hold the ring' in trade disputes for the foreseeable future.

THE ROYAL COMMISSION

The report of the Dunedin Commission was not implemented but remains of interest as representing contemporary establishment values.[25] It is worth recalling that the bill originally introduced by the incoming Liberal government was very much based on the Commission's report. The composition of the commission was a matter of some controversy:

> The inclusion of Sir William Lewis, who had a fair claim to be considered the leading industrial opponent of trade unionism, was provocative, and the chairman, . . . Lord Dunedin . . . had recorded his vote against the motions in the House in May 1902 and again in 1903. The balance might have been redressed by the fact that two of the three remaining members were Sidney Webb and Sir Godfrey Lushington, neither of whom was hostile to the unions. But Webb had made public his view that the unions would not be justified in claiming the restoration of complete immunity from legal proceedings, while Lushington had called Taff Vale 'just and salutary law.' The

---

[24] See, for instance, C Fairfield 'State Socialism in the Antipodes' in T MacKay (ed) *A plea for Liberty* (London: J Murray, 1891).

[25] Report of the Royal Commission on Trade Disputes and Trade Combinations (Cd 2825).

fifth member was Arthur Cohen . . . a lawyer of similarly conventional views.[26]

The Commission approached their remit in a decidedly legalistic fashion. Moreover, their outlook was profoundly conservative in that their underlying premise was that industrial action was legitimate to the extent it did not give rise to common law liabilities. It might be asked how the Commission would have justified section 3 of the 1871 Act which freed trade unions from the doctrine of restraint of trade! The answer, although it involved a fundamental inconsistency, was that such existing statutory concessions were also seen as legitimate. Accordingly, a key question was whether the decision in *Taff Vale* contravened the 1871 settlement. The Commission was of the view that it did not:

> the law laid down by the House of Lords involved no new principle and was not inconsistent with the legislation of 1871.[27]

The practical difficulties of suing an unincorporated association explained the previous absence of litigation: the 'long practical immunity . . . was simply the result of defects in general legal procedure . . .'[28] This explanation is wholly unconvincing. The 'practical difficulties' in 1871 were so immense that if Parliament had intended that unions be capable of being sued it would have been obliged to provide for incorporation. Nevertheless, since *Taff Vale* was regarded as being consistent with the intention of Parliament it would be inappropriate to change the law. A position which, in any event, was seen as being correct on policy grounds:

> that vast and powerful institutions should be permanently licensed to apply the funds they possess to do wrongs to others, and by that wrong inflict upon them damage, perhaps to the amount of many thousands of pounds, and yet not be liable to make redress out of those funds would be a state of things opposed to the very idea of law and order and justice.

Taff Vale allowed the law of tort to discharge its key functions of deterrence and compensation. The evidence of employers to the Commission had been to the effect that Taff Vale had made

> trade unions much more careful than heretofore in seeking not to infringe the law with the result that strikes have been less frequent, that in the

[26] Clegg, above n 8, pp 324–25.
[27] Dunedin, above n 25, at para 60.
[28] *Ibid* at para 31.

conduct of trade disputes there has been less violence and intimidation, and that the disputes themselves have been easier to settle than was the case before the law was authoritatively laid down.[29]

Whilst the Commission did not endorse this evidence as such, the tenor of the report can be seen as indicating acquiescence.

As I have indicated, the Commission based their recommendations on the premise that the 'right to strike' should exist but only to the extent permitted by the common law. The limitations of this formalistic approach are perhaps most glaringly illustrated by the fact that the Commission did not regard it as appropriate to recommend that an immunity be granted in respect of the tort of inducing breach of contract.[30] This was despite the fact that it was acknowledged expressly that, where trade unions were concerned, their 'chief strength must necessarily lie in collective action.'[31] The Commission had, however, viewed the boundaries of legitimate industrial action as being marked out by statutory concessions as well as common law liabilities. Respecting the former boundary led to a number of recommendations being made to 'tidy-up' the legal position. With regard to the law on the economic torts, it seems to have been accepted that *Quinn v Leatheam* had left the standing of *Allen v Flood* in some doubt. It was, therefore, suggested that the legislature declare that an individual shall not be liable for doing any act not in itself actionable in tort only on the ground that it is an interference with another person's trade, business or employment. Moreover, *Quinn* was also seen as disrupting the 1875 reforms. At that time, the crime of conspiracy had largely been removed from the industrial relations scene.[32] The Commission were of the view that it would be inappropriate to, in effect, re-impose such a liability in a civil form. Thus, it should be provided that a conspiracy in contemplation or furtherance of a trade dispute should not give rise to a civil action unless indictable.

The Commission discussed the position in relation to picketing given the decision in *Lyon v Wilkins*. This caused a measure of difficulty. On the one hand, the act of picketing was thought likely to transcend the boundaries of legitimate behaviour given that it might well give rise to common law liabilities such as nuisance. Moreover, picketing was perceived as a form of anti social behaviour:

[29] *Ibid* at para 39.
[30] *Ibid* at para 60.
[31] *Ibid* at para 57.
[32] See above at p 22.

watching and besetting for the purpose of peacefully persuading is really a contradiction in terms . . . it is obvious how easy it must be to pass from the language of persuasion into that of abuse, and from words of abuse to threats and acts of violence.[33]

On the other hand, given that the legitimacy of industrial action was accepted, persuading workers to strike, of itself, was unobjectionable. In the result, it was recommended that the 1875 Act be amended. Accordingly, before Section 7 was infringed a defendant would have to act

in such a manner as to cause a reasonable apprehension in the mind of any person that violence will be used to him or his family, or damage be done to his family.[34]

Two further recommendations were made by way of concession to the union movement. First, it was suggested that

means shall be furnished whereby the central authorities of a union may protect themselves against unauthorised and immediately disavowed actions of branch agents.[35]

The latter recommendation displayed some understanding of the nature of trade union organisation. At this point in time, the application of the law of agency to trade unions had not dominated the case law. However, there had been indications that there was a good deal of scope for union liability to be accentuated by it.[36] Nevertheless, it appears that the recommendation may well have been as much inspired by an assessment by the Commission of the nature of trade union organisation as by judicial decisions. The view was taken that trade unions at national level often had limited control over their constituent elements:

[branches] . . . are often in a semi-independent position to the union as a whole or its central executive. It is not unnaturally looked on as a hardship

---

[33] Dunedin, above n 25, at para 48.
[34] *Ibid* at para 60.
[35] *Ibid* at para 36.
[36] In *Taff Vale* at p 433 Farwell J had held that the law as stated in *Barwick v English Joint Stock Bank* (1867) LR 2 Ex 259 was applicable to trade unions. In *Barwick* it had been held that an employer is answerable for torts committed by an employee in the course of employment and for the employer's benefit, even in the absence of an express command. The approach of Farwell J was followed in *Giblan v NALU* [1903] 2 QB 600 which held that a union would be liable for acts which were not ultra vires of the union but only of its officers.

that the funds of the whole union may be rendered liable by the unauthorised act of some branch agent.[37]

The second concession came by way of a grant of protection for trade union funds which were held for benefit purposes: the law should

provide for the facultative separation of the proper benefit funds of trade unions, such separation if effected to carry immunity from those said funds being taken in execution.[38]

It is clear that implementation of the foregoing recommendations would have improved the lot of workers in a most limited way. There was no desire to shield unions from the key common law liabilities such as inducing breach of contract, let alone from the evolution of the common law. The taking of industrial action by workers would, in most instances, give rise to the risk of liability in damages being incurred by trade unions. Union funds were only to be protected to the extent that they were held for benefit purposes. Finally, the Commission also recommended that

facultative powers be given to the Trade Unions, either (a) to become incorporated subject to proper conditions, or (b) to exclude the operation of section four of the 1871 Act, or of some one or more of its subsections, so as to allow Trade Unions to enter into enforceable agreements with other persons and with their own members.[39]

The reasons behind this were not elaborated upon in the report of the Commission but the recommendation is consistent with their legalistic stance. The natural inclination of the Commission, to the extent that trade union affairs were not already regulated through law, was to suggest reform that would facilitate legalisation. Incorporation would have led to internal and external union relations being regulated through the law of contract. The Commission would have endorsed the view of the Webbs that

The trade unions should forego their position of being outside the law, and should claim, instead, full rights, not only citizenship, but actually of being duly authorised constituent parts of the social structure, lawfully fulfilling a recognised function in industrial organisation.[40]

---

[37] Dunedin, above n 25, at para 36.
[38] *Ibid* at para 60.
[39] *Ibid* at para 66.
[40] S & B Webb, *The History of British Trade Unionism, 1866–1920* (Edinburgh: Printed by the authors for the trade unionists of the United Kingdom, 1920 edn), p 605.

Taff Vale had brought the unions into line in respect of tort liability, the same should happen in respect of contractual capacity. Incorporation would facilitate legally enforceable contracts being entered into by trade unions and employers or employers associations.

As we have seen the initial trade union reaction had been somewhat mixed. However, attitudes were to harden. A significant factor in all of this was the cumulative impact of judicial decisions. Had *Taff Vale* stood alone it might have been viewed as an unfortunate, but isolated, incident. However, it did not stand alone. It followed the Court of Appeal decision in *Lyon v Wilkins* and preceded the House of Lords decision in *Quinn v Leatheam*. The potential of *Taff Vale* to decimate union finances also quickly became glaringly apparent. *Taff Vale* itself was settled out of court for £23,000, a very significant sum of money in 1903. Moreover, the dispute had not been a national one but merely one concerning a railway company in South Wales. The later case of *Glamorgan Coal v SWMF* resulted in damages being awarded against the union as a result of inducement of breach of employment contracts[41]—a tort which it was difficult to avoid committing in the course of organising a trade dispute. The consequences of the combination of the change in union legal capacity and the impact of the economic torts (whose scope was rapidly expanding) became clear:

> What is often missed in the discussion of the Taff Vale case is that other unions began to be mulcted for damages in cases brought against them.[42]

Judicial decisions apart, the stance of the Government was less than conciliatory and was not conducive to promoting a spirit of compromise. In any event, many trade unionists believed that the 1871 Act had been intended to put them 'outwith the law' and that the passage of time had accorded a 'prescriptive right' to this immunity. Indeed, the Attorney General was to state in the Commons that

> without fear of challenge from either lawyer or constitutional historian Parliament in 1871 or 1875 intended to create this immunity, and according to the general assent of the politicians and lawyers of the day, and of a whole

---

[41] [1905] AC 239.
[42] Saville, above n 1, at p 15, n 16.

generation of their successors, down to the year 1901, this immunity had, in fact, existed and had authority.[43]

Distrust of the judiciary played its part in union insistence on restoration; the view being expressed in the Commons that 'Trade unions had very good difficulty in getting level justice in a court.' Ultimately, the underlying motivation was basically the pragmatic belief that the 1871 settlement had worked and that the sensible thing to do was to restore it—a view further reinforced by the general feeling of trade unionists that the immunity was a basic right.

THE LIBERAL GOVERNMENT

As we have seen, there were three possible avenues of reform in vogue at the time. One could restore the pre *Taff Vale* position, one could mitigate the effects of *Taff Vale* by amending the law of agency, or one could incorporate. Why was the latter not favoured? An argument that had proved significant in 1871 arose again; to give trade unions full legal personality would rekindle the controversy as to the enforcement of the union rule book. Much of the discussion seems to have been based on the assumption that incorporation would result in the repeal rather than amendment of section 4; albeit that, a priori, this need not have been the case. Indeed, the Dunedin Commission had, at one point in their report, distinguished between a trade union's internal and external relations. The Webbs, however, noted that repealing section 4 would require 'a great advance in public opinion' and the Government certainly did not wish to see injunctions being issued against strike breakers, etc. Robson, the Solicitor General, commented as follows:

> a trade union would be able, would be entitled then to go, and to go with a very good case, to the court of chancery and ask that injunctions should issue against certain of its workmen who in breach of their contract with the union proposed to go back to work . . . The trade unions having got those injunctions, what follows? Imagine the case of some great strike with, it may be, hundreds of thousands of workmen, under pressure of starvation, desiring to return to work. They have been forbidden by law. We hear a great deal about watching and besetting and picketing. That would become an obsolete controversy then, because the trade union would be entitled to go before the court and demand to receive the aid of the law and their pickets

---

[43] Parl. Deb., HC, 5.11.1906, vol 164, col 162.

would be the police, and, if need be, perhaps the military. I wonder what we should hear then about peaceful persuasion.[44]

Thus the fact that to provide for incorporation was assumed to involve a repeal of section 4 counted against it. Again, as in 1871, it was argued that trade unions were essentially voluntary associations and, while this might have become a good deal less convincing, this argument still seems to have carried some weight.

The bill as introduced to the Commons by the Government was very much based upon the recommendations of the Royal Commission. Clause 1 provided an immunity where simple conspiracy was committed in contemplation or furtherance of a trade dispute. Clause 2 amended the law on picketing in a way very similar to the eventual enactment. Clause 3 provided, for the avoidance of doubt, that mere interference in the trade or business of another did not give rise to liability. Clause 4 of the bill, as introduced to the Commons, amended the application of the law of agency. The Royal Commission had stated that

> It is not unnaturally looked on as a hardship that the funds of the whole union may be rendered liable by the unauthorised act of some Branch. Agent. We recommend that means shall be furnished whereby the central authorities of a union may protect themselves against unauthorised and immediately disavowed actions of branch agents.[45]

Clause 4 provided that

> Where a committee of a trade union . . . has been appointed to conduct on behalf of the union a trade dispute, an action whereby it is sought to charge the funds of the union with damages in respect of any tortious act committed in contemplation or furtherance of the trade dispute, shall not lie, unless the act was committed by the committee or by some person acting under their authority.[46]

However, clauses of this nature could provide only marginal help in terms of the problem caused by *Taff Vale*. Certainly, the clause offered a way of ameliorating the risk, of liability in damages, arising from unofficial action. However, the fundamental problem of the exposure

---

[44] Parl. Deb., HC, 25.4.1906, vol 155, cols 1486–87.

[45] Dunedin, above n 25, at para 36.

[46] The clause went on to provide that a person shall not be deemed to have acted under the authority of the committee if the act was an act or one of a class of acts expressly prohibited by a resolution of the committee, or by the committee by resolution expressly repudiating the act as soon as it is brought to their knowledge.

of union funds to meet tortious claims would have remained. It is important to appreciate that there was to be no immunity in respect of inducing breach of contract. Moreover, in some quarters at least, there was instant scepticism over an agency approach:

> The law of agency . . . was a continuation of judge-made law, it was useless for all practical purposes as a means to enable them to escape from one set of legal difficulties, to invite them to take another equally dangerous and to a considerable extent an unknown path, subject to the legal subtleties of the courts.[47]

The legislative scheme that was actually enacted was much more favourable to trade unions, and prompts one to ask why the Government moved, from an approach based on the law of agency, to the privilege contained in section 4? Section 4 prohibited actions in tort against trade unions except in certain circumstances. One technical reason for dropping the 'agency approach' was a desire for clarity and certainty:

> there was less risk of actual litigation on disputed questions going to Court of Law, passing from one stage of appeal to another, and involving loss of temper, money and time, by adopting the perfectly simple and common sense method imported in the alternative clause, than if they were to lay down in regard to industrial combinations a new code of the law of agency.[48]

The foregoing is very much a partial explanation and the real reason somewhat more difficult to fathom. However, it is undoubtedly the case that the decision to opt for complete immunity owes a great deal to the personal initiative of Campbell-Bannermann. In a speech to the Commons on 30th March 1906, after the announcement of the Government's proposals and apparently without consulting colleagues,[49] he announced, in a radical departure, that he favoured complete immunity. In the process he observed that

> I have never been and I do not profess to be now very intimately acquainted with the technicalities of the question, or with the legal points involved in it.

---

[47] Parl. Deb., HC, 30.3.1906, vol 155, col 23.
[48] Parl. Deb., HC, 3.8.1906, vol 162, col 1713.
[49] C Cross, *The Liberals in Power 1905–14* (London: Barrie and Rockliff, 1963) p 32, J Wilson, *A Life of Sir Henry Campbell-Bannermann*, p 505. Wilson also points at p 572 that Campbell-Bannermann behaved in a very similar fashion over the Workmen's Compensation Bill. And see KD Brown, 'Trade Unions and the Law' in CJ Wrigley (ed) *A History of British Industrial Relations 1875–1914* (Brighton: Harvester, 1982) p 127.

The great object then was, and still is, to place the two rival powers of capital and labour on an equality so that the fight between them, so far as fight is necessary, should be at least a fair one . . .[50]

The reason the Prime Minister changed his mind remains something of a mystery:

the lack of direct evidence reduces explanation to the level of speculation in which few have been willing to indulge.[51]

Having said that, it seems safe to say that the Prime Minister was well disposed to the interests of labour.[52] His biographer said of him 'that he was essentially a man of the left.'[53] In passing, it is also worth mentioning that Brown makes the intriguing suggestion that neither the Prime Minister

nor his followers regarded the matter as one of prime importance. It had certainly not been a major Liberal concern during the election campaign.[54]

The change of heart by the Prime Minister swung the momentum in favour of those who desired the restoration of the pre *Taff Vale* position. However, it is not a sufficient explanation as to why restoration took place. After all, the Liberal government were themselves divided with a majority of the Cabinet opposed to offering absolute immunity; the position of the Liberal backbenchers is also clearly highly relevant. It has been suggested that 'large numbers of Liberal MPs were under electoral obligation to support the changes in law that were being demanded.'[55] It is not, however, absolutely clear that this was the case. One historian has concluded that

Analysis of election manifestos suggests strongly that most Liberal candidates had in mind a moderate bill of the sort first introduced by David Shackleton in 1903.[56]

What is perhaps most certain is that there was a great deal of sympathy for the cause of labour within the ranks of Liberal MPs at this time. Campbell-Bannerman's belief in the importance in achieving a greater balance of power between the two sides of industry was held more widely:

[50] Parl. Deb., HC, 30.3.1906, vol 155, cols 51–52.
[51] Brown, above n 49, at p 128.
[52] J Wilson, above n 49, at p 506.
[53] *Ibid* at p 635.
[54] Brown, above n 49, at p 128.
[55] Saville, above n 1, at p 31.
[56] Brown, above n 49, at p 128.

One of the most essential things to the well-being of this country is the condition of the industrial classes. Trade unions are an essential safeguard
against this country's being turned into the paradise of the sweater. It is the
greatest mistake in the world to suppose that a matter affecting the vital
interests of the industrial classes is not an intensely national question. We
cannot injure them without injuring ourselves, for we are all members of one
another.[57]

There was a fear that the burden of litigation might severely weaken
the unions and grossly restrict their bargaining power. Some wondered
if workers would remain union members if their subscriptions were to
be 'confiscated by the lawyers.' It may also have been relevant that the
last body to have looked at industrial relations in the round, the Royal
Commission of 1894 which reported in the wake of the industrial relations difficulties of the early 1890s, did not recommend a move away
from the settlement of 1871. There would also appear to have been an
absence of organised opposition on the part of employers and, as a consequence, a lack of lobbying of MPs and Ministers.

The volte-face over trade union immunity should not be allowed to
obscure other significant changes to the bill as introduced to
Parliament.[58] Dilke displayed a great deal of vision in proposing a
number of important amendments. Thus, he proposed, successfully,
that an immunity be provided against liability for inducing breach of
contract in contemplation or furtherance of a trade dispute.[59] In comparison to the blanket immunity offered by section 4 this amendment
was something of a secondary measure but, nevertheless, a very important secondary measure. It is also striking that the amendment had not
been pressed for by the labour movement. Dilke also proposed an
amendment in relation to picketing to deal with the possibility of pickets being found liable, despite the 1906 Act, for nuisance.[60] He suggested that the words 'and such attending shall not be held to be a
nuisance' should be added to the tabled clause.[61] The Government
viewed the amendment as unnecessary and were not prepared to accept
it. However, it was a noteworthy attempt to clearly demarcate the
boundary between action legitimate under the statutory scheme and

[57] Parl. Deb., HC, 25.4.1906, vol 155, col 1494.
[58] It might seem surprising to note that the bill introduced by government did not contain a definition of trade dispute. Instead such a definition was added during the course
of parliamentary proceedings.
[59] Saville, above n 1, at p 34.
[60] *Ibid* at p 36.
[61] Parl. Deb., HC, 3.8.1906, vol 162, col 1655.

behaviour which would otherwise give arise to liability at common law. If the Dilke amendment had been passed it might have served to offer an adequate basis, in law, for the act of picketing.

Responding to the 1906 Act

Section 3 of the 1906 Act provided immunity in respect of certain specified torts. No consideration appears to have been given to offering protection against others heads of common law liability that might, in the future, be deployed against trade unionists. The most likely explanation for this would appear to be that the scheme of the 1906 Act very much involved the enactment of specific solutions to contemporary problems. For instance, given that trade unions had been sued for directly inducing breach of employment contracts, an immunity was called for.[62] Nevertheless, it is striking that, but for the Dilke amendment, one would not have been provided. Against this backdrop, it was clear that Parliament would be much less likely to provide an immunity in respect of torts which had not yet been utilised by employers. As a consequence, the legislative scheme left trade union organisers vulnerable to attack from either torts that had not hitherto been deployed against them or to refined versions of existing torts. However, in the years immediately following the enactment of the 1906 Act, there was little attempt made to develop the common law of economic torts. What explanation might be offered for this? This is a difficult question to answer but part of the explanation undoubtedly centres on the immunity contained in section 4. Given the width of that immunity plaintiffs would not be assisted in a damages action against a trade union by discovering a new economic tort. On the other hand, the fact that, for example, section 3 provided immunity against inducing breach of employment contracts but not commercial contracts might have been thought to have suggested possible lines of attack to plaintiffs in pursuit of trade union organisers. It is something of a mystery that such issues do not appear to have been raised until the 1952 case of *Thomson v Deakin*.[63] On occasion, the unavailability of a defendant

---

[62] What of *Temperton v Russell* [1893] 1 QB 715 where the plaintiff sued after the union persuaded his suppliers not to fulfil their contracts?
[63] [1952] Ch 646.

with the means of meeting a damages award would have been an important consideration.

Given the foregoing it is clear that developments in the law of the economic torts offer a limited means of assessing the judicial response to the 1906 Act. An alternative way of doing this is to look at the way in which the Act was interpreted. The reported cases between 1906 and 1914 reveal a variety of attempts by plaintiffs to restrict the scope of the protection afforded by the statute. One question which arose was whether the presence of an ulterior motive could cause a defendant to forfeit the protection of the immunities. In the Court of Appeal in *Conway v Wade* the Master of the Rolls (Cozens-Hardy) had thought not: 'the motive of the act, as distinct from its purposes, seems irrelevant.'[64] The House of Lords thought differently and took the view that the words used imported motive:

> If, however, some meddler sought to use the trade dispute as a cloak beneath which to interfere with impunity in other people's work or business, a jury would be entirely satisfied in saying that what he did was done in contemplation or furtherance, not of the trade dispute, but of his own designs, sectarian, political or purely mischievous, as the case might be.[65]

By insisting on a defendant acting from proper motive the courts allowed themselves a means of control should they wish to restrict the ambit of lawful industrial action. Certainly the requirement of proper motive might be argued to be a gloss on the statute.[66] To obtain the protection of the immunities a defendant might have felt that he merely had to show that a trade dispute existed and that he had acted in furtherance of it. The dicta of the Law Lords show a reticence to accept the will of Parliament. On the other hand, it should be said that the dicta in *Conway* on motive were obiter. It is important to appreciate that when the issue again arose in the Court of Appeal in *Dallimore* the relevance of motive was doubted.[67]

[64] [1908] 2 KB 844 at p 850. And see Kennedy LJ at p 862 to the same effect.

[65] [1909] AC 506 at p 512, per Lord Loreburn LC at p 512. This obiter dictum was concurred in by Lord Gorell at p 520 and Lord MacNaghten at p 513.

[66] KD Ewing, 'The Golden Formula: Some Recent Developments' (1979) 8 *ILJ* 133 at p 134. Motive might also be in issue at the earlier stage of determining whether or not there was a trade dispute in existence at all. In *Conway*, above n 64, at pp 520–21 Lord Shaw of Dunfermline observed that

> I cannot see my way to hold that trade dispute' necessarily includes . . . every case of personal difference between any one workmen and one or more of his fellows.

[67] 1912 (29) TLR 67 at p 68, per Cozens-Hardy MR.

A second potentially restrictive point of interpretation was reviewed by the House of Lords in *Vacher v London Society of Compositors*.[68] The issue was whether the trade union immunity from actions in tort, provided by section 4(1), was limited to instances where the union was acting in contemplation or furtherance of a trade dispute. In holding that the subsection was not so limited it might be thought that their Lordships were merely arriving at an inevitable conclusion. Apart from anything else, the first three sections of the Act were stated expressly only to apply to actions in contemplation or furtherance of a trade dispute. The fact that, in contrast, the subsection at issue contained no such qualification would appear to offer the strongest of indications that none should be implied. Indeed Lord Moulten was to remark, of the argument for the plaintiff, that

> This contention appears to me to be directly contrary to the most elementary principles of the construction of statutes.[69]

This decision by the House of Lords, in such a clear cut case, might be thought to furnish very little in the way of evidence of judicial attitudes. Nevertheless, one might go on to ask why the plaintiffs appealed at all having already lost before the Court of Appeal. It may be that, within the legal community, the prevailing mood encouraged the belief that there was always a good chance of achieving a result 'against the odds' should a trade union be the defendant. Certainly Farwell LJ (dissenting) had held against the union in the Court of Appeal:

> I think myself at liberty therefore, and indeed bound, to try and find some fair construction that will avoid the conclusion that section 4 has given trade unions a charter of absolute immunity for the consequences of all tortious acts, and has thereby encouraged and induced the commission of torts.[70]

Such an approach from Farwell LJ is not too surprising. However, Channell J had refused to strike out the action against the union at an earlier stage in the proceedings. Moreover, in *Rickards v Bartram*, Darling J had arrived at the same conclusion as Farwell LJ.[71]

A third point of interpretation arose over the issue of who might properly be parties to a trade dispute within the meaning of section 5(3)

---

[68] [1913] AC 107.
[69] *Ibid* at p 129.
[70] [1912] 3 KB 547 at p 558.
[71] 1908 25 TLR 181. He had, however, previously arrived at the opposite conclusion in *Bussy v ASRS* 1908 (24) TLR 437.

of the Act. The latter definition section encompassed 'any dispute between employers and workmen, or between workmen and workmen . . .' Where did this leave a trade union? At first instance in *Dallimore v Williams* the judge had ruled that there was no trade dispute within the wording of the statutory definition but merely a dispute between the trade union and the employer. This approach was rejected by the Court of Appeal who adopted a purposive approach to this question of statutory interpretation.[72] The foregoing approach acknowledges the practicalities of trade disputes whereby trade unions will act on behalf of the membership. An obiter dictum in *Conway v Wade* went the other way:

> where . . . an intruder . . . interfered, and by threats and molestation stirred up strife and disputes which neither employer nor workmen thereto thought of, he should [not] be made irresponsible because of the very mischief he intended and hoped to stir up . . .[73]

The Osborne Judgment[74]

The Act of 1871, wholly intentionally, did little to regulate the internal affairs of trade unions. Moreover, access to the courts was restricted by virtue of section 4. As time progressed, it appears that the courts became less inhibited by that section in the granting of judicial orders. In terms of interference in trade union internal affairs, matters were to come to a head in two cases dealing with union financial support for parliamentary activities. In *Steele v South Wales Miners' Federation* rule 3 dealt with the objects of the union and paragraph 12 stated that one object was to

> provide funds wherewith to pay the expenses of returning and maintaining representatives to Parliament and other public councils and boards, and to request them to press forward by every legitimate means all proposals conducive to the general welfare of the member of the federation.[75]

The union sought to raise money for a parliamentary representation fund and Steele sought an injunction to restrain the union from

[72] 1912 (29) TLR 67.
[73] Op cit per Lord Atkinson at p 518. However, Lord Loreburn at p 512 took a different view: 'the section cannot fairly be confined to an act done by a party to a dispute.'
[74] For detailed discussion of the case and the subsequent legislation, see KD Ewing, *Trade Unions, The Labour Party and the Law* (Edinburgh: Edinburgh University Press, 1982).
[75] [1907] 1 KB 361 at p 362.

misapplying union funds by returning representatives to, or maintaining them in, Parliament. It was argued that rule 3(12) was ultra vires in that its purpose did not fall within the statutory definition of a trade union. The Divisional Court, however, were of the view that

> the definition was not intended to be exhaustive, or to prevent an association from lawfully doing other acts beyond those there mentioned.[76]

In any event, Darling J was of the view that even if the definition had been exhaustive the purposes mentioned in rule 3(12) fell within those specified in section 16:

> it seems to me that one of the ways of regulating relations between workmen and masters, or workmen and workmen, or masters and masters, is to get laws passed by Parliament for their regulation, and that one of the first steps towards getting those laws passed would be to send a representative to Parliament to promote a bill for that purpose.[77]

This view was endorsed by Lord James in the House of Lords in *Osborne v Amalgamated Society of Railway Servants*.[78] The view propagated in *Steele* was to prove very short lived. *Steele* was overruled by *Osborne* which also dealt with the legality of a levy for the purposes of parliamentary representation. There is a clear thread running between *Osborne* and *Taff Vale* in terms of the judicial conceptualisation of a trade union. The latter treated a trade union as having some kind of quasi-corporate status and *Osborne* extends this by applying the ultra vires rule:

> it is true that the Act does not make the trade union a corporation; but, taking the only distinctive word used, a 'combination', it can hardly be suggested that it legalises a combination for anything, and if some limit must be placed on its powers, one can only apply the same rules that were agreed to in . . . [Ashbury].[79]

Applying a statutory version of ultra vires was arguably wrong but is at least consistent with the approach in *Taff Vale*. Interestingly enough, Lord Shaw, perhaps influenced by pluralist thought, had difficulty with the corporate analogy:

> Long before the statutes of 1871 and 1876 were enacted trade unions were things in being, the general features of which were familiar to the public

---

[76] [1907] 1 KB 361 at p 367.
[77] *Ibid.*
[78] [1910] AC 87 at p 98.
[79] *Ibid* at pp 92–93.

mind. They were associations of men bound together by common interests for common ends. Statute did not set them up and, speaking for myself, I have some hesitation in so construing language of statutory recognition as a definition imposing such hard and fast restrictive limits as would cramp the development and energies and destroy the natural movements of the living organism.[80]

Having adopted a statutory based concept of ultra vires the next question to consider was whether the proposed expenditure was intra or ultra vires. The House of Lords took the view that it was ultra vires:

> there is nothing in any of the Trade Union Acts from which it can be reasonably inferred that trade unions, as defined by Parliament, were ever meant to have power of collecting and administering funds for political purposes.[81]

However, no real explanation is given for this position by the Law Lords. Turning to the judgments of the Court of Appeal a number of reasons emerge. In the first place, in interpreting the statutory definition of a trade union, account was taken of the nature of trade union activity in 1871 and it was noted that the 'maintenance of parliamentary representation was no recognised object of trade unions.'[82] In the second place the view was taken that Parliament cannot have intended that trade unions pursue political activities because their membership may embrace individuals of all political persuasions:

> I cannot think it was the intention of the Legislature that it should be competent to a majority of the members to compel a minority to support by their votes, still less by their subscriptions, political opinions which they may abhor, under penalty not only of being expelled from the union, and thus losing all chance of benefit, but also the risk, and in some cases very serious risk, of not being able to find employment in their trade in consequence of the refusal of trade union members to work with non-union members.[83]

Third, there was the role of the trade union immunities:

> I cannot bring myself to believe that the Legislature intended to allow a combination whose purposes were to a considerable extent trading or political propagandism or any other of the lawful purposes which one could mention, which have nothing to do with the relations of masters and workmen,

[80] *Ibid* at pp 107–8.
[81] *Ibid* at p 97.
[82] [1909] 1 Ch 163 at p 186 per Fletcher Moulton LJ and at p 174 per Cozens-Hardy MR. And see Lord MacNaghten in the House of Lords at [1910] AC 87 at p 98.
[83] *Ibid* at p 175.

to obtain for itself such a statutory immunity by including within its purposes some regulations such as those adopted by genuine trade unions.[84]

Lord James and Lord Shaw did not find against the union on grounds of *vires* but, instead, on constitutional grounds. Lord James' objection arose from the fact that Labour MPs were subject to the party whip:

> I construe this condition as meaning that the member undertakes to forgo his own judgment, and to vote in Parliament in accordance with the opinions of some person or persons acting on behalf of the Labour Party. And such vote would have to be given in respect of all matters, including those of a most general character, such as confidence in a Ministry or the policy of a budget—matters unconnected, directly at least, with the interests of labour.[85]

This view was based on an anachronistic view of political life which did not allow for party politics. Lord Shaw's judgment delved into much more sweeping constitutional issues: 'Take the testing instance: should his view as to right and wrong on a public issue as to the true line of service to the realm, as to the real interests of the constituency which has elected him, or even of the society which pays him, differ from the decision of the Parliamentary party and the maintenance by it of its policy, he has come under a contract to place his vote and action into subjection not to his own convictions, but to their decisions. My Lords, I do not think that such a subjection is compatible either with the spirit of our Parliamentary constitution or with that independence and freedom which have hitherto been held to lie at the basis of representative government in the United Kingdom.'[86] Lord Shaw's position was also based on the existence of the union rule which provided that candidates were to be 'responsible to and paid by the Society.' Ewing comments on the rule as follows:

> In a parliamentary democracy the . . . condition would clearly be intolerable if it meant that the member of Parliament was to act at the bidding of his union. The member is a representative of his electors, not of interest groups which canvass his support or to which he has any personal loyalty. But on examination it is difficult to believe that this is what was intended by the union rule. It simply stated that there was a responsibility of candidates to the union, without specifying what that meant. It certainly did not say that members of Parliament would be responsible to the union.[87]

---

[84] [1909] 1 Ch 163 at p 185.
[85] *Osborne*, above n 78, at p 99.
[86] *Ibid* at p 111.
[87] Ewing, above n 74, at p 30.

Whilst *Osborne* might be viewed in a similar vein to *Taff Vale,* it is open to the same criticism that the attribution of quasi-corporate status was contrary to the intention of Parliament. In addition, it was further contrary to the legislative scheme by interfering in trade union internal affairs. The minority in 1871 had said that

> Trade Unions are essentially clubs and not trading companies, and we think that the degree of regulation possible in the case of the latter, is not possible in the case of the former. All questions of crime apart, the objects which they aim for the rights which they claim and the liabilities which they incur, are for the most part, it seems to us, such as courts of law should neither enforce, nor modify nor annul. They should rest entirely on consent.[88]

Osborne and subsequent cases on political funding[89] served to confirm the existence of a judicial unwillingness to accept a non-interventionist role. In response to the decision in *Osborne* the trade union movement wished to see a complete restoration of the previous position whereby trade unions could incur political expenditure provided the contract of membership was observed.[90] The Liberal government was unwilling to accede to this. Instead they were willing to legislate on the basis that political expenditure was only legitimate if a number of safeguards were adhered to. The Trade Union Act 1913 provided that expenditure on political objects to which it applied could only take place provided such expenditure had been approved by a majority vote of the membership. The political objects to which the Act applied were, inter alia, the expenditure of money on a Parliamentary candidate's election expenses and on the maintenance of any person who was an MP. Following a vote authorising such expenditure a union had to have rules in force, approved by the Registrar of Friendly Societies, providing (a) that any payments in the furtherance of those objects were to be made out of a separate fund (the political fund), and for the exemption of any member of the union from any obligation to contribute to such a fund if he gave notice that he objects to contributing; (b) that a member who was exempt from the obligation to contribute to the political fund of the union shall not be excluded from any benefits of the union, or placed in any respect either directly or indirectly under any disability or at any disadvantage as compared with other members of the union by reason of his being so exempt, and that contributions to the

---

[88] Royal Commission on Trade Unions (Cd 4123, 1869), at p lix.
[89] Ewing, above n 73, at pp 32–37.
[90] TUC Annual Report (1912) p 12.

political fund of the union shall not be made a condition for admission to the union. Aggrieved individuals had the right of complaint to the registrar. Where the registrar upheld the grievance he had power to 'make such order for remedying the breach as he thinks just in the circumstances.' Once such an order was registered in court it became enforceable as if it was a court order. The importance of the role given to the registrar is further demonstrated by the fact that an order emanating from him was

> binding and conclusive on all parties without appeal and shall not be removable into any court of law or restrainable by injunction.

Arriving at an assessment of judicial attitudes in the wake of *Taff Vale* is not particularly straightforward. It would, of course, be easy to fasten upon extravagant statements by particular judges and point to them as demonstrating judicial reluctance to accept the policy underpinning the 1906 Act. Farwell LJ remarked that 'The Legislature cannot make evil good, but it can make it not actionable.'[91] In a similar vein Darling J regarded the 1906 Act as placing trade unions 'super legem, just as the medieval Emperor was super grammaticam.'[92] Such dicta cannot, and should not, be ignored but too much focus upon them can give rise to a distorted picture. As we have seen, the enactment of the 1906 Act seems to have curtailed, for a while at least, the expansion of the economic torts. There are, however, indications that judges turned to exploring means of statutory interpretation through which the protection afforded by the immunities might be restricted. One might draw comparison here with the activities of the Court of Appeal during the late 1970s.[93] However, it is of note that the only restrictive device which remained intact by 1914 was that of withholding the protection of the immunities to those acting out of improper motives. Even that was in doubt given that the discussion of this issue was obiter in *Conway* and the views to the contrary expressed in *Dallimore*. On the other hand, *Osborne* and the decisions on political funding which followed can be viewed as a continuation of the attack on the settlement of 1871. Such decisions suggested that judicial respect for statutory protection of trade unions was very fragile. It is notable that, if the legislature had intended the 1906 Act to serve, in part, as a

---

[91] [1908] 2 KB 844 at p 856.
[92] *Bussy v ASRS*, above n 71, at p 437.
[93] KD Ewing, above n 66.

judicial rebuke following *Taff Vale,* then that went unheeded by the House of Lords in *Osborne.*

RIGHTS, IMMUNITIES AND NON-INTERVENTION

Let us turn to the question that has provoked much contemporary discussion. Why was a scheme not introduced based on rights? Wedderburn attributes this to the nature of the labour movement in the formative period of UK labour law. On his analysis that period

> saw a unique conjunction of three elements in Britain: (i) a relatively strong but wholly industrial labour movement; (ii) the absence of a working-class political party, with the political ideology of which the unions might have been associated; and (iii) the first, but gradual extensions to men of political franchise.[94]

One might wish to cavil with the second point of the foregoing analysis at a descriptive level. After all, one of the consequences of *Taff Vale* was the emergence of the Labour Representation Committee who were in favour of complete immunity.[95] In any event, in terms of explanation as to why the UK favoured immunities it seems less than convincing. It might be inferred from Wedderburn's second point that detachment from 'political ideology' made a 'rights' system less likely. This is confirmed by his observation that

> In other European countries trade unions were part of a labour movement that included an ideology and a political party or parties and therefore strove to achieve positive legal rights—rights to associate, to bargain, to strike.[96]

This meant that the British Labour Movement 'made pragmatic not ideological demands.'[97] However, both the 1871 and 1906 legislation were heavily influenced by intellectuals sympathetic to the labour movement. Positivists had provided the thinking behind the former settlement. Sir Charles Dilke had a significant part to play in 1906.[98] Dilke lobbied hard to persuade the TUC parliamentary committee that the

---

[94] Wedderburn, above (1980), n 2, p 71.
[95] Clegg, above n 8, at p 322.
[96] 1978 Is LR 435 at 436–67.
[97] *Ibid* at p 437.
[98] S Gwynn and GM Tuckwell, *Sir Charles Dilke* (London: J Murray, 1917) pp 365–67.

pre *Taff Vale* position be restored. He also was a vigorous critic of the wording of the 1906 Bill and the mover of important amendments. It must be the case that such individuals supplied the sort of input that, had the political scene been different, might well have flowed from party intellectuals/ideologues. Moreover, by the time we get to 1906 knowledge of other systems was much more extensive and it would have been possible to have based reform on this. It may be that a significant factor was the absence of a written constitution in the UK and, as a consequence, a lack of a tradition of bestowing positive rights. Given such a culture, the enactment of a positive right to strike would not been viewed as an option. Furthermore, and probably much more importantly, viewing matters through 1906 eyes, the 1871 settlement had been regarded as largely successful up until the decision in *Taff Vale*. The way forward would have seemed to be one of amending the existing scheme in order to repair the damage done by the judges, rather than contemplating a completely new approach. Whether a scheme involving positive rights would have made a difference to the way in which the judiciary viewed trade disputes cases is open to argument. It may well be that, since legislation protecting industrial action would inevitably conflict with the common law, there would have been little in the way of practical consequences.[99]

If the absence of a rights based system can be explained, in part, by the enduring strength of the settlement of 1871 then so can the policy of non-intervention. It might well be said that the

> whole policy of the Bill was founded on the established right of workmen for any reason which they in their judgment thought sufficient to abstain from work. . .They were the best judges of that.[100]

Nevertheless, the Parliamentary debates in 1906 contain references to moves to restrict immunity to primary strikes and to render employee-only disputes illegitimate. Such proposals tended to be rather summarily discussed and met with little enthusiasm, the debate in Parliament being concentrated around the proposed clause 4 and the law on picketing. In later years controversy over the proper ambit of the purposes

---

[99] The wording of the section on picketing might be usefully considered at this stage. It is expressed somewhat differently from the sections that surround it in that it commences with the words 'it shall be lawful.' Why this should be so is not entirely clear. Wording along these lines appears to have first emerged in the 1903 Bill. The fact that it remained in the version which was enacted may, to some extent, illustrate the lack of coherent thinking in the drafting of the 1906 Act.

[100] Parl. Deb., HC, 27.7.1906, vol 162, cols 141 and 161.

for which industrial action may be taken arose in relation to 'political' strikes. This was not an issue in 1906 though the Government believed 'that trade disputes should be limited to those concerned with questions of employment and conditions of employment.'[101] Their concern was presumably to prevent personal grudges etc from masquerading as trade disputes.

CONCLUSIONS

From the enactment of the 1906 legislation until 1982 trade union funds were immune from actions in tort.[102] The 1906 Act, and section 4 in particular, was of great importance to trade unions. There is some evidence to suggest that *Taff Vale* had had an impact on the extent of industrial action.[103] The lasting success of the Act is in some ways surprising when one considers that its content was determined, much more by the cut and thrust of parliamentary proceedings, and not by the coherent vision of the great statesmen of the day. The *Taff Vale* case may well have afforded an opportunity to move to a much more legally regulated system; any such opportunity was not seized. The Conservative government lacked the vision, and almost certainly the desire, for legislation of this sort. It was, of course, the case that the attention of Balfour's administration was taken up with other issues—such as tariff reform. A Royal Commission report might have filled the gap but, partly on account of its composition, the one which did report was overly concerned with technical legal points. There was little prospect of the Commissioners involved offering anything in the way of industrial relations policy. Having said all of that, had Balfour foreseen the steps that Campbell Bannermann was prepared to take, he might have acted more positively. Once the 1906 Act was placed on the statute book it was going to be very difficult to effectually control industrial action through law. A tradition was being allowed to develop whereby trade unions could pursue such activities with minimal restraint by the law. Again, as time went on, more unions became stronger and the prospect of legal regulation would be less likely to be viewed by them as bringing sufficient advantages to outweigh the disadvantages.

---

[101] Parl. Deb., HC, 5.11.1906, vol 164, col 232.

[102] Apart from the period 1971–1974 when the Industrial Relations Act was in force.

[103] See the review of the evidence in Clegg, above n 8, at pp 326–28.

5

The Impact of War 1914–1918

INTRODUCTION

T HE OUTBREAK OF the First World War posed a military challenge
on an unprecedented scale for British government. It soon became
apparent that a similar challenge to the administrative resources of the
state would arise. In the course of the war two new ministries which
had involvement with industrial relations were established: the
Ministry of Labour and the Ministry of Munitions. As part of the
mobilisation for war movement towards tripartism occurred. With
the effluxion of time state interventions in many areas steadily
increased. For instance, state action was taken to direct and control the
economy. Such intervention went beyond anything that would have
been envisaged before the war. Moreover, as the war progressed the
extent of such intervention grew. A similar trend was seen in the industrial relations field.[1]

From virtually the beginning of the war, Government realised that
the co-operation of both sides of industry would be vital. In response
to Government appeals and exhortations a number of joint meetings,
between employers' organisations and unions, were held where the
issues for discussion were topics such as the relaxation of restrictive
practices. The latter was regarded as a sensitive issue:

> The suspension of restrictive rules and customs was justly regarded by the
> workman as imperiling the most highly valued and hard won safeguards of
> his standard of living.

One of the practical results of such government appeals was that, at the
end of August 1914, the trade union movement resolved

> That an immediate effort be made to terminate all existing trade disputes,
> whether strikes or lock-outs, and whenever new points of difficulty arise
> during the war period, a serious attempt should be made by all concerned to
> reach an amicable settlement before resorting to a strike or lock-out.[2]

---

[1] On this period see GR Rubin, *War, Law, and Labour* (Oxford: Clarendon Press, 1987).
[2] Official History of the Ministry of Munitions (hereafter OHMM), vol I, Pt II p 31.

In the months to follow the level of strikes fell dramatically but began to rise again from early in 1915.

Progress on negotiations over matters such as the suspension or relaxation of restrictive practices proved to be painfully slow and the Board of Trade became involved with a view to expediting the proceedings. Their involvement had a limited impact and in March 1915 the Government became more heavily involved by setting up a conference 'with a view to reaching some general understanding with them about the suspension of restrictive rules and practices.' This involved a meeting between a number of members of the Government including the Chancellor (Lloyd George) and union representatives. The result was the Treasury Agreement whereby the unions agreed to recommend to their members that for the duration of the war there should be no stoppage of work on munitions or other war work. Where a dispute could not be resolved through the normal channels it was to be referred to arbitration. Paragraph 3 of the agreement provided for the establishment of an advisory committee, representative of organised workers, for the purposes of facilitating the carrying out of these recommendations and for consultation by the Government of the workmen concerned. The unions also agreed to recommend that restrictive practices be relaxed to increase the output of munitions and war equipment. This was, however, conditional on Government requiring the contractors involved in such production to give an undertaking which, amongst other things, made clear that any departure from existing practice was only for the duration of the war. The Treasury agreement proved to be very much a dead-letter and perhaps the main reason for this was the absence of any restriction on profits. In the event, in the three months immediately following the agreement, strikes increased in number.[3] The history of all this also illustrated the growing gap between union officialdom and the rank and file.

Having become frustrated by reliance on voluntary means the Government then turned to legislation. The Munitions of War Act 1915 enshrined the provisions of the Treasury agreement but also sought to control profits made by employers. Those engaged in war production were not allowed to resort to a strike or lock-out. Trade disputes were to be resolved by means of compulsory arbitration. Greater restrictions existed in controlled establishments where wages and profits were to be controlled and restrictive practices suspended.

[3] H Wolfe, *Labour Supply and Regulation* (Oxford, 1923) p 120.

THE 1915 ACT

Compulsory Arbitration

The Act sought to ensure continuity and efficiency in the production process. Thus the right to strike was curtailed; restrictive practices were suspended. The Act was also concerned with the supply and movement of labour. Part one of the Act dealt with trade disputes involving workers employed in war production. In particular, the Act applied to those employed in the manufacture of munitions, armaments etc. By royal proclamation it could also be extended to other employments

> on the ground that in the opinion of His Majesty the existence or continuance of the difference is directly or indirectly prejudicial to the manufacture, transport or supply of Munitions of War.

Opposition from the miners and cotton operatives meant that the arbitration provisions of part one would only apply to them in the event of a proclamation being issued. Where the Act was applicable the dispute mechanisms of the Act applied to differences between any employer and person employed or between any two or more class of persons employed over certain subject matters. The Act only covered

> differences as to rates of wages, hours of work, or otherwise as to terms or conditions of or affecting employment . . .

It can also be seen that the legislation did not extend to action taken against the government qua government rather than qua employer.

Part one provided that where a dispute was not determined by the parties directly concerned either party was entitled to report the matter to the Board of Trade. In a sense the process was voluntary at this stage. In fact, a significant element of indirect compulsion existed in that, where a relevant dispute existed, a failure to refer meant that the right to resort to industrial action was curtailed. The Board were under an obligation to consider any difference so reported and to take any steps, which seemed expedient, to promote a settlement of the difference. This might include encouraging the parties to engage in further collective bargaining. In any case in which they thought fit, the Board was empowered to refer the matter for settlement either in accordance with the provisions of the first schedule to the Act or, if in their opinion suitable means for settlement already existed, in pursuance of any agreement between employers and persons employed, for settlement in accordance with those means. A reference under the schedule involved referral to an arbitration tribunal, which might be constituted in one of three forms: the Committee on Production; a single arbitrator agreed upon by the parties (in the absence of agreement the Board of Trade would appoint); a court of arbitration consisting of an equal number of persons representing employers and persons representing workmen with a chair appointed by the Board of Trade. Should a reference be made under the schedule, the form of the tribunal were to be determined by agreement between the parties or, in the absence of such an agreement, by the Board of Trade. Arbitration was most likely to be undertaken by the Committee on Production or by a single arbitrator. It was the former body whose influence was by far the more pervasive. In effect, for the duration of the war, it became a national arbitration tribunal.

The Committee on Production was reluctant to interfere in the pre-war basis of wages and awards would normally be on the basis of increases in the cost of living which, in any event, were the main factor in pay claims. A common clause in an award of the committee being:

> The amounts hereby awarded are to be regarded as war advances intended to assist in meeting the increased cost of living, and are to be recognised as due to and dependent on the existence of the abnormal conditions now prevailing in consequence of the War.

The influence of the committee is demonstrated by the strong tendency for its awards to be followed, in trades related to those in respect of which awards were made, and for government departments with any responsibility for wages to take a lead from it. The original composition of the committee was the Chief Industrial Commissioner (Askwith) and a representative of the War Office and the Admiralty. One reason for the frequent resort to this particular form of arbitration was said to be respect for the committee's competence and impartiality. The latter must have been put under a great deal of strain when, in late 1915, Government sought to restrain the level of pay rises and sent the following communication to the Committee of Production:

> His Majesty's Government have given earnest attention to the financial position of the country, to the great and increasing demands which will still be made upon its resources to meet the needs of the war and to the imperative need for economy in all forms of expenditure and consumption, both public

and private. They have also had regard to the general advances of wages that have already been given since the beginning of the war and to the measures already taken to tax or limit the profits of undertakings. HM Government have come to the conclusion that in view of the present emergency any further advance of Wages (other than advances following automatically from existing agreements) should be strictly confined to the adjustment of local conditions, where such adjustments are proved to be necessary.[4]

The Committee allowed themselves to be influenced by this for a number of months, which caused a great deal of resentment. After all, the quid pro quo for the loss of the right to strike had been access to impartial arbitration and not Government diktat over wages. The analysis of the official history is worthy of note:

> The embargo was indeed a fundamental breach of the principle on which the regulation of wages had been based. In effect it reduced the Committee on Production to the position of an instrument of the Executive Government, and substituted control by administrative instructions for unfettered arbitration.[5]

The saga does demonstrate that, much as Government may desire industrial peace, the price may be too high to pay.

The work of the Committee

> did much to regularise Industrial Relations by awards which served as general precedents for the conditions of the wage contract, such as the settlement of overtime rates in different industries . . . and the rates of payment for work at night.[6]

The Committee also contributed to an increase in the extent of national pay bargaining. Dealing with cases on the basis of claims caused by rises in the cost of living led to a great deal of repetition when claims were submitted on a local or district basis. As time wore on awards became more and more identical—in effect becoming national in nature. The Committee was quite content to endorse a move towards national pay awards. Thus, in early 1917, the engineering unions and the employers' federation were to enter into a national agreement at the instigation of the Committee on Production. Similar national agreements rapidly emerged in other industries. This process was backed up by the enactment of a common rule provision to catch the

---

[4] OHMM, vol V, pt I, p 70.
[5] *Ibid* at p 73.
[6] *Ibid* at p 87.

non-federated firm.[7] The issue of a national award was frequently not the end of the matter as questions of application etc. might well remain. This administrative burden was largely taken up by the labour department of the Ministry of Munitions.

Inherent in any form of compulsory arbitration is some constraint on the taking of industrial action. Prior to the enactment of the 1915 Act the Government considered three options:

> (1) The total prohibition of strikes and compulsory arbitration. This method, while it would entail a considerable organisation for arbitration and invite a flood of applications for settlement, could be largely simplified if it could be established that pre-war controversies (eg recognition of unions) must not be raised (2) some measure like the Canadian Act, which prevents strikes and lock-outs pending investigation by an independent authority with recommendation of terms of settlement. This would obviate all sudden strikes (3) To make it a condition of employment that one month's notice must be given before work could be left, with penalties for breach. This would really be an extension of the Conspiracy and Protection of Property Act 1975 (clause 4), which protects gas and water undertakings from sudden strikes, and could be made applicable to irregular attendance.[8]

It was also suggested that

> the penalty to be imposed on persons guilty of resorting to a strike or lock-out, or of leaving work without a month's notice, should be imprisonment up to three or six months, fines being useless.[9]

The Munitions Act adopted the first option and section 2 imposed a prohibition on strikes and lock-outs in industries concerned in war production. Employers were forbidden from declaring, causing or taking part in lock-outs and employees were forbidden from striking, in connection with any dispute, unless it had been reported to the Board of Trade, and 21 days had elapsed since the date of the report, and the difference had not during that time been referred by the Board of Trade for settlement. Thus a strike would only be lawful in the event of both the Board of Trade having failed to make a reference and 21 days having elapsed. Breach of these provisions was a criminal offence. In addition, an award made under the Act was binding on both employers and employed and might be retrospective; again breach of an award constituted a criminal offence.

---

[7] See below at p 144.
[8] OHMM, vol I, pt IV, p 10.
[9] *Ibid* at p 12.

The Act came into force on 2nd July 1915 and it was not long before the efficacy of the prohibitions on strikes was tested. A wages dispute had existed in the mines of South Wales since early March 1915. By the end of June a strike seemed inevitable and on 12th July the delegate conference of the South Wales Miners' Federation called for a strike. The 1915 Act was extended to the dispute by royal proclamation the following day. This made it an offence, under the Act, to take part in a strike. The proclamation was completely ignored and the entire work-force of some 200,000 miners went on strike. Within a matter of days the Government was forced to back down and a settlement was arrived at which met most of the miners' demands. In the words of the official History of the Ministry of Munitions:

> In effect the miners obtained nearly everything they had demanded, and it was mutually agreed between the parties that no one should be penalised for the part he had taken in the dispute. The strike demonstrated the impotence of legal provisions for compulsory arbitration where a large body of obstinate men were determined to cease work rather than surrender their claims.[10]

Industrial strife in the South Wales coalfield continued throughout most of 1916 and industrial action over the two main wage claims during this period was only averted by government intervention and the settlement, in full, of both claims.

Later that same year the efficacy of the Act was again called into question over a dispute involving a Glasgow shipbuilding firm. Following a strike a number of ringleaders was prosecuted and fined heavily; several individuals refused to pay and were imprisoned. Imprisonment led to considerable unrest and industrial action seemed likely. The Government responded by setting up an enquiry into the unrest on the Clyde; the terms of reference were to 'inquire into the causes and circumstances of the apprehended differences affecting munition workers in the Clyde District.' An interim report was produced within a matter of days but the response of the labour movement was uncompromising and it seemed likely that, unless the men were released, there would be a complete stoppage of work on the Clyde. The Government too was reluctant to back down but, at the same time, could not afford the loss of production that would be the result of a strike. A letter from Lloyd George reveals his view that release of the men 'would mean . . . that the Munitions Act would become a dead

---

[10] vol IV, pt II, p 9.

letter. Yet it is my last resort short of imprisonment.' The Government found a way out of the situation by persuading the unions to pay the fines involved and, hence, securing the release of the men. The sequence of events bears significant similarities to events during the life of the Industrial Relations Act. Formally the law was upheld but only as a result of executive interference in the administration of justice. Certainly on Clydeside itself the sequence of events can only have reduced respect for the rule of law. Again in 1917 a number of shop stewards were arrested and imprisoned for inciting strikes. The act of imprisonment only served to render dispute resolution more problematic. When the shop stewards next appeared in court the Attorney-General asked for leave to withdraw the charges, a course of action which caused him considerable anxiety as he felt that the criminal law was being used, wholly inappropriately, as a 'pawn in industrial strife.'

The overall impact of the legal prohibition on striking is difficult to assess. On the one hand, the number of working days lost was significantly lower than in the period both before and after the war. On the other hand, this was also true of industries to which the provisions were not extended. Rubin has argued that the impact of the statutory prohibitions was diminished by the limited number of successful prosecutions:

> the number of workers convicted of illegal striking up till July 1916 was just over 0.2 per cent of those actually participating in such strikes.[11]

Perhaps though, any reduction in the number of working days lost was worthy of note given that

> the occasions of disputes were multiplied. The novel power which the leaving certificate gave to foremen and managers, the suspension of trade union customs, the introduction of non-unionists into union shops, dilution, the mistakes of the recruiting authorities and the smouldering suspicion of victimisation, the rise in the cost of living, the discomfort of mean and crowded lodgings, and the strain of overwork all contributed to set the temper of the worker on edge and offered daily temptations even to the loyal and steady to throw down their tools.[12]

Curiously enough the 1915 Act did not deal with the position of those seeking to induce others to take part in a strike. Nevertheless, anyone inciting a strike may well have been found to have committed

---

[11] Rubin, above n 1, at p 247.
[12] OHMM, vol IV, pt II, p 10.

the common law crime of conspiracy to commit an unlawful act.[13] It was also the case that wide-sweeping powers existed under regulations made under the Defence of the Realm Act (DORA). Lloyd George stated, in the debates on the Munitions Act, that

> If a man works short-time he could not be prosecuted under the DORA, but if he went about organising short-time work amongst the workers and persuading workmen not to work full-time, or if he deliberately took part in an organisation to impede the output of munitions he could be prosecuted under the Defence of the Realm Act.[14]

Regulation 42 provided that

> If any person attempts to cause mutiny, sedition or disaffection . . . among the civilian population, or to impede or restrict the production, repair or transport of war material or any other work necessary for the prosecution of the war, he shall be guilty of an offence against these regulations.

It should also be mentioned that regulation 14 allowed the military authorities to deport persons suspected of acting in a manner prejudicial to the safety of the realm. Under this provision six members of the Clyde Workers committee were deported in 1916.

MOBILITY OF LABOUR

Mobility of labour was also a problem for Government with skilled labour being highly sought after by employers. As a result of poaching by employers wages rose and disruption to production occurred through movement of labour. In wartime the Government was not content to allow free reign to market forces. They first sought to tackle the problem by issuing regulation 8(B) under DORA. This prohibited the occupier of a factory engaged in war production from inducing

> (a) any person employed in any other factory or workshop, being a person engaged on work for any Government department or otherwise serving war purposes, to leave his employment; or (b) any person resident in the UK at a distance of more than 10 miles from the occupier's factory or workshop to accept employment therein, otherwise than by notifying vacancies to a Board of Trade Labour Exchange.

---

[13] A possibility referred to by the Secretary of State for the Home Office (Sir John Simon); Parl. Deb, HC, 1.7. 1915 vol 72, col 1965.
[14] Parl. Deb., 4.1.1916, HC, vol 77, col 879.

Breach of this regulation was a criminal offence but it did not have much effect. It did not prevent poaching by employers who were not involved in war production and 'inducing' did not appear to cover the simple tactic of paying higher wages and allowing potential employees to hear of this by word of mouth. Evidence that other methods of inducement had been used proved difficult to come by. Indeed the Board of Trade did not succeed in bringing a single prosecution although 'the evil was a matter of general complaint.'

The Government then resorted to the enactment, by way of section 7 of the 1915 Act, of the device of the leaving certificate. The measure sought to restrict the movement of labour. Many workers being motivated to move from one employment to another by the prospect of higher wages. Section 7 proved to be, perhaps, the least popular element of the wartime legislation. It provided that a person was prohibited from employing a workman who had, within the previous 6 weeks, been employed on or in connection with munitions work, unless he held a certificate from the employer by whom he was last so employed that he left work with the consent of that employer. Where an employer refused to grant a certificate a workman could apply to a munitions tribunal, who would grant a certificate if they felt that the consent of the employer had been unreasonably withheld. The provision was enacted

> to prevent the dislocation of munitions work by the migration of the workman from one workshop or shipyard to another. The shortage of skilled mechanics conferred on them a monopoly of which they naturally took advantage, and the instinct to sell in the dearest market was not restrained by the general belief that capital was exploiting to the full the needs of the country. Incidentally, therefore, the embargo on freedom of movements limited the advance in wages which in a variety of forms had become prevalent.[15]

The provision, however, had a much more severe impact on workers than the legislature intended. A number of employers used it as a disciplinary measure by suspending or dismissing an employee and then refusing to grant a certificate. Again other employers were slow to issue certificates. Such behaviour resulted in a great deal of hardship and consequent resentment. Respect for the provision cannot have been assisted by the fact that that it was not state practice to bring prosecutions against firms which were in breach. Instead enforcement was left

---

[15] OHMM, vol IV, pt 2, p 14.

up to the other employer and, as a result, a very limited number of prosecutions took place.

The right of appeal was of limited value to workers. There appears to have been a reluctance on the part of tribunals to grant certificates. This remained true even where a 'sweated' rate of wages was being paid. Again, the fact that grossly excessive hours were being worked was no guarantee of an appeal being successful. There was also no right of appeal from the tribunals other than the theoretical possibility of judicial review. Section 5 of the Munitions of War Act 1916 sought to alleviate some of the concerns over the operation of leaving certificates. The section empowered the Minister to make rules prohibiting any statement on a certificate other than the simple fact that the worker was free to accept other employment. This was to prevent some employers from using leaving certificates as 'character notes' and also to conceal whether an employer or a tribunal had issued the certificate. Section 5(2) dealt with another concern by providing that where an employee was dismissed the employer must provide a leaving certificate straight away. Where the employer failed to do so a munitions tribunal was empowered to order the employer to make a payment of up to £5 to the employee as well as issuing a leaving certificate.[16] The use of suspension without pay was also hit at, in that the benefits of subsection 2 were extended to any employee who applied for a certificate on the ground that he had for a period of more than two days been given no opportunity of earning wages.[17] Guidance was also given to munitions tribunals in that, when deciding whether the grant of a certificate has been unreasonably refused, a tribunal was obliged to take into consideration certain matters specified by statute. These included whether the employer's terms and conditions complied with the terms of the Fair Wages Resolution.

One of the main complaints regarding leaving certificates was that, while workers might be prevented from working for up to 6 weeks, at the same time, it was possible for employees to be instantly dismissed. Section 5(3) provided that where an employee was dismissed with less than one week's notice (or wages in lieu thereof) a munitions tribunal was empowered to award a sum, not exceeding £5, by way of payment

[16] The employee could not, however, benefit from this provision where he was guilty of misconduct for the purpose of obtaining dismissal.
[17] The subsection also extended to any employee who left his employment on account of conduct on the part of the employer which would justify the immediate termination by the employee of his employment contract.

in lieu. The provision did not apply where the tribunal was of the opinion that, owing to the discontinuance or temporary nature of the employment or misconduct of the workman, the employer had reasonable cause for dismissing the workman without a week's notice.

The Government viewed leaving certificates as one of the most fundamental elements of the wartime legislative scheme. They were very much aware of the strong discontent that existed but offered merely palliatives, such as those introduced in 1916, by way of response to specific grievances. Subsequently, the possibility of the repeal of the leaving certificates scheme became a bargaining counter, in 1917, as Government sought to persuade the labour movement of the wisdom of extending the scope of dilution. Section 2 of the Munitions of War Act 1917 gave power to the Munitions Minister to repeal the leaving certificate provisions provided that he was satisfied that to do so would be consistent with the national interest. Should such an order be made safeguards existed to prevent employees moving away from munitions work. It was provided that it was unlawful for a person, without the consent of the Minister, to give employment to a workman who had been employed on munitions work where the work on which he was to be employed was work of a different nature. Breach of this provision amounted to a criminal offence. A defence existed where the employer could prove that

> he did not know that, and had taken all reasonable steps to ascertain whether, the workman had been so employed.[18]

It may be noted that the section did not prevent workers migrating between different munitions firms. In supplement to section 2 was section 3 which provided for a mandatory minimum period of notice in relation to employment contracts in the munitions industry. Such a contract was not determinable by either party except by a week's notice or a payment of a sum equal to an average week's wages under the contract. Not surprisingly, the section did not apply in the case of the termination of the contract on the ground of such misconduct, on the part of either party, as would justify the immediate termination of the contract by the other party.[19]

Once section 7 was repealed it was thought likely that workers in particularly dangerous jobs might seek to move. It was also clear that

---

[18] In addition, it may be noted that only the Minister of Munitions or the Admiralty could institute a prosecution.

[19] S 3(1)(c).

employers had lost a significant sanction to reinforce workplace discipline. In the parliamentary debates it was said that

> there are many reasons, when these leaving certificates are abolished, why men should move. They will move from a more onerous to a less onerous employment. They will move in search of higher wages. They will move to some extent, perhaps through love of change. But I am advised that the most serious form in which movement could take place is a movement from the skilled to the semi-skilled form of labour.[20]

The effect that repeal would have on wages was difficult to predict though the Government was certainly concerned about the possibility of poaching of labour.[21] They had originally intended inserting a clause in the bill prohibiting

> the employment of a workman at a higher rate than the employer was paying other men for similar work, unless the man was already receiving a higher rate.[22]

Ultimately, it was decided that resort would be had to powers under DORA if necessary; power existed to place an embargo on employment of additional labour. The concern that skilled workers might move to unskilled work was a real one. Anomalies had developed between skilled workers paid on time rates and other employees paid on a piece rate basis; the solution adopted was the enactment of section 1 of the 1917 Act. Section one gave the Minister power to give directions as to the remuneration of certain classes of workers.[23]

The order to repeal section 7 was promulgated on October 1917, once an order under section 1 had been made to protect the position of skilled workers. In the event, at least initially, repeal did not lead to movement of labour to anything like the extent feared but, certainly by 1918, the ability of workers to move employment much more readily was forcing wages up. Government circulars were issued to discourage poaching of labour with the proviso that if this was not successful resort would be had to the powers provided by DORA. The provision which the Government had in mind was regulation 8A(b) which empowered the Minister

---

[20] Parl. Deb., HC, 15.8.1917, vol 97, col 1305.

[21] One helpful factor, from the point of view of Government, was the movement by this time towards national wage agreements and, hence, the reduction in scope for divergence between different districts.

[22] OHMM, vol VI, pt II, p 13.

[23] See below at p 144.

to regulate or restrict the carrying on of any work in any factory or work-shop or other premises, or the engagement of employment of any workmen.

Further pressure to remain at work was provided by a new measure which made anyone who had been unemployed for more than 14 days liable to be called up into military service, unless that individual could show that there was reasonable cause for the lack of employment.

Restricting freedom of movement was a major concern for Government. On occasion, on the other hand, the public interest lay in increasing the mobility of labour. Early in the war the Government had launched the War Munitions Volunteers scheme. By virtue of the scheme a body of volunteers was enrolled who could then be required to proceed to any employment where their services were required for the purpose of expediting or increasing the output of war material. In 1918 the Government proposed to expand the scheme with the aim of increasing the mobility of labour. Such was the nature of the proposals that the use of the word volunteer was less than apposite:

> If, however, it is found that workmen who are not War Munitions Volunteers are surplus to an establishment, or their skill is not being fully utilised, or if on other general grounds, in the opinion of responsible officers, they should be transferred elsewhere, they should be required to enrol as War Munitions Volunteers.

The Government proposed that dilution officers should be responsible for deciding who would be required to enrol, though a right of appeal on grounds of personal hardship would be provided. Where a man refused to enrol, and any appeal was unsuccessful, the recruiting authorities would be informed that 'he might if of military age, be called up for military service.' At the end of the day, however, sufficient men enrolled as War Munitions Volunteers on a voluntary basis and the element of compulsion did not need to be applied.

Earlier in the war the Government, by circular, had sought to restrict employers in the hiring of labour. However, by 1918 resort was had to regulation 8A(b). As a result employers, in the sheet metal trade, were not allowed

> without the written authority of the Minister, to engage or employ any skilled sheet metal workers in excess of the total number in your employ-ment on the date of this communication.

In addition, such employers were not permitted 'to engage or employ any skilled sheet metal workers at a rate of wages other than the [prescribed rate].' In June 1918 the Government announced its intention to make much greater use of the foregoing embargo scheme.

Wage Control

Some of the most important provisions of the 1915 Act were to be found in part two. As we have seen, the failure to control profits was the main reason for the demise of the Treasury agreement. Part two of the Act sought to attain such control whilst, at the same time, regulating labour. By virtue of section 4 the Minister could categorise an establishment as a 'controlled establishment' where he considered

> it expedient for the purpose of the successful prosecution of the war that any establishment in which munitions work is carried on should be subject to the special provisions as to limitation of employers' profits and control of persons employed . . .

However, the total number of controlled establishments never exceeded 6,000 even 'when the engineering firms alone of the many trades engaged on munitions work numbered not less than 32,000.'[24] The excess profits of such an establishment had to be paid over to government. Of greater interest to the labour lawyer were the statutory restrictions on wage increases; a proposed wage variation in a controlled establishment had to be referred to the Minister of Munitions who was entitled to veto the mooted increase or decrease. The Minister expected that, prior to any reference to him, both sides in industry must have agreed to the increase. Where a proposed variation was vetoed an aggrieved party was entitled to refer the matter to arbitration within the meaning of schedule 1 of the Act (ie normally the Committee on Production). Alternatively, the Minister, without having decided the matter, could directly so refer. The right of veto was exercised with considerable restraint. One instance where it was likely to be exercised was where employees of one firm sought to increase wages significantly in advance of the district rate.[25] One of the main reasons for restraint was the fact that reference might be made to the Committee on Production. The Committee was the most influential body in this area

---

[24] OHMM, vol V, pt 1, p 100.
[25] Wolfe, above n 3, at p 251.

and, knowing this, the Ministry sought to co-ordinate its activities so as not to veto an increase that the Committee might agree to. The committee had clear ideas on the reasons for an increase being necessary and the legitimate extent of a resulting increase.

The legal restrictions on wage increases were arguably ineffectual. For instance, the measure did not apply to individual increases. The Ministry was also very cautious in its use of the veto and was 'driven . . . by the pressure of Supply Departments to agree to rates which the Committee . . . would have resisted.'[26] Control of wage increases was only one concern of Government; maximising war production was another. The Ministry was also aware of some means of evasion:

> it was, indeed possible for firms to engage fresh labour at rates much above the district level without recourse to the Ministry, and the prevention of this was discussed during the discussions of the Munitions of War Bill, 1918. Further, employers could evade the need for official sanction by giving occasional unauthorised bonuses for good time-keeping etc . . . Such evasions . . . were probably neither serious nor numerous, so long as the power of the workpeople to exploit the shortage of labour was limited by the leaving certificate . . .[27]

The inter-locking nature of so much of the wartime legislation is demonstrated by the fact that once the leaving certificate provisions were abolished the section 4 provisions 'became almost inoperative.'[28] Employers lured employees from other firms by the offer of higher wages. The official history quite frankly notes

> evasions of the standard rate became more frequent and more serious in their effects. The Department was hampered in its efforts to check them, partly by the difficulty of discovering them until it was too late to take action, and partly by the wholly inadequate penalties which the courts inflicted when prosecutions were instituted. It had, therefore, sometimes to connive at, and even to suggest, time-keeping bonuses or other additions to the standard rate as the only way of enabling firms to retain essential men.[29]

Dilution

Part two also dealt with restrictive practices. From early in the war union restrictive practices were targeted by politicians as an obstacle to

[26] Wolfe, above n 3, at p 254.
[27] OHMM, vol V, pt 1, p 109.
[28] Wolfe, above n 3 , at p 254.
[29] OHMM, vol V, pt 1, p 110.

the war effort. Concern was regularly expressed that the alleged greater efficiency of German industry would prejudice the prospect of military success. The treasury agreement had dealt with dilution but its practical results were minimal and the 1915 Act sought to bring about dilution in controlled establishments:

> Any rule, practice or custom not having the force of law which tends to restrict production or employment shall be suspended in the establishment, and if any person induces or attempts to induce any other person . . . to comply, or continue to comply, with such a rule, practice or custom, that person shall be guilty of an offence . . .

The Act also empowered the Government to regulate by subordinate legislation

> the general ordering of the work in the establishment with a view to attaining and maintaining a proper standard of efficiency and with respect to the due observance of the rules of the establishment.

The owner of a controlled establishment was deemed to have entered into an undertaking that any departure from existing custom should only be for the duration of the war. Breach of the undertaking was a criminal offence and no civil remedy appeared to be available, an unsuccessful attempt being made during the enactment of the 1916 Act to furnish such a remedy. The employer was also deemed to have entered into an obligation to consult:

> Due notice shall be given to the workmen concerned wherever practicable of any changes of working conditions which it is desired to introduce as a result of the establishment becoming a controlled establishment, and opportunity for local consultation with workmen or their representatives shall be given if desired.[30]

Experience was to demonstrate just how important meaningful consultation was to the achievement of dilution. Where it did not take place dilution might still occur but, even if changes were acquiesced in at the time, 'they contributed in no small degree to intensify the unrest which broke out in 1917.'[31] Outside controlled establishments regulation 8A of the DORA regulations could be resorted to:

> It shall be lawful for the Admiralty, Army Council, or the Minister of Munitions (a) to require any work in any factory or workshop to be done in

---

[30] Schedule II, Munitions of War Act, 1915.
[31] OHMM, vol V, pt 1, p 89.

accordance with the directions of the Admiralty, Army Council, or the Ministry of Munitions, given with the object of making the factory or work-shop or the plant or labour therein as useful as possible for the production of war material, and to require returns as to the nature and amount of work done in any factory or workshop.

Little use, in the event, was made of these powers over matters of dilution.[32]

Returning to the position in controlled establishments one must ask what effect would the statutory declaration of the suspension of restric-tive practices have on the shop floor? The barriers in the path of the legislation were considerable:

> In order to succeed, dilution required the willing co-operation of manage-ment, the foreman and the skilled workmen. Even a neutral attitude on the part of any of these would cause a scheme technically feasible to fail.[33]

The Act did not compel employers to introduce new methods of work. Accordingly, without an employer taking the initiative to amend work-ing practices, nothing would happen and it would be perfectly possible for work to continue in the customary way. The Ministry also took the view that the statutory power to make regulations with respect to the general ordering of work

> was limited to workshop rules on such matters as time-keeping and proper conduct in the works, and did not extend to the coercion of the employer if he refused to carry out a scheme of dilution prescribed by the Ministry.[34]

As a result, the provision was not used to promote dilution. It soon became clear that an employer who did try to bring about dilution in the workplace might well meet with resistance. This was far from sur-prising:

> the skilled workman saw that the policy of dilution meant not merely the admission of unskilled men and women into the workshops, but a re-organisation of the factory and new methods of production, entailing the subdivision of complex and varied processes into their simple elements, specialisation and repetitive work.

Whatever assurances were given there was understandable scepticism that such changes would be reversed. An early illustration of the diffi-

[32] They were used, in the main, in connection with an embargo on the hiring of skilled labour which was introduced in 1918.
[33] OHMM, vol 6, pt X, p 86.
[34] *Ibid* at p 84.

culties that might be faced was provided by Scottish experience. An attempt was made in early August 1915 to introduce female labour to the firm of Lang at Johnston but the employer did not succeed in the face of union opposition. Over the following two months a series of discussions took place between the Amalgamated Society of Engineers (ASE) and the Government. It was only at the end of October that the Council of the ASE agreed to cooperate with the introduction of dilution into controlled establishments where circulars L2 and L3 were observed.[35] Women were subsequently introduced at Langs but shortly thereafter management was informed by shop stewards that the introduction of any more women would prompt industrial action. No further progress appears to have been made at Langs until the arrival, nearly two months later, of the Clyde Dilution Commission. One lesson to be drawn from the dispute was the fact that the authority of union hierarchies may be very limited vis-a vis the grass-roots.

The possibility of industrial relations strife acted as a deterrent to employers who might otherwise have been interested in dilution and, in October 1915, the president of an employer's association wrote to the Minister of Munitions in the following terms:

> We sympathise and approve most heartily of the terms of the instructions, which we shall do our utmost to carry out wherever possible. But it is impossible to expect us or any other firm to give effect to such instructions in the face of the declared hostility of the trade unions to such action on the part of employers, and their defiance of their arrangements with the Government, notably in that notorious instance of the works of Lang and sons . . . No employer is going to imperil the continuity of his work or run the risk of a stoppage by acting upon the terms of your circular, as long as the trade unions are permitted to flout the Government's instructions and treat their solemn engagements with the Government as so much waste paper.[36]

Employers were more interested in maintaining the level of output and dilution schemes tended not to have high priority—particularly if employee resistance was likely to be forthcoming.

Government had appreciated from the outset that employer cooperation might not be automatic; accordingly a great deal of administrative support and direction was provided. A tripartite advisory

---

[35] L2 and L3 were circulars which were issued containing recommendations as to the pay of women, semi-skilled and unskilled workers. They later gained the status of statutory instruments; see below 'Further Wage Control'.

[36] OHMM, vol V, pt IV, pp 100–1.

committee, the Central Munitions Labour Supply Committee, was established in September 1915 and was instructed to furnish a dilution scheme. It was intended that it

> should not only provide advice on the methods of effecting dilution and obtaining the skilled labour required to staff the new factories, but should also assist in investigating and settling disputes and grievances arising out of dilution and the administration of the Act by Munitions Tribunals.[37]

In addition, local labour advisory boards were set up in the main industrial centres; one of their duties being to ensure that employers carried out the statutory undertaking to honour the provisions of schedule II of the Munitions of War Act, to report all cases of failure to the labour officer or the National Advisory Committee for action by the Ministry and to record or verify changes of workshop practice.[38] These boards appear to have made a limited impact.[39]

One of the first tasks of the Central Committee was to consider the question of wages for semi-skilled and unskilled workers performing work which had previously been done by skilled workers. This was viewed as urgent lest union concern over the undermining of wage levels obstructed dilution. Two circulars were issued—L2 and L3. L2 set out wage levels for women employed on munitions work of a class which prior to the war was not recognised as women's work in a district where such work was customarily carried out. L3 applied to work performed by unskilled and semi-skilled men. A more general circular (CE1) was issued urging employers in controlled establishments to make the most effective and economical use possible of all available machinery and skilled labour. The circular also required certain information to be returned to enable an assessment of progress to be made. The information revealed made disappointing reading and the Ministry of Munitions realised it would have to become much more actively involved at ground level. A dilution department was established within the Ministry of Munitions and dilution officers were deployed at local offices. The latter were to visit munitions firms to exhort the furtherance of dilution and to provide expert advice. The Central Labour Supply Committee also produced circular L6, which was then issued by the Minister, providing a model procedure to be followed when any change was to be made in working practices. The

---

[37] OHMM, vol IV, pt 1, p 51.
[38] *Ibid* at p 55.
[39] GDH Cole, *Workshop Organisation* (London: Hutchinson, 1973) p 122.

circular placed a great deal of emphasis on consultation with trade unions. The extent of government involvement is indicated by the following paragraph from the circular:

> Any difficulties experienced by either employers or workpeople should be at once referred to the Ministry, in order that an immediate endeavour may be made to find a satisfactory solution.

Whilst a number of circulars were destined to be elevated into subordinate legislation the Ministry of Munitions refused to take this step with L6. This was despite the fact that many employers disregarded it which resulted in a 'good deal of friction . . . caused by attempts to introduce dilution without workshop consultation.' Nevertheless

> the general effect of the various schemes of dilution was to compel most employers to concede some sort of de facto recognition to the shop stewards and workshop committees set up in their works.

In the post-war period such concessions proved to be reasonably durable.

The establishment of the dilution department meant that civil servants harangued employers with recommendations and instructions and government representatives arrived in a number of districts seeking to further the policy of dilution. On the Clyde a three-man dilution commission was appointed. The procedure adopted by them placed a tremendous amount of emphasis on consultation with the parties involved. Initially, in consultation with the firm and an outside engineer, a draft dilution scheme was drawn up. After this extensive consultation with both shop stewards and union officialdom followed. As part of a finalised scheme the Commission insisted on the formation of a shop committee (comprised of shop stewards) to resolve any difficulties in the operation of the scheme with management. Such schemes were comprehensive and included

> full details of the processes on which less skilled labour was to be introduced, the rates to be paid, the measure of recognition to be accorded to shop stewards and Trade Union representatives in the working of the scheme and so on.[40]

The technical difficulties were great:

> great care was necessary in adapting the general principles of dilution to circumstances. Differences in machinery, differences in scale of production,

---

[40] *Ibid* at p 49.

> differences in respect of accommodation and room for extension, all affected the employment of women . . . dilution could only be effected by an elaborate investigation of particular works and the individual consideration of the men and machines involved.

Given that dilution was taking place in the engineering industry, the traditional heartland of dynamic bargaining, it emerged that 'dilution was not a process which could be effected at one stroke, but required continual readjustment.' It was also said that

> no small part of the success of the Clyde Dilution Committee was due to their practice of bringing employers and workmen into joint consultation on schemes of dilution and the difficulties arising from it.[41]

Devoting considerable administrative resources to the implementation of dilution appears to have been reasonably successful. Progress, however, being both slower and less radical than Government would have desired. Cole's conclusion that dilution 'advanced rapidly indeed and was applied to every branch of munitions production in which it was practicable' is not supported by a number of other commentators. The statistics do, however, show that the proportion of women to men in essential industries increased very considerably.

In controlled establishments persuasion was greatly relied upon, but elsewhere it was the sole means used since the Munitions of War Act did not apply. The knowledge that resort might be had to regulation 8 of DORA may have had some effect. Outside controlled establishments there was no statutory guarantee of the subsequent restoration of pre-war practices if dilution took place. Nevertheless civil servants visited non-controlled establishments and sought to promote the adoption of dilution schemes. The Government also sought to influence employers by issuing leaflets relating to specific trades which indicated the manufacturing processes where a dilution scheme would be likely to be beneficial. The Treasury agreement applied to a number of workers other than munition workers and subsequently a number of national and local collective agreements were entered into, relating to such workers, which provided for dilution subject to guarantees on the restoration of trade practices. By late 1916 the Government wished to see dilution taking place to a much greater extent in commercial and private work. They believed that the way to do this was by encouraging the signing of collective agreements and, to promote this, the

---

[41] OHMM, vol 4, pt IV p 90.

Government consulted with trade unions in engineering and shipbuilding. The initial union reaction was not warm and one of labour's greatest concerns was that they should have a real share in the administrative control of dilution. Unions were disillusioned with government assurances in general and were discontent with the limited role of advisory committees. To meet these concerns a detailed scheme, the terms of which were broadly similar to those applying to munitions establishments, was put forward by Government. It was accepted that, were dilution to come about, on the ground joint machinery, at local level, on which workers representatives were adequately represented would be essential. Negotiations over the scheme proved to be difficult and protracted and were ultimately unsuccessful. The reasons for the lack of success are revealing.

The ASE displayed great reluctance regarding entering into an agreement. One of their main objections was the lack of a statutory guarantee on restoration of trade practices. To meet this problem the government proposed to legislate and a bill emerged which, in effect, proposed to extend the range of industries to which the 1915 Act applied. Before the bill could become law, however, a large number of unofficial strikes broke out in May 1917. In a number of cases the strikers were motivated by disquiet at the attempt to apply dilution to commercial work. However, there was no single explanation for the strikes and the underlying reasons were plentiful. The Government attempted to secure a return to work through a variety of tactics. A number of trade unions were persuaded to issue statements encouraging their members to return to work. The Government also relied upon a propaganda campaign, through its control of the press, and by the dissemination of information through posters and other means. The foregoing measures began to produce the desired effect only for a fresh round of strikes to break out. The Government's response was, on this occasion, much more hard-hitting and eight ring-leaders were arrested under DORA for inciting workers to strike. The use of the tactic of arrest is difficult to assess. On the one hand, Cole was of the view that the prospect of further arrests was a factor in inducing the stewards to retreat. On the other hand, the unofficial actions had been very much on the wane in any event and it appears that the arrests may have had the effect of prolonging the disputes in a number of districts.

By July the Government had abandoned its attempt to extend dilution by legislation. The following month a heavily revised Munitions Bill was enacted. It had become clear that even if the union executive of the ASE could be persuaded by the merits of Government proposals they would be unable to carry the membership with them. The May strikes had served to illustrate the nature of trade union organisation and the limits of hierarchical control. In the process the extent to which Government could expect to restrain and discipline trade union members by acting through the union emerged. The official history recorded that

> the extension of dilution to private work . . . was rendered more difficult and hazardous by the relative discredit into which the executives of the trade unions had fallen.[42]

Government took consolation from the belief that dilution schemes would not work in the absence of local individual agreements. Failure to arrive at a centrally agreed scheme (whether embodied in legislation or not) was perhaps not the greatest of blows.

Further Wage Control

Statutory powers introduced in 1916 brought the state into the business of the fixing of actual wage rates. Up until this point government had not set wage rates though, on occasion, it had provided for the legal enforcement of wages set by bodies such as trade boards and the Committee on Production. Section 6 provided that where female workers were employed on, or in connection with, munitions work the Minister of Munitions should have power by order to give directions as to the rate of wages, or as to hours of labour, or conditions or employment of the female workers so employed. Section 7 provided a similar power in relation to semi-skilled and unskilled men employed, in any controlled establishment, on munitions work being work of a class which, prior to the war, was customarily undertaken by skilled labour. Breach of an order made under either section was a criminal offence. Both the measures were brought forward as a result of much union pressure and, ultimately, were conceded as part of the government's campaign to achieve dilution. It was hoped that the enactment of the sections would help in winning union support for dilution by ensuring that the use of female and semi-skilled labour would not lead to the undermining of wage scales. The administrative burden assumed by Government was a significant one.

[42] OHMM, vol VI, pt 1, p 93.

The powers contained in section 6 were also used in response to the problems posed by women doing work which was not 'men's work.' A statutory instrument was issued to set wage rates for munitions work of that sort.[43] The order specified time rates and also guaranteed fixed time payments to piece workers and premium bonus payments. Promulgation of the order was inspired by the

> need to recruit women for munitions work away from their homes, and to the sense that the government should be a model employer directly and indirectly, or should at least secure a reasonable wage to workers from whom the leaving certificate regulations removed in the public interest the power to move freely from ill-paid occupations.[44]

The difficulty for Parliament was that there were no fair-wage standards in the different districts because the work was never undertaken before. As a consequence there was no standard to apply in the case of female workers. Collective bargaining was unlikely to furnish the standards as it was unlikely to regulate the terms and conditions of employment of occupations which were not normally performed by men. A section 6 order was, therefore, used to fill the gap. A further order was subsequently issued to deal with additional payments in respect of overtime.[45] The regulation sought to make use of current standards where relevant standards could be invoked; such standards might, but would not necessarily, be collectively agreed. The order provided that

> where no custom providing for such additional payments exists in the establishment, such additional payments shall be made at the rates and on the conditions prevailing in similar establishments or trades in the district. Where there are no similar establishments or trades in the district, the rates and conditions prevailing in the nearest district in which the general industries are similar shall be adopted.

In the last resort the amounts would be fixed by the State:

> In the absence of any custom prevailing in the establishment, or in the district, or elsewhere, such additional payments shall be made at such rates and on such conditions as the Minister of Munitions may direct.

Orders made under the 1916 Act involved a radical new departure in that central government determined actual wage rates. Such a process involved

[43] SI 1916/447.
[44] OHMM, vol V, pt II, p 57.
[45] SI 1916/618.

an elaborated administrative organisation, comprising not only a central department issuing the Orders, but local agents to enquire into questions of applications, and, some judicial authority to decide on disputed cases.[46]

Moving from auxiliary to regulatory legislation in respect of wages was seen by government as a temporary expedient:

> while there would seem to be scope for a considerable extension of State enforcement of standard rates, the actual fixing of the rates is best done by the representatives of people who pay and receive wages.[47]

The expression of such sentiments would appear to indicate support for collective bargaining yet more could have been done, for example, to link orders made under section 6 with collective bargaining. Women trade unionists complained that there was no incentive to organise because the statutory rates were standard and not minimum ones. Again one regulation stated that

> piece work prices and premium bonus time allowances shall be fixed by mutual agreement in accordance with these directions . . . between the employer and the worker or workers who perform the work.[48]

Trade unionists lobbied, unsuccessfully, to have the regulations amended so that trade unions would be party to the negotiations.

Further piecemeal reform of the law on wages took place in 1917. Section 1 of the Munitions of War Act 1917 was enacted to solve problems caused by the position of the skilled time worker who, by this stage in the war, might well be at a financial disadvantage compared to semi-skilled workers paid by the piece. The section empowered the Minister of Munitions to give directions as to the remuneration paid to time workers on munitions work where he considered it necessary in order to maintain the output of munitions. Orders made by virtue of section 1 once again involved government in fixing the actual rate of wages. Section 1 was, in part, a response to the repeal of the leaving certificate. It enabled the government to discourage skilled workers from moving by raising their wages. The 1917 Act contained a further important provision in respect of wages. Section 5 was a provision of the common rule type and was aimed at the non-federated employer. Such employers would sometimes, but by no means always, be caught by the Fair Wages Resolution. Prior to enactment Government had

[46] OHMM, vol V, pt II, p 121.
[47] *Ibid* at p 124.
[48] *Ibid* at pp 116–17.

applied a degree of administrative pressure to secure compliance and had suggested that, should a measure along the lines of the eventual section 5 be required, it was likely that it would be retrospective. A limited number of orders were issued under section 5 and 'the desired extension of general awards was achieved far more by department circulars.'[49] It is worthy of mention that orders made under the section sometimes applied to national awards as part of the movement towards national collective agreements. Breach of an order was a criminal offence. It may be noted that

> the intrinsic difficulties of giving effect to the principle under normal conditions, especially the demarcation of trades to which different awards were to apply, and the administrative enforcement of awards in marginal cases, were never fully tested.[50]

By 1918 the Government was moving towards exercising much wider and closer control over wage increases. They were approaching the view that they could only exercise effective control over wages 'if they were empowered to control wages completely.'[51] Had the war gone into 1919 it was likely that further legislative powers would have been sought. The industrial relations background to this was the failure to control wage inflation. The repeal of the leaving certificate provisions had contributed to the inflationary pressures. It has already been noted that the controls contained in section 4 of the 1915 Act had been rendered superfluous. For several months following the repeal there appeared to be a rather limited impact but the picture changed in 1918. State intervention over wages had also taken the form of the provisions of part one of the 1915 Act . However, part one was predicated on the basis that the problem to be addressed was industrial action. As the war wore on Government became increasingly concerned about inflation. However, the provisions were not designed to combat wage increases that were perceived to be against the public interest; nor were they overly successful in doing so. It was true that they were utilised to considerable extent—some 8,000 awards being made. It was also the case that the awards tended to be accepted by both sides of industry. Nevertheless 'wages drift' evidently still occurred; particularly as a result of the frenzied competition for skilled workers. Furthermore, it

---

[49] OHMM, vol V, pt I, p 120.
[50] *Ibid.*
[51] *Ibid* at p 64. And see above at p 132 where reg 8 A(b) prevented employment at a rate of wages other than the prescribed amount.

is crucial to appreciate that, where both sides had collectively agreed an increase, a reference under part one was not required. By October 1918 an internal Munitions Ministry memorandum went so far as to say that

> the policy of restricting changes in wages to general advances to meet increases in the cost of living and, apart from these, maintaining recognised pre-war standard rates and conditions had broken down. Bargaining had been freed by the abolition of the leaving certificate; competition for labour was constantly forcing wages up: standard rates had disappeared.[52]

A further difficulty with wage control was that government departments did not speak with one voice. Supply departments had other goals and allowed contract prices to rise with the effect that it was easier for firms to raise wages. The inflationary spiral was thus furthered.

The position had been reached whereby the acquisition of sweeping powers of control by the state in respect of wage regulation could realistically be contemplated. Progress down such a road could be envisaged because the intervention of the state in society had reached such a degree that it was possible to view the state as the real employer: 'private employers and work-people only trustees for it.' It was also now realised that government had not yet taken sufficient statutory powers to attain effective control over wages: neither the statutory framework nor the administrative machinery existed to achieve systematic control of wages.

CONCLUSIONS

The lessons to be drawn from wartime experience were considerable. It did appear that legal regulation of wages might lead the State into an ever-increasing involvement. When the State first became involved with wages issues it sought to interfere with voluntary arrangements to a limited extent. It is true that, under the first round of legislation, the normal operation of the collective bargaining process was restricted; for example, industrial action was no longer a permissible sanction in trade disputes in certain industries. Nevertheless, the fixing of wage rates was by and large left to voluntary mechanisms. Under section 1 of the 1915 Act the Board of Trade could not commence dispute resolution on their own initiative but were obliged to rely upon a reference by

---

[52]   OHMM, vol 5, pt I, pp 61–63.

one of the parties. In the event of a reference to arbitration under schedule 1 of that Act, the constitution of the arbitration tribunal was to be
determined by agreement between the parties. With regard to controlled establishments the minister exercised his power of veto with
much restraint and, in addition, insisted on prior agreement between
the industrial parties before agreeing to a variation. A variation to
bring wages into line with the fair wages resolution could not be
vetoed. As time went on, the extent of involvement was to increase
both in extent and nature. This was partly because

> the relation between the wages of different classes and grades of worker is
> so intimate that interference at one point is bound to have reactions at
> others.[53]

As a result, the 'choice lay between the control of wages generally and
a policy of abstention from the fixing of any rates.'[54] In the event, the
evolution of the law on wages showed a tendency for the State to
become further and further involved. The taking of further control
only fuelled the craving for a yet more regulated system. The Official
History concluded from the experience of legal control of wages
during wartime that

> To establish statutory bodies for collective bargaining, like the Trades
> Boards . . . to make the determinations of such Boards and of voluntary joint
> bodies mandatory on whole trades, to assist collective bargaining by pro-
> viding facilities for conciliation and arbitration, are all in line with this pol-
> icy, and great extension of such activity is possible . . . But with the actual
> fixing of rates in normal times . . . no Government that has studied the expe-
> rience of the Ministry of Munitions and can by any means avert that neces-
> sity, will be inclined to meddle.[55]

The verdict on the compulsory arbitration provisions is somewhat
mixed. The State provided a mechanism for arbitration which
appeared to operate reasonably satisfactorily. The Committee on
Production turned out to be the most important adjudicatory body;
their credibility was only called into question during the period when
they followed a policy of pay restraint at the behest of government.
The awards of the Committee appear to have been respected. The
Committee's impact on industrial relations was long term given its part
in promoting national collective bargaining. However, the limitations

[53] *Ibid* at p 229.
[54] *Ibid.*
[55] *Ibid* at p 143.

of the law were clearly exposed through the law's inability to deter any sizeable group of workers from withdrawing their labour. Rubin has noted that by the latter stages of the war hardly any prosecutions took place in 'any stoppage of national significance': 'prosecutions for minor infractions of the law against strikes were all that might be risked.'[56] Moreover, penal sanctions had the capacity to prolong disputes and render dispute resolution more difficult. Executive interference in the legal process was, on occasion, necessary to get workers back to work and production resumed. It was not difficult to draw the conclusion that if workers could not be deterred, by such a scheme, from striking in wartime then they would be far less likely to be so deterred in peacetime.

Restricting the movement of labour proved to be highly problematic. Government found that such restrictions on the exercise of a traditional freedom provoked considerable resentment. However, the resentment arose, in part, on account of the nature of the legislative scheme. It is interesting to compare the much more balanced approach of the Essential Works Order some 25 years later.[57] In contrast, in World War I the government was slow to realise that restrictions on individual freedom would only be palatable if there were corresponding benefits. Whilst restricting the movement of labour presented great difficulty so did restricting the movement of wages. Despite the restrictive regime imposed on controlled establishments evasion was to prove an on-going problem. This is perhaps not surprising when both employer and employed often shared a common interest in agreeing to a wage increase.

Government consulted with trade unions over industrial policy on a scale never before encountered. Such dialogue was often successful in securing the cooperation of union executives. However, the potential for control over rank and file members by such a corporatist route was much more problematic. Nevertheless, progress on matters such as dilution was shown to be dependent on the active involvement of trade unionists; consultation was a crucial part of that process. Dilution could not be imposed from above and required the full cooperation of those immediately involved.

---

[56] Rubin, above n 1, at p 176.
[57] See ch. 8 below.

6

The Aftermath of War 1918–1921

INTRODUCTION

T HE DEMANDS MADE by the Government on the British people over the course of the First World War were on a scale hitherto unknown. Consensus in society was fostered by Government which became increasingly desperate in its attempts to maximise the war effort; its vision of post-war society became a crucial means of inspiring the populace to greater endeavours. Lloyd George stated in 1917 that

> there is no doubt at all that the present war . . . presents an opportunity for reconstruction of industrial and economic conditions of this country such as has never been presented in the life of, probably, the world. The whole state of society is more or less molten and you can stamp upon that molten mass almost anything so long as you do it with firmness and determination . . .[1]

Post-war planning began well before the end of hostilities. The Whitley Committee was established in 1916, as was the Ministry of Labour, and the Ministry of Reconstruction in July 1917;[2] legislation on matters such as trades boards and trade union amalgamations was enacted before the end of the war. The winning of the armed conflict had resulted in the state intervening in numerous aspects of society and the economy and to an extent that was wholly unparalleled. As we saw in the last chapter, in the field of labour law drastic measures, such as prohibitions on strikes and the imposition of compulsory arbitration, were brought in. The first glimmers of corporatism also emerged as the Government sought to enlist the co-operation of key interest groups. When thoughts turned to reconstruction one might suggest that policy makers had very much a clean sheet in that notions of what was politically feasible had changed so radically. This chapter seeks to explore the avenues of development that were opened up for the regulation of industrial relations and why, at the end of the day, certain options were

---

[1] Quoted in BB Gilbert, *British Social Policy 1914–1939* (London: Batsford, 1970) p 5.
[2] The Ministry was wound up in June 1919.

pursued and not others. As well as examining proposed changes to the law, the role of collective bargaining will be considered, along with plans for the nationalisation of industries. At the end of the war the Government took the view that it would be foolish to allow wartime controls to expire immediately. Thus the Wages (Temporary Regulation) Act 1918 was brought in to maintain the level of wages though the Minister of Labour wished it to be known that

> the Government are particularly anxious to encourage each industry to deal with wages and allied questions for itself as soon as practicable.[3]

One particular concern was that demobilisation would flood the labour market leading to a rapid drop in wage levels. The Act was originally to last for a mere six months but ultimately it was extended until the end of September 1920. In place of the Committee on Production, the wartime national tribunal, the Act provided for an Interim Court of Arbitration to settle any differences. At the same time it also abolished the prohibitions on strikes and lock-outs. The after-math of the wartime policy of dilution was addressed and a 1919 Act provided for the restoration of pre-war customs and practices within two months of the passing of the Act.[4] Once restored the employer was obliged to maintain the custom in question for one year.[5] Complaints of infringements of the Act were brought before munitions tribunals and were punishable by fine. Both individual workers and trade unions were entitled to institute proceedings. It was further provided that any custom or practice could be modified by agreement between the employer and the trade union concerned. In the event pre-war practices seem to have been restored remarkably readily. At the same time a number of prosecutions did take place under the 1919 Act but they were few in number. The success of such transitional legislation might have been thought to augur well for the prospect of more permanent measures.

---

[3] Parl. Deb., 18.11.1918, HC vol 110, col 3311.

[4] The Restoration of Pre-War Practices Act 1919. In the main the Act applied to munitions establishments.

[5] At the end of that year the custom could not be enforced under the Act but it is arguable that it could be enforced through contractual remedies. This would depend upon the custom satisfying the standard tests for incorporation.

PLANNING FOR THE FUTURE—PROMOTING COLLECTIVE BARGAINING

The Whitley Committee, the body charged in 1916 with planning for reconstruction in the sphere of industrial relations, was given the following terms of reference:

(1) To make and consider suggestions for securing a permanent improvement in the relations between employers and workmen. (2) To recommend means for securing that industrial conditions affecting the relations between employers and workmen shall be systematically reviewed by those concerned, with a view to improving conditions in the future.[6]

The membership of the committee included employers and trade union officals, as well as economists and social workers. The Committee, adopting a somewhat unitary perspective, stressed the benefits that could be gained from co-operation between the two sides of industry:

The feature which gives the Whitley scheme a definite place in the history of industrial relations, lies in the emphasis placed on the community of interest of all engaged in the industry.[7]

Whitley and his colleagues placed much faith in the improvement and expansion of joint decision-making. At the same time at least some of the Whitley Committee were convinced of an inherent conflict of interest in industrial relations. So, despite the wisdom of improving collective bargaining,

a complete identity of interests between capital and labour cannot be thus effected, and . . . such machinery cannot be expected to furnish a settlement for the more serious conflicts of interest involved in the working of an economic system primarily governed and directed by motives of private profit.[8]

If joint regulation was the desired goal how was this to be furthered? Central to the Whitley report was the concept of the Joint Industrial Council (JIC):

the establishment for each industry of an organisation, representative of employers and workpeople, to have as its object the regular consideration of matters affecting the progress and well-being of the trade from the point

---

[6] H Clay, *The Problem of Industrial Relations* (London: 1929) p 149.
[7] Ministry of Labour, Report on the Establishment and Progress of Joint Industrial Councils (1923), p 2.
[8] Final Report on Relations Between Employers and Employed, Cd 9153, appendix.

of view of all those engaged in it, so far as this is consistent with the general interest of the community, appears to us necessary.[9]

It was hoped that the JICs would

> secure the largest possible measure of joint action between employers and workpeople for the development of the industry as a part of the national life and for the improvement of the conditions of all engaged in that industry.[10]

While the issue was not discussed at length in any of the reports, it appears that worker representation was to be channelled through trade union machinery and not by any other means. Whitley was wary of making recommendations that might lead to conflict with trade unions or employers' associations.[11]

In the better-organised trades and industries, where bargaining structures were already satisfactory, it is difficult to see what difference Whitley's JICs would have made. Very little attention was paid to this by Whitley, though in an appendix to the report one finds the statement that

> In most organised trades there already exist joint bodies for particular purposes. It is not proposed that the Industrial Council should necessarily disturb these existing bodies. A council would be free, if it chose and if the bodies concerned approved to merge existing committees etc in the Council, or to link them with the Council as sub-committees.[12]

Subsequent events were to suggest that perhaps greater attention should have been paid to this issue. While 73 JICs were formed in the period 1917–1922[13] a 1923 Ministry of Labour report found that

> For various reasons—partly on account of the prior existence of adequate joint machinery, partly because the Whitley Scheme was not considered by the trade unions concerned as suitable to the realisation of their industrial policy,—the formation of JICs on the lines laid down by the Whitley Committee was not undertaken in certain industries where the recognition of trade unionism was most completely established.[14]

[9] Interim Report on Joint Standing Industrial Councils, Cd 8606, para 5.
[10] R Charles, *The Development of Industrial Relations in Britain 1911–1939* (London: Hutchinson, 1973) p 148.
[11] Supplementary Report on Workshop Committees, Cd 9001, para 4.
[12] Interim Report, above n 9, appendix.
[13] Report on the Establishment and Progress of Joint Industrial Councils, above n 7, at p 3. However, by 1922 15 of those were no longer functioning.
[14] *Ibid* at p 24.

Some of the most important and well-organised industries, such as coal and steel, did not establish JICs. Looking to the other end of the spectrum experience was to show that JICs established in industries where organisation was weak might well falter.

The Government adopted the Whitley report as early as 1917 and employers and unions were circulated and asked to implement it. The Ministry of Labour publicised the scheme, and encouraged and assisted its implementation. Assistance took a wide variety of forms and ranged from the publication of model constitutions to permission to use Government buildings for meetings of JICs. One means of encouragement was to emphasise the importance of the role envisaged for JICs; a Ministry circular made clear that Government saw the councils as

> the official standing consultative committee to the Government in all future questions affecting the industries which they represent.[15]

Equally the Ministry was prepared to threaten the establishment of a trade board to bring about the formation of a JIC. In 1919 one outcome of an internal reorganisation within the Ministry was the creation of a Joint Industrial Councils division charged with promoting implementation of Whitleyism.[16] The Government found it more difficult to practice what it preached but, despite initial reluctance, it was pressurised into implementing the scheme for the civil service.

Whitley paid some attention to the question of the role of law. Proposals for compulsory arbitration were emphatically rejected:

> there is no reason to believe that such a system is generally desired by employers and employed and, in the absence of such general acceptance, it is obvious that its imposition would lead to unrest. The experience of Compulsory Arbitration during the war has shown that it is not a successful method of avoiding strikes, and in normal times it would undoubtedly prove even less successful.[17]

The report continued:

> For the same reason we do not recommend any scheme relating to conciliation which compulsorily prevents strikes or lock-outs pending inquiry. But it is obviously possible and desirable that in some instances arrangements should be voluntarily made in organised trades for holding an inquiry before recourse to extreme measures; and we suggest that the Ministry of Labour

[15] Ministry of Labour circular of 20.10.1917 quoted in Seymour, *The Whitley Councils Scheme* (London: PS King & Son) p 19.

[16] Subsequently abolished as part of the cuts of the 1920s.

[17] Report on Conciliation and Arbitration, (Cd 9099), para 2.

should be authorised to hold a full inquiry when satisfied that it was desirable, without prejudice to the power of the disputing parties to declare a strike or lock-out before or during the progress of the inquiry.[18]

This element of Whitley led to part two of the Industrial Court Act 1919.

There was also the question of whether agreements entered into by JICs should be legally enforceable. Whitley was opposed to any scheme which sought to compel legal enforceability but believed that consideration should be given to making the necessary legislative changes which would allow the parties to enter into such agreements should they so wish. Legislation to regulate the relationship of the collective parties was not a favoured mode of approach. This ties in with Whitley's vision of the State's role in industrial relations:

> It is fundamental to the idea of a JIC that it is a voluntary body set up by the industry itself, acting as an independant body and entirely free from all State control.[19]

In cases where industrial organisation was adequate Whitley saw no justification for external interference: 'our proposals are that the content of State assistance should vary inversely with the degree of organisation in industries.'[20] Where government intervention was required its function should be to promote voluntary institutions. In effect the Committee was calling for auxiliary legislation:

> We do not . . . regard Government assistance as an alternative to the organisation of employers and employed. On the contrary, we regard it as a means of furthering the growth and development of such organisation.[21]

In the light of the endorsement of auxiliary measures Whitley's discussion of the trades boards deserves attention. The Committee believed that the scheme of JICs was inappropriate where unorganised and badly organised industries were concerned. In those areas it would be more profitable to set up Trade Boards until there was suffcient organisation to allow collective bargaining. The Committee stated in their second report that

> Trade Boards should be regarded . . .as a means of supplying a regular machinery for negotiation and decision on certain groups of questions dealt

---

[18] Report on Conciliation and Arbitration, (Cd 9099), para 3.
[19] Industrial Councils and Trade Boards, Cd 9085, para 5.
[20] Second Report on Joint Standing Industrial Councils, Cd 9002, para 21.
[21] *Ibid*, para 2.

with in other circumstances by collective bargaining between employers' organisation and trade unions.[22]

It had already been noted that

The Trade Board Act was originally intended to secure the establishment of a minimum standard of wages in certain unorganised industries . . .[23]

The Whitley report therefore saw collective bargaining as the primary way of conducting industrial relations. This placed the report in line with earlier studies such as the 1894 Royal Commission on Labour[24] and the 1913 Industrial Council inquiry into collective agreements,[25] as well as anticipating much later ones such as Donovan. While Whitley might therefore be seen as saying relatively little that was new the response of Government was worthy of note. As we have seen the Government adopted the report but, more to the point, thereafter behaved consistently with that decision. One might argue that, at least from this point onwards until 1979, the State regarded collective bargaining as the primary way of conducting industrial relations. The degree of support offered would, however, vary significantly.

Before the war was over a number of legislative reforms were made. These included amendments to the trades boards legislation which, while they were in line with Whitley, had existed in draft prior to the establishment of the committee. The Minister of Labour, Roberts, put forward his vision of the new scheme in the following way:

I would like to regard the wages boards as a temporary expedient facilitating organisation within the industry, so that, in the course of time, the workers or their employers will not have need of the statutory regulations, but that their organisation will have then developed into a JIC, whereby the affairs of the industry will be controlled and managed by the people concerned in industry themselves, without any recourse to any legislative expedient.[26]

By 1918 experience of the operation of the existing regime had led to the belief that, in practice, trade boards actually encouraged organisation in the industries concerned. Thus employers' associations were formed in order to get agreed policies and to nominate representatives for the employers' side of the board. From the trade union side of the

[22] *Ibid*, para 11.
[23] *Ibid*.
[24] See ch. 2.
[25] See ch. 3.
[26] Parl. Deb., 17.6.1913, HC, vol 107, col 70.

fence there was evidence of a rapid upsurge in membership in certain industries after the formation of a trade board. There was also some empirical basis for the belief that trade boards would lead to full-blooded collective-bargaining; in the course of parliamentary debate it was pointed out that in a large number of trade board industries the average rate of wages was considerably above the rate set by the trade board. Furthermore, in some cases

> the employers and their workmen have jointly agreed to rates of wages which are considerably in excess of the rates established under the Trade Board Act.[27]

It therefore seemed legitimate to view the 1918 Act as part of an industrial relations structure which upheld '. . . the voluntary principle of negotiation . . . [whereby] . . . employers and workers should continue to manage their own affairs.'[28]

As well as being seen as a stimulus to organisation trade boards were, by this point, viewed as being benefical in other ways to industrial relations. Contact between the two sides of industry through the medium of the board was seen as conducive to better understanding and mutual respect. The better employers recognised the role the boards played in protecting against undercutting. Nevertheless, one contemporary commentator took the view that there was a real chance that industry would not, in the future, wish to abandon the protection a trade board afforded against a non-federated employer:

> it is difficult to believe that those who have experienced the advantages of the legal authority of the statutory trade board will consent to abandon it for the moral persuasion of the voluntary industrial council.[29]

AFTER THE ARMISTICE

Once the Armistice was signed expectations of social reform were high:

> The aspirations for a better social order which have been quickened in the hearts of My people by the experience of the war must be encouraged by prompt and comprehensive action . . . since the outbreak of the war every party and every class have worked and fought together for a great ideal . . . we must continue to manifest the same spirit. We must stop at no sacrifice

27 Parl. Deb., HC, 17.6.1913, vol 107 at col 116.
28 Parl. Deb., HC, 17.6.1913, vol 107. at col 71.
29 Willis, *Trade Boards* (London: WA Willis, 1920) p 7.

of interest or prejudice to stamp out unmerited poverty, to diminish unemployment, to provide decent homes, to improve the nation's health and to raise the standard of well-being throughout the country.[30]

The electoral roll for 1918 contained 8 million additional names since the previous general election and the existence of this new mass electorate obviously added to the pressure on government. Fear of revolution also weighed on the minds of the establishment and, for example, Churchill saw the value of minimum wage legislation in the following way:

> the real answer of ordered society to Bolshevism was the frank recognition of minimum standards and open access to the highest posts in industry.[31]

By what means were the 'aspirations for a better social order . . .' to be furthered? In the sphere of industrial relations, a policymaker in November 1918 might well have taken the view that implementing the Whitley report would be nowhere near enough. Collective bargaining might well be a highly appropriate means of conducting industrial relations but it would not necessarily bring about the substantive gains in terms and conditions sought by workers. Where a union was recognised for bargaining purposes but lacked bargaining power, what could it realistically expect to achieve? One option beyond Whitley was quasi-Keynsian economics:

> The right sort of policy was above all, the policy of full employment and high wages and it was to take the depression, another war and a revolution in economics and politics before this could be achieved.[32]

Other options included greater use of regulatory legislation and, on a much more radical note, nationalisation.

In trying to determine which legislative options might realistically have been considered one must take into account past, and especially wartime, experience. Understandings, which attracted a good deal of consensus, were being built up as to the limits of the law in industrial relations. Neither compulsory arbitration, nor a prohibition on taking industrial action, were going to be on the legislative agenda given the difficulties involved in operating such measures even in wartime.[33] The complexities of wage legislation were such as to rule out the possibility

---

[30] (1963) *Past and Present*, vol 24, 43 at p 46.
[31] Johnson, *Land Fit For Heroes*, p 382.
[32] Charles, above n 10, at p 235.
[33] See ch. 5.

of any comprehensive measure on this topic. Equally they were not of such an overwhelming nature as to exclude the possibility of minimum wage legislation; indeed shortly after the armistice Lloyd George spoke of 'the necessity for a minimum wage, which would ensure to every honest worker a decent standard of living.'[34] Maximum hours legislation might have been thought to be even more of a possibilty as a result of wartime experience since it could be seen as being in the interests of both sides of industry. It had become very clear that working excessive hours could result in diminished output.[35] Moreover, as a result of gains already made, or likely to be, through collective bargaining, a legal maximum of 48 hours a week would have a limited impact and would function more as a safety net for workers with weaker bargaining power. The prospects for greater use of regulatory legislation were enhanced by the report of the National Industrial Conference (NIC). This had been called by Government in early 1919 in the face of considerable industrial unrest. The delegates were from trade union and employers' associations and a sub-committee produced a report containing a number of suggestions for reform.

The report of the NIC sought to promote the interests of employees by, amongst other things, the use of regulatory legislation and in so doing went beyond Whitley. The International Labour Organisation (ILO) and the Versailles treaty also added to the legitimacy of such demands.[36] The Government's response to the report was positive; in general the recommendations of the NIC were accepted. Moreover, the Minister of Labour

> said he would not have attended the second meeting of the Conference had he not been prepared to see the government accept its main recommendations.[37]

In May 1919 the Prime Minister was to speak effusively of the proposals:

> I cannot commit myself to every detail, as many of them are complex and technical. I may say at once that I fully accept in principle your recommendations as to the fixing of maximum hours and minimum rates of wages. As regards hours, a bill is now being drafted to give effect to your recommendations and will, I hope, be introduced at a very early date.[38]

[34] The Times 13.11. 1919.
[35] Fisher, *Wages and Their Regulation in Great Britain since 1918* (London: PS King & Son, 1926) p 42.
[36] See below at p 160.
[37] Charles, above n 10, at p 244.
[38] LAB 2/775/3.

The Prime Minster did go on to express a measure of caution in respect of the recommendations as to wages:

> The question of the best method of doing this, however, is complex and full of difficulties, and I do not think it would be possible to frame legislation until a scheme for carrying out the principle of minimum rates has been fully worked out.[39]

On hours of work the NIC recommended that the legal maximum should be 48 hours per week. However,

> where an agreement has been arrived at between representative organisations of employers and employed in any trade and by such agreement provision is made that the number of working hours per week for that trade shall be lower than the maximum established under the Act, the Secretary of State . . . shall, if he has no reason to deem it contrary to the public interest, make an order prescribing the lower number of hours as the maximum for that trade.[40]

A parallel provision existed whereby the legal maximum might be raised but this should not happen

> unless and until the appropriate authority is satisfied either that the rate of wages payable in the trade is fixed on such a basis as to take into account, for payment at an enhanced rate, any extra hours worked, or that provision is made for the payment, as overtime, of all hours worked over 48.[41]

On the subject of wages the NIC came out in favour of a legal minimum wage. The level of that wage was to be determined by a commission consisting of 'an equal number of representatives of employers' associations and trade unions, with a chairman nominated by the government.'[42] The NIC also made a recommendation that a common rule provision be enacted:

> Where an agreement is arrived at between representative organisations of employers and trade unions in any trade laying down a minimum rate of wages, the Minister of Labour shall have power, after investigation, to apply such minimum rate, with such modification as he thinks fit, to all employers engaged in the trade falling within the scope of the agreement.

---

[39] *Ibid*
[40] Report of Provisional Joint Committee Presented to Meeting of National Industrial Conference, Cmd 139, p 7.
[41] *Ibid* at p 8.
[42] *Ibid* at p 9.

There was also an international dimension to all of this in that one of the ideas mooted as part of post-war reconstruction was international agreements on labour standards. International labour conventions predated the war and during it there was much talk of an expanded international framework. Statements by Lloyd George indicated that labour questions would be raised at any peace conference. The British delegates were, in fact, to play a prominent part in securing the labour chapter of the peace treaty. However, their vision of the chapter was that it would be procedural and organisational in nature:

> (1) It is impossible that the Peace Conference itself should consider specific proposals e.g. the proposal for a universal eight-hour day. The most that it can do is to establish a machinery for dealing with such matters. (2) It is important that the principle of international agreements on such questions should be adopted and suitable machinery established.[43]

The setting up of a permanent international organisation was central to British thinking:

> Such an organisation . . . would be able to exert a powerful pressure on backward countries to bring up their conditions to the standard of the recognised 'international minimum'; it would facilitate the adoption of improved conditions in all countries by arranging for simultaneous action, thereby excluding unfair competition; it would co-ordinate scientific investigation into labour questions in all countries and, finally, it would act as the authority to report upon the observance of agreements in the different countries.[44]

The result was that the ILO came into being; its first general conference took place in Washington in October 1919 and adopted a convention on hours of work. The central provision stated that, subject to exceptions, the hours of work of any person should not exceed eight in the day and forty-eight in the week. The UK Government was a signatory and indicated its intention to ratify.

THE END OF THE DREAM

In the period immediately after the war Britain experienced an economic boom. By the end of 1919, however, there were warning signs that all was not well with the economy. The Government responded by

---

[43] J Shotwell (ed), *The Origins of The I.L.O.*, vol 1, p 90.
[44] *Ibid* at p 91.

raising interest rates in November 1919 and again in April 1920. Matters continued to deteriorate throughout 1920 however and by the end of the year it was clear that the economy was descending into full-scale slump. The Government, prompted by the economic orthodoxy of the Treasury, resorted to the traditional weapon of deflation and public spending on social reforms was no longer a likely option. An early victim of this process was the trades boards system. The Treasury refused to sanction the expenditure required to allow an expansion in the number of boards.[45] The view was expressed that any such increase might lead to an increase in the number of unemployed workers.[46] A number of reforms put forward by the NIC would not have involved any significant increase in public expenditure; but conventional economics was relevant here too in that it was assumed that regulatory legislation would add to employers' costs and thereby both divert resources away from investment and render British products less competitive. By early 1920 it was clear that the report of the NIC would not be implemented; nor, indeed, was any form of regulatory legislation likely to appear on the statute book. It is also noteworthy that despite the fact that the UK was a signatory to the Washington Convention it did not ratify it. Why the change of heart? It is tempting to attribute this to the decline in the economic position but it is suggested that that can be at most a partial explanation.

It is probable that, by the end of 1919, when the economic difficulties were still relatively minor, the Government had decided not to implement the regulatory legislation favoured by the NIC.[47] Trades boards, on the other hand, continued to expand until 1921. The most cynical explanation is that the Government, no longer so concerned about industrial unrest, felt that it could renege without fear of the consequences.[48] It does seem likely that this was by far the most important factor, though the whole truth is much more complicated. All the parties involved (employers, unions and Government) had internal differences over the way to proceed. A number of leading trade unions refused to participate in the NIC (those being the Amalgamated Society of Engineers, the Iron and Steel Trades Federation and the unions of

[45] A decision taken in early 1921.

[46] LAB 2/8331/1.

[47] Johnson, above n 31, pp 471–73. R Lowe, 'The failure of consensus in Britain: the National Industrial Conference, 1919–21' (1978) *Historical Journal* 649.

[48] This is reinforced by the saga of the demise of proposals for nationalisation of the railways and mines.

the Triple Alliance). The major omission from the employers' side was the absence of representation from the coal-owners. The employers' side reflected a variety of views but one of the most influential was Sir Allen Smith (of the engineers) who was a hardliner. Any government will reflect a range of opinions on issues of controversy and in the case of the 1918/22 Government this was graphically reflected in the fact that it was actually a coalition. The majority party within Government was the Conservatives and it seems that Lloyd George came increasingly under their dominance as time went on. The Conservative response to the state control of the war years was to advocate vehemently non-intervention.

Anyone hoping for full implementation of the proposed labour law reforms of the NIC would have looked for the backing of a strong and committed Ministry of Labour. The reality was that the Ministry was a very new Ministry (formed in 1916) and possessed very little in the way of political clout. The position would obviously have been very different had senior figures in the Government chosen to lend their backing to any such programme. However, it was simply not realistic to expect that the Ministry would be able to push through Cabinet a comprehensive programme of labour law reform. Indeed, as we have seen the Ministry was not successful in defending the trades boards programme against government cuts. This was despite the fact that there were those within the Ministry who believed that

> the argument that the statutory regulation of wages in unorganised trades should be suspended in a time of trade depression is one that the Government cannot possibly accept; for it is at such times that some safeguarding machinery is most required by unorganised workers.[49]

The Ministry's weakness was also evidenced in other ways. Between its inception and October 1922 it was headed by as many as four ministers but, with the exception of Sir Robert Horne,[50] the individuals concerned were not overly talented. Horne himself appeared to have had a limited store of sympathy for the cause of labour. Two civil servants of the utmost distinction, Beveridge and Askwith, left the ministry in 1919, and their successors were not of the same level of ability. Again, the 'two main departmental heads, Horace Wilson and FW Bowers, were both treasury-minded economists.'[51]

---

[49] LAB 2/8331/1.
[50] Minister of Labour, Jan 1919–Mar 1920.
[51] Morgan, *Consensus and Disunity* (Oxford: Clarendon Press, 1979) p 52.

Aside from any issue regarding the Ministry's capacity to provide greater institutional support there was a significant question mark over the Ministry's commitment towards the suggested reforms of the NIC Within the Ministry there were very different views as to the way in which the development and reform of industrial relations should proceed.[52] Thus there were those who saw collective bargaining as the normal means of regulation within industry and were reluctant to countenance any alternative. One finds Shackleton, Permanent Secretary between 1916 and 1920, stating, in discussion on the principle of maximum hours legislation, that it is 'a matter which must be decided by the trades concerned.'[53] The Ministry found it much easier to throw its weight behind auxiliary as opposed to regulatory legislation, as can be seen by its treatment of trade boards. The latter received genuine support from the Ministry and in 1919 funding was obtained to establish more boards; in the period 1919–1921 38 boards were established. The Ministry's attitude was conditioned, in part, by belief in the value of the trade board system in itself. Trades Boards were seen as fostering both collective bargaining and better industrial relation. In addition, Ministry support stemmed from the more negative perspective that if trades boards did not exist then a universal minimum wage would be required. The potential political difficulties involved in this troubled the Ministry; as did the concern that a universal wage might be determined without reference to the conditions prevailing in any particular trade.[54]

It can be seen that a number of factors stood in the way of a move to a system with greater legal regulation. In addition, there were detailed arguments against specific proposals. Take the demands for a legally enforceable minimum wage which the Government appeared willing to concede in the earlier part of 1919.[55] The Ministry of Labour had grave reservations about this. One concern was over the principles by which wages would be set; would it be according to the needs of the worker or by the ability of the employer to pay? More surprisingly the Ministry perceived a conflict between minimum wages/maximum hours legislation and the endorsement and implementation of the Whitley report. The underlying reason seemed to be that regulatory legislation was not compatible with 'self-governance' in industry, presumably on the basis

[52] See R Lowe, *Adjusting to Democracy* (Oxford: Clarendon Press, 1986) ch 4.
[53] Fisher, above n 35, p 71.
[54] LAB 2/8331/1.
[55] Lowe, above n 47 at p 656.

that such legislation might undermine collective bargaining. This is surprising when it is considered that the levels likely to be set by legislation would only have affected the position of workers in the less well organised trades. One might contrast the contemporary 'floor of rights' legislation, where express provision is made for contracting-out by the collective parties.[56] Why was this view held? The answer is not clear, but it may be that the Ministry's real objections were on other grounds and were perhaps part of the backlash against state interference. Again a number of Ministry officials were former trade unionists who may have been concerned to protect the autonomy of collective bargaining. The Minister of Labour was also not slow to draw attention to the potential difficulties involved in common rule legislation:

> Not only would complicated questions of demarcation and trade definition inevitably arise, but the question of the extent to which any given group of employers or employed represented a large majority of the trade would require close examination. There is the further difficulty that certain wage settlements affect an industry, while others affect a craft extending through a number of industries.[57]

More fundamentally, Horne also suggested that legislation of this type was inconsistent with a position whereby collective agreements were not legally enforceable between the collective parties.[58] However, such agreements, subject to incorporation, were and are legally enforceable at the level of the individual employment contract. Legislation of the common rule type merely seeks to extend enforceability at the individual rather than the collective level.

While the NIC had recommended a minimum wage law the unanimous support of either employers or trade unions could not be assumed. Some of the latter would be concerned lest such a reform functioned as a dis-incentive to organise. It might be readily assumed that a significantly larger proportion of employers would be opposed since state setting of wage levels would stop them falling to the level naturally determined by the market. By 1920, with the commencement of the steady descent into slump and a rising number of unemployed, further arguments were adduced against reform. Classical economics taught that unemployment could only be tackled by a reduction in wage levels.

[56] See, for instance, s 110 of the Employment Rights Act 1996.
[57] Parl. Deb., HC, 8.3.1920, vol 126, cols. 950/1.
[58] *Ibid.*

Maximum hours legislation met a similar fate though, as has been indicated, prospects had perhaps been better here and indeed initial reservations had been at the margins. Horne, for instance, noted that 'there were obvious difficulties in meeting the case of farm workers, seamen and domestic servants,'[59] and he assumed that any bill would have to allow for exemptions and variations. Subsequently, the same sorts of objections that were raised against minimum wage legislation emerged. Matters were further complicated by differences between the NIC recommendations and those which emerged from the Washington conference.

State endorsement of the primacy of collective bargaining remained solid throughout the inter-war period. The willingness to support it by a degree of auxiliary legislation, on the other hand, tended to fluctuate. Perhaps the best illustration of this is the administration of the trades boards. As early as 1920 the boards came under the malevolent attentions of the Treasury which was anxious to reduce the running costs of the boards. More fundamentally, and alarmingly, the Treasury believed that the trades boards system interfered with the prospects of economic recovery since it prevented wages falling to their natural level. Thus the Treasury

> frustrated the creation of new boards throughout 1920 and 1921 by limiting the number of investigating officers (who established an industry's need for a board) and undermined the effectiveness of existing boards by reducing the number of enforcement inspectors.[60]

Even more drastically the Cabinet in 1921 decided to prohibit the creation of any new boards. Employers too had begun to question the value of the boards and even the Ministry of Labour was internally divided on this issue. Admittedly the Ministry fought against the attentions of the Treasury but in June 1921 it appeared to be bowing to the tide when it 'evaded its statutory responsibility to confirm minimum rates in the grocery trade.'[61] One should perhaps make a distinction between 'pure' auxiliary legislation such as the Industrial Courts Act 1919[62] and auxiliary legislation which, while its primary purpose might be to promote collective bargaining, has a secondary regulatory

[59] Johnson, above n 31, p 382.
[60] R Lowe, 'The Erosion of State Intervention in Britain, 1917–1924' (1978) *Econ Hist Rev* 270 at p 279.
[61] R Lowe, above n 52, at p 100.
[62] See below at p 166.

function. Trades Boards clearly fell into the second category and indeed, as originally enacted, had been viewed as purely regulatory.

DISPUTE RESOLUTION AND CONTROL

In 1919 the Industrial Courts Act was passed, part one set up the Industrial Court. In a sense this was a successor body to the Committee on Production. It implemented Whitley's recommendation that there be 'a standing arbitration council for cases where the parties wish to refer any dispute to arbitration.'[63] Unlike the Committee on Production, the court operated on an entirely voluntary basis. As a result, the Minister could only refer a dispute where both parties consented and any award made was not compulsory. Moreover, where collectively agreed dispute procedures existed in a trade or industry,

> the Minister shall not, unless with the consent of both parties to the dispute, and unless and until there has been a failure to obtain a settlement by means of those arrangements, refer the matter for settlement . . .[64]

It was hoped that the court would take an overview of wage settlements across different industries in arriving at decisions, and also that it would develop a body of principles to inform those decisions. Such concerns are likely to have been attributable to knowledge and experience gained during wartime and the realisation that the State had to be at least conscious of the impact that a wage settlement in one industry might have on others.

Part two of the Act gave the Minister power to set up a Court of Inquiry to which he could refer any matters connected with or relevant to a dispute.[65] This provision was aimed at disputes which had the potential to have a major impact on the community at large. Strikes in industries such as mining and the railways might disrupt other major industries severely. Whitley had recommended that

> there should be means by which an independent inquiry may be made into the facts and circumstances of a dispute and an authoritative announcement made thereon . . .[66]

---

[63] Report on Conciliation and Arbitration, above n 17, para 16.
[64] S 2(4).
[65] S 4(1).
[66] Report on Conciliation and Arbitration, above n 17, para 6.

The inquiry could be in public or in private, but any report had to be laid before both Houses of Parliament.[67]

The Act gave very little indication as to what a report should contain, though in practice most Courts of Inquiry felt it appropriate to go beyond a fact-finding role. The Board of Trade already possessed powers of inquiry under the 1896 Act but proceedings under part two of the 1919 Act were more public in nature; this was regarded as a key difference. The notion of the public as the ultimate arbiter, particularly in serious disputes, had been raised on numerous occasions over the years, the idea being that fully and properly informed public opinion would produce strong pressure for a settlement. A further difference was the acknowledgement that Government had an interest in the outcome of major disputes and might in fact be one of the parties:

> A body which is itself a party to a dispute cannot be an arbitrator. Its views are no longer accepted as impartial; its judgments are considered to be biased.[68]

In contrast the public were said to be 'eminently fair and just.'[69] The issue of how public opinion was to be divined was simply not raised. A healthy note of cynicism was introduced into the parliamentary debates by Askwith[70] who expressed the view that

> In 999 out of 1,000 cases the public does not want to know anything about them and does not care.[71]

Part two was not entirely voluntary in that it allowed for the passing of subordinate legislation which would empower the inquiry to compel the attendance of witnesses and the production of documents.[72] More significantly, on the other hand, there were no powers to prevent industrial action until the conclusion of the inquiry. It seems to have been assumed that if resort to an inquiry was used sparingly, then any held might make a genuine impact. In fact only 20 Courts of Inquiry were appointed between the passing of the Act and 1939 and 16 of those took

[67] Ss 4 and 5.

[68] Parl. Deb., 6.11.1919, HC, vol 120, col 1734.

[69] Parl. Deb., 6.1.1919, HC, vol 120, col 1715.

[70] Askwith had immense experience of industrial conciliation and arbitration. He had held a number of positions in this field, including that of Chief Industrial Commissioner to the Board of Trade.

[71] Parl. Deb., 18.11.1919, HL, vol 37, col 314.

[72] It seems that no regulations were made under this provision. See IG Sharp, *Industrial Conciliation and Arbitration in Great Britain*, 1st edn (London: Allen & Unwin, 1950) p 361.

place in the first 6 years.[73] Over the years the establishment of a Court of Inquiry was to evolve into 'another technique for dispute development, half-way between conciliation and arbitration . . .'[74]

The Act was a classic example of auxiliary legislation; indeed it is noteworthy that the bulk of cases referred to the Industrial Court came from the less-organised trades.[75] The Act might have included a provision whereby employers in an industry who were not party to an award were, by force of law, nevertheless bound by it. At one stage, during the course of parliamentary proceedings, clause 5 provided that where the Minister of Labour considered that a substantial number of workmen were affected by a particular award in an industry the Minister should have power to extend that decision to other businesses and other workman in the same industry.[76] The Ministry seemed wary of the concept of the 'common rule.' This was partly for technical reasons, such as the difficulty of defining and distinguishing particular trades and industries. However, the Ministry also suggested that trade unions would not welcome such a reform. Union opposition was not surprising when the Minister of Labour was of the view that any enactment of the common rule should be accompanied by

> provisions which made it obligatory upon trade unions to observe the decision, that is to say, made it illegal for them to pay strike pay to those on strike against the decision, and made those responsible for any such act amenable to the law.[77]

It must be said that prior to such statements there seems to have been trade union support for a common rule provision, and indeed the NIC had been in favour of this. The Minister's view was based on the premise that unless there was the possibility of sanctions against the trade union, any common rule provision was biased against the employer in that sanctions could only lie one way. This was quite erroneous since common rule provisions normally operate by way of implication into the individual employment contract, hence allowing for the possibility of litigation between employer and employee. The employer also benefits by way of protection against undercutting.

---

[73] IG Sharp, *Industrial Conciliation and Arbitration in Great Britain*, 1st edn (London: Allen & Unwin, 1950) at p 363.
[74] McCarthy and Clifford, (1966) BJIR 39 at p 56.
[75] Sharp, above n 72, pp 357–58.
[76] Parl. Deb., 6.11.1919, HC, vol 120, col 1761.
[77] Parl. Deb., 6.11.1919, HC, vol 120, col 1711.

In February 1919 the Cabinet set up a new committee, the Industrial Unrest Committee,

> to make the necessary arrangements for dealing with any situation that might arise from industrial unrest both at the present moment and in the future.[78]

The Committee looked at questions such as coal distribution in the event of a miners' strike, and the use of troops to guard essential services. The Industrial Unrest Committee evolved into the Supply and Transport Committee and that body's work included the drafting of the Emergency Powers legislation. Civic Commissioners were also appointed to co-ordinate the military, the police and so on. Drafting of the bill which became the Emergency Powers Act began early in 1920. The Act was part of the response to the considerable amount of industrial unrest in the period immediately after the war. Some members of government were sufficently alarmed to regard trade union activity as potentially revolutionary. A more widely shared concern was the impact of major disputes in certain areas. The Act did not aim to regulate or control organisation of, or participation in, industrial action, but instead sought to diffuse its impact. The legislation allowed for the proclamation of a state of emergency where

> any action has been taken or is immediately threatened by any persons or body of persons of such a nature and on so extensive a scale as to be calculated . . .

by interfering in prescribed ways 'to deprive the community, or any substantial portion of the community, of the essentials of life . . .' Thus the legislation could only be deployed in response to human action and did not cover the problems posed by natural disasters. The fact that the power to issue a proclamation was contingent on the prospect of the community being deprived of the essentials of life was important to the government's ability to legitimise its use of the Act. Government could always make the claim that the well-being of the public justified the promulgation of any proclamation, and not the wish to defeat a strike. A proclamation could only be made where the interference would arise in prescribed ways; that is to say 'by interfering with the supply and distribution of food, water, fuel or light, or with the means of locomotion . . .' Given the background of alarm over the might of the Triple Alliance, it would seem that the Act would cover industrial action by any of those unions. The Government's power to make regulations was very wide indeed but two important amendments were

[78] K Jeffery and P Hennessy, *States of Emergency* (London: Routledge & Keegan Paul, 1983) p 10.

made during the committee stage. First, it was provided that the Act did not include power to impose any form of industrial conscription. At the same time the Government made clear that the possibility of voluntary assistance was not ruled out. Second, to protect the right to strike, it was provided that no regulation should make it an offence for any person or persons to take part in a strike, or peacefully to persuade any other person or persons to take part in a strike. As we have seen, legislation of this sort had been in the pipeline for some time but it was eventually introduced during the middle of the 1920 miners' strike and then rushed through both Houses of Parliament.[79] The manner of enactment aroused more controversey than the principle of such legislation, which was accepted by both sides of the House.

Both Acts were predicated on the basis that a prohibition on strikes would be futile, though in all other respects they were very different measures. The Industrial Courts Act 1919 can be viewed as evolving from measures such as the 1896 Act. It is essentially about dispute resolution and assumes that normally the parties' own machinery will resolve conflict but that on occasion additional procedures/machinery will be required. Legislation of this type had become an accepted part of the industrial relations system. The 1920 Act was introduced to counter the impact of strikes in key industries. Its enactment must be set against a background of government deliberations over the use of troops in trade disputes and the setting up of administrative apparatus to deal with strikes in vital industries. Troops were used in a number of disputes in the period but, even within establishment circles, their role was controversial. The Army saw its role as minimal, confined to the likes of guarding essential installations.

The Emergency Powers Act 1920 might be viewed as an acknowledgement of the changes brought about by the war. The State had come to appreciate that it now had a more interventionist role and that a complete return to the position pre-1914 was not realistic. The growth in trade union membership[80] and the corresponding increase in union power had also to be taken into account. Changes in the level at which collective bargaining was conducted meant that national disputes were also much more likely. Some members of government believed that a new breed of trade dispute had come into being:

[79] It was introduced on 20.10.1920 and received the Royal Assent one week later.

[80] In 1914 the total trade union membership in the UK stood at 4,145,000 and this had increased to 6,533,000 by 1918. By 1920 the figure was 8,334,000. See Clay, above n 6, p 143.

It is no doubt true that the character of industrial disputes and of strikes has materially altered within quite recent memory.[81]

Bonar Law was at pains to stress that the Act would only affect such disputes and not those of a traditional variety:

> This bill is not intended to apply, and could not by any possibility apply, to any ordinary industrial dispute between employers and workmen, on any question affecting strikes to raise the conditions of their lives.[82]

However, the Act would clearly apply to, for example, a pay dispute in the mining industry and what is 'new' is in fact the impact caused by national strikes called by certain unions. Thus the real issue for government was whether at least some unions had acquired an unreasonable degree of power. One government supporter was of the view that union demands might now, on occasion, be framed in the following way: 'We will inflict great inconvenience or hardship on the whole community unless our particular demands are conceded.'[83] Noone believed that the Government could retain the statutory powers it had possessed in wartime but clearly it was more than likely that some alternative would be enacted.

STATE CONTROL OF INDUSTRY

Before the First World War a goal for many trade unionists was the end of private control of industry. At the same time various individuals had somewhat different visions of the future; some sought nationalisation while others attached themselves to the syndicalist camp. Such goals must have seemed immeasurably closer to realisation after the State took over the running of a number of key industries such as coal and rail during the war. Once the war was over, demands for change in the running of industry intensified. It is a powerful testament to the impact the war had on political thought that support for nationalisation could be found on most points on the political spectrum. Those seeking nationalisation had a number of aims; for example that public utilities should be run for the benefit of the community as a whole and not simply private shareholders. There was, moreover, a clear industrial relations dimension in that nationalisation was seen as a route whereby

---

[81] Parl. Deb., 28.10.1920, HL, vol 42, col 108.
[82] Parl. Deb., 25.10.1920, HC, vol 133, col 1399.
[83] Parl. Deb., 25.10.1920, HC, vol 133, col 1431.

terms and conditions of employment would be raised to satisfactory levels. Indeed some in the union movement had a distinctly prosaic vision of what nationalisation might achieve; for example, the engineers were not interested because they

> did not have the same problems of badly underpaid members, accidents, and recognition which faced the miners and railwaymen, and which they hoped to solve through nationalisation.[84]

There was also the issue of worker representation; were it to occur at the level of the boards of nationalised concerns industrial democracy would be facilitated. A typical nationalisation bill of the period provided that

> A nationalised industry was to be run by a board, chaired by a minister, and consisting of equal numbers of ministerial appointees and of representatives of the trade unions which organised the workers, and the same pattern of men appointed from above along with workers' representatives, was to be followed in managerial bodies at lower levels.[85]

For a variety of reasons, not least the matter of industrial muscle, nationalisation of the mines loomed large in the immediate post-war period. A miners' conference in January 1919 sought further legislation on working hours and nationalisation of the mines. A draft bill, which provided for the running of the mines by a Mining Council, had already been prepared by the union. The Minister of Mines was to be president of the Council and a board of twenty members would consist of, inter alia, ten members nominated by the miners' federation. The bill addressed the role of unions in the industry post-nationalisation. A union's ability to bargain collectively and take industrial action was not to be impeded. A union of mineworkers could

> do anything individually or in combination which the members of a trade union or a trade union may lawfully do. Provided further that notwithstanding any Act, order, or regulation to the contrary, it shall be lawful for any person employed under this Act to participate in any civil or political action in like manner as if such person were not employed by his Majesty, or by any authority on his behalf.[86]

---

[84] Pribicevic, *The Shop Steward's Movement* (Oxford: Blackwell, 1959) p 42.
[85] Clegg, *Industrial Democracy and Nationalisation* pp 9–10.
[86] Quoted in Arnott, *The Miners: Years of Struggle* (London, 1953) p 220.

Subsequently, in evidence to Sankey one witness stated that

> I think it is quite true that we must retain the strike weapon. At the same time I think that the incentive to use it will be largely taken away under nationalisation.[87]

The bill embodied a statutory duty of recognition:

> The Mining Council, before making or altering any regulations or conditions of employment, including wages, as affects workmen engaged in the mining industry, shall consult with the association known as the Miners' Federation of Great Britain, and in the event of such representatives and the Mining Council failing to agree, the matter in dispute may be referred to arbitration on such terms as may be mutually agreed.[88]

In February 1919 the miners were balloted on industrial action over wages, hours and nationalisation and the result was overwhelmingly in favour of taking action but implementation was postponed for several weeks to allow the Royal Commission to produce an interim report.[89] A judge, Mr Justice Sankey, chaired a 12 man commission whose composition is worthy of note. Four members of the commission were appointed by the MFGB and two more were agreed upon by the MFGB and the Government. Of the remainder three were government nominees and only three were appointed by the coal-owners. A single interim report could not be agreed upon but nevertheless a substantial majority were in favour of amending the 1908 Act to reduce the number of hours worked.[90] The same majority agreed that private ownership should not be allowed to continue but were divided as to exactly what should replace it. The Government announced that it accepted Sankey 'in the spirit as well as in the letter'[91] and the union then balloted its membership on acceptance of the government's proposals. The union was convinced that the Government had conceded the principle of nationalisation. The miners heeded an Executive recommendation of acceptance and voted to call off the threat of industrial action.

The Sankey Commission reported on 20th June 1919 and again unanimity proved elusive.[92] However, the report produced by the

---

[87] Coal Industry Commission, Reports on the Second Stage of the Inquiry (Cmd 360), evidence of W Straker, p 965.
[88] Arnott, above n 80, p 223.
[89] Coal Industry Commission, Reports on the First Stage of the Inquiry (Cmd 359).
[90] This led to the Coal Mines Act, 1919.
[91] Parl. Deb., 20.3.1919, HC, vol 113, col 2346.
[92] Coal Industry Commission, above n 87.

chairman himself was backed by six of the commission (subject to reservations) and that report was uncategorically in favour of nation-alisation. Sankey found that

> the relationship between the masters and workers in most of the coalfields in the U.K. is, unfortunately, of such a character that it seems impossible to better it under the present system of ownership. Many of the workers think they are working for the capitalist and a strike becomes a contest between labour and capital. This is much less likely to apply with the State as owner, and there is fair reason to expect that the relationship between labour and community will be an improvement upon the relationship between labour and capital in the coalfields.[93]

Post-nationalisation Sankey wished to see worker control along lines similar to that proposed by the MFGB. There were, however, a number of significant differences. The National Mining Council was to be advisory and, in addition, its composition was to be tripartite. One third of the members were to represent consumers. It is also worthy of note that whilst the National Council was to be advisory no national alteration of wages was to be made without the consent both of the Minister of Mines and the Council. Similarly at district level the composition of the District Council was to be modified to include consumer representation. The role of the Council was not insignificant:

> Subject to the direction of the Minister of Mines, the District Mining Council shall manage in its district the entire coal extraction, the regulation of output, the discontinuance of or opening out of mines, trial sinkings, the control of prices and the basis of wage assessment, and the distribution of coal.'

Nationalisation was seen as potentially bringing a number of benefits which would accrue not just to miners. Focusing on the industrial relations dimension the Sankey scheme could be viewed as a form of industrial democracy. One advantage of this was that management would be more efficient once workers lent their expertise:

> For a generation the colliery worker has been educated socially and technically. The result is a great national asset. Why not use it?[94]

Other anticipated advantages were improved industrial relations and a commensurate fall in the strike rate. Secure in the knowledge both that they were no longer working to increase the wealth of private mine-

---

[93] Coal Industry Commission, above n 87 at p vii.
[94] *Ibid* at p ix.

owners and that their representatives had a genuine share in decision-making there was every reason to look forward to industrial harmony. Industrial democracy was seen as worthwhile not simply for the improvements it would bring but also because it would be fairer:

> the man who gives his labour to the industry has, at least, an equal right to executive powers in every department of the industry with the man who put his capital into it . . .[95]

Sankey reported on June 20th but in August, in what to the union movement at least was an astonishing volte-face, the Government declared that it rejected nationalisation. One reason for this was the lobbying which had been done on behalf of the coal-owners. One might have then expected an early ballot of miners with a view to taking industrial action; instead the union's first line of attack was to seek the support of the Trades Union Congress (TUC) and the general public. By 1920 the miners were much more inclined towards industrial action but by an overwhelming vote of 3,732,000 against 1,050,000, a special TUC decided against a general strike and in favour of political action in the form of intensive political propoganda in preparation for the next general election. Arnott writes that

> [t]he miners were indignant. They knew what the decision meant. Nationalisation of mines, as an immediate aim, had been shelved for the time being. A General Election was not in sight . . . So they drew the necessary conclusions. With nationalisation postponed to an indefinite future, they would now bend their activities to the question of wages and prices.[96]

In the end all that emerged in terms of worker control was part two of the Mining Industry Act 1920. This set up a hierarchial structure of joint bodies comprised of representatives of both sides of industry: pit committees, district committees, area boards and a national board. The function of these bodies was to discuss and make recommendations with respect to a variety of matters, including disputes as to wages. In the matter of wages, the area boards had a pivotal position in that they were charged with the duty of formulating

> at such intervals and on such principles as may be prescribed by the National Board, schemes for adjusting the remuneration of workers within the area
> . . .

---

[95] *Ibid* at p 944, evidence of W Straker.
[96] Arnott, above n 86, p 218.

A recommendation made by one of the aforementioned joint bodies, other than a pit committee, could be referred to the Board of Trade which had power to make it legally binding. Breach of such an order led to criminal penalties. Under the legislative scheme, to have the status of a recommendation a decision had to be arrived at by a majority of both sides of the relevant joint body.

The aim of the legislation was to give employees an opportunity to have an input to decisions about their working lives. The underlying philosophy of the scheme was in line with Whitleyism and government thinking in general on the value of joint decision-making in industry:

> The representation of employers and workmen according to the methods which are there suggested [ie in the bill] is one of the fundamental ideas upon which the whole labour policy of the Goverment has been based.[97]

The catalyst for this particular scheme was Sankey and the view of the representatives of the employers was that such a scheme 'would be a means of bringing us closer together than we used to be before the war . . .'[98] More realistically, for mine-owners it was infinitely preferable to the prospect of nationalisation. Given that there was no compulsion to participate one might well ask why the scheme could not have been established by voluntary means. Horne suggested that one reason for this was that

> you could never have in a voluntary scheme, an arrangement by which recommendations made by representatives of employers and workmen may obtain the formal sanction of the Minister, and by that means become part of the law of the land . . .[99]

It is submitted that this does not follow; after all, wartime legislation had made collective agreements binding on employers who were not party to the relevant agreement. One suspects that the real reason for the enactment of part two was that the Government was anxious to be seen to be doing something in the light of the retreat from nationalisation.

The scheme came to nothing. While it contained elements of compulsion there was, as we have seen, no mechanism to compel either side to participate. Initially the miners would not co-operate on the basis that the role given to the area board conflicted with their aim of secur-

---

[97] Parl. Deb., 20.3.1919, HC, vol 131, col 588.
[98] Parl. Deb., 20.3.1919, HC, vol 131, col 570.
[99] Parl. Deb., 20.3.1919, HC, vol 131, col 588.

ing national pay bargaining. After the lock-out of 1921 they abandoned their opposition only for the employers to declare that the machinery provided for in the Act was now 'unnecessary.' Given that the owners no longer feared nationalisation they had no incentive to offer anything by way of compromise; instead the view prevailed that 'industries should be absolutely free from all inteference that is not essential on the part of the executive powers of the country . . .'[100]

A second industry where nationalisation seemed, for a time, to be within the grasp of the workforce was the railways. The unions had had that aim since 1894; the National Union of Railwaymen (NUR) reaffirmed this shortly before the end of the war by passing a resolution demanding

> complete nationalisation of all the railways in the United Kingdom with equal representation both national and local for the N.U.R. on the management.

This aspiration was encouraged by a statement to the TUC from Lloyd George and by the following statement from a Commons Select committee:

> The main railway systems of the United Kingdom should be brought under unified ownership and managed as one system if the question of the improvement and development of the internal transport facilities is to be considered from the standpoint of economy and effcency.[101]

Shortly before the election of 1918 several Cabinet ministers declared that the railways were to be nationalised. The coalition government introduced the Ministry of Ways and Communications Bill; clause 4 gave the Minister power to nationalise the railways but intensive parliamentary lobbying led to the deletion of the clause. (One may note that 45 MPs were railway directors.) The response of the railwaymen to this seems to have been somewhat muted; energies were perhaps diverted by the wages dispute of 1919 and the ensuing national strike.

For the time being nationalisation was off the agenda but the attentions of government were not removed from the railways. Wartime controls were to be abandoned in time (ultimately in August 1921), but the position would not be allowed to revert to the pre-war one. A

---

[100] Correspondence between the Mines Department and the Mining Association of Great Britain, p 6, Cmd 1551.
[101] Second Report of the Select Committee on Transport.

White Paper was published in 1921[102] which contained proposals for the re-organisation of the industry. In particular it was suggested that the railway companies be amalgamated, by compulsion if need be, into a mere six/seven companies. The White Paper also contained the following recommendation on worker participation in management:

> The composition of the Board [of Management] is considered to be of the greatest importance, and whilst in the past the directors of railway companies have all been appointed by the shareholders, the Government are of the opinion that the time has arrived when the workers, both offical and manual workers, should have some voice in the management.[103]

Under the proposals shareholder-directors would still be in a majority on the board. Of the worker directors

> 1/3 might be leading administrative officals of the group, to be co-opted by the rest of the board, and 2/3 members elected from and by the workers on the railway.[104]

This proposal was approved, in general terms, by the unions.

The legislation which ultimately emerged was the Railways Act 1921, part four of which dealt with labour relations. In essence it encapsulated in legal form the collectively agreed negotiating machinery of the industry, which had recently been agreed. What it did not contain was provisions on worker directors. The superficial explanation for this omission was that part four sought to enact what had been agreed between the two sides of industry, the unions having abandoned their support for boardroom representation in the course of talks about negotiating machinery. The change in union stance may have been brought about by employer opposition, but the unions themselves were divided internally as to the desirability of boardroom representation. Some union members took the view that such proposals would only be acceptable in the event of nationalisation of the industry:

> it will only require a little reflection to realise that the position of representative employees on the board of directors which were running the railways primarily for dividends and only secondarily for the public service would be untenable.[105]

---

[102] Ministry of Transport, Outline of Proposals as to the Future Organisation of Transport Undertakings in Great Britain (Cmd 787).
[103] *Ibid* at p 2.
[104] *Ibid* at p 3.
[105] Bagwell, *The Railwaymen* (London: Allen & Unwin, 1963) p 410.

There are some indications that the Government genuinely regretted the demise of this proposal, although amendment of the Bill was not a serious possibility in the light of the knowledge that the employers would withdraw from the negotiating machinery if any changes were to be made. Under the procedure in the absence of agreement between management and labour, disputes as to pay and conditions of service were to be referred to the Central Wages Board (CWB) or on appeal, the National Wages Board (NWB). The CWB contained an equal number of representatives from both sides of industry. The NWB was similarly constituted but, in addition, contained representatives of the users of railways, with an independent chairman nominated by the Minister of Labour. The four representatives of the users were to be nominated as follows: one by the TUC; one by the co-operative Union; one by the Association of British of British Chambers of Commerce; and one by the Federation of British Industries.

Despite this legislative intervention into the industrial relations of the railway industry no statutory obligation was placed on either management or labour apart from the duty of referral. Accordingly any agreement reached would be purely voluntary in import. The unions had earlier agreed that no industrial action was to be taken until one month after a dispute had reached the NWB, but this provision did not find its way into the legislation. Finally, either side could terminate the procedures by giving twelve months' notice (though such notice could not be given before January 1923). The result of resorting to law was to give a statutory basis to certain institutions of the industry.

Compared to worker representation on the Board, let alone nationalisation, part four seems of little significance. Flanders has expressed the view that

> Given the pre-war resistance of most of the companies to full recognition of the unions, they felt more secure in having their agreements supported by law.[106]

In the light of the non-compulsory nature of the legislative scheme, it is questionable whether labour felt more secure by virtue of its existence. Admittedly the scheme put union recognition on a statutory basis but one may doubt whether a return to the pre-war position was ever a serious prospect. While it has been said that

---

[106] (1974) BJIR 352 at p 356.

on the whole the machinery worked exceedingly well over a very difficult period and was a great improvement on the pre-war position[107]

the impact of the law was arguably negligible.

CONCLUSIONS

During the immediate post-war period it appeared, for a while, that a position would be reached whereby industrial relations would be regulated to a significant extent by several different means. Collective bargaining was always going to be of importance but it had seemed that legal regulation of wages and hours of work was also likely to occur. Nationalisation of certain industries also seemed a distinct possibility and in its wake that might have carried industrial democracy for those industries. It would also have been assumed that a nationalised industry would act as a model employer with regard to the terms and conditions that it offered. If such a system had emerged it would have been difficult to view it as anything other than a hybrid. The reasons why such a system did not emerge are complex but it is important to note that the predominance of argument was not about the impracticability or inappropriateness of legal regulation.

It is difficult to review this period and feel anything other than cynicism over the behaviour of government. This is not to question the good faith of individual ministers and leading civil servants. Nevertheless, the motivating factors on the part of government all too often seemed to be based on narrow considerations of expediency. One is left to wonder what might have been attained, in the realms of legal regulation and public ownership, had there been greater resort to industrial action in the first half of 1919. Trade union leaders may well have shown far too much in the way of good faith.

During the period under discussion the significance of collective bargaining in industry continued to increase.

> No change in kind, no innovation in principle is to be discerned, but a wide extension and elaboration, in a single decade, of practices and methods, devised by the empirical wisdom of workpeople . . .[108]

Moreover, by its endorsement of the Whitley report the State accepted that collective bargaining was the best way, in general, to conduct

---

[107] Sharp, above n 72, at p 253.
[108] Clay, above n 6, p 143.

industrial relations. At the same time this clearly allowed for the possibility of auxiliary legislation and did not exclude the use of regulatory regulation. But the Government was to waver over the extent of support it was prepared to give to collective bargaining; the position of the trades boards illustrates this very well. At times even auxiliary legislation seemed to be regarded as an unacceptable degree of intervention.

7

Labour Law Between the Wars

INTRODUCTION

T HE PERIOD IMMEDIATELY after the war, covered in the last chapter, was one in which the role of labour law might have become much more extensive. It was also one, where, for a time, there appeared to be a real prospect of a significant expansion of individual employment rights. The 1920s saw a return to a much more laissez-faire approach to industrial relations by Government. This, however, did not mean that the government viewed collective bargaining as anything other than a highly appropriate way to conduct industrial relations and institutionalise conflict in the process. The Balfour Committee commented (towards the end of the 1920s) as follows:

> on the whole the methods of collective negotiation and settlement of wages questions, which have grown up spontaneously in accordance with the varying circumstances of different trades, are vastly preferable to any uniform cast-iron system imposed by law.[1]

The flexibility of the collective bargaining process drew praise: 'defects or errors can be corrected by the same method by which the original agreement was arrived at.'[2] Indeed, more widely, trade unions were seen as contributing to the stability of society. Middlemas writes that

> an awareness had emerged, across the whole field of government, among Ministers and civil servants, of the need for formal organisation of industrial politics.[3]

It is also extremely noteworthy that, despite the adverse economic conditions which existed between the wars, employers did not seek to abandon collective bargaining. Clegg writes that

> The new system of collective bargaining had been tested by the two most severe economic depressions since the hungry forties of the last century.

[1] Final Report of the Committee on Industry and Trade (Cmd 3282), p 89.
[2] *Ibid* at p 93.
[3] K Middlemas, *Politics in Industrial Society* (London: Deutsch, 1979) p 160.

There had been a few defections, but the system as a whole had survived in remarkably good order. It could not have done so without firm support from employers' organisations, and their attachment to it had been demonstrated during the depression from which the country was beginning to emerge.[4]

It is worth highlighting that the coverage of collective bargaining increased by approximately threefold between 1910 and 1933—despite coverage having dropped somewhat since 1920.[5] Moreover, there was a further significant increase in coverage between 1933 and 1939.[6]

Collective bargaining may have continued to be viewed favourably but how did labour law evolve? A limited number of new measures were enacted between the wars; easily the best known, and easily the most controversial, of which was the Trade Disputes and Trade Union Act 1927. However, that Act was decidedly limited in its scope. Other measures enacted tended not to be of general application but, instead, related to particular trades or industries; eg the Agricultural Wages Act 1924, the Cotton Manufacturing Industry (Temporary Provisions) Act, 1934 and the Baking Industry (Hours of Work) Act 1938. Nevertheless, a significant number of further proposals for reform were brought forward (mainly in the areas of hours and wages). The explanation why a greater proportion of them did not become law is not a straightforward one.

LABOUR LAW IN THE 1920S

The 1920s began very much as they would go on with the report of the Cave Committee (the committee which had been appointed in 1921 to inquire into the impact of the trade boards legislation reported in 1922).[7] The tenor of the report was far removed from the philosophy of Whitley and did not seek to underpin collective bargaining by way of legal measures. More particularly, the report was not sympathetic to the trades boards system or, to be more precise, to the reforms which had taken place in 1918. One of the main complaints by employers had been that boards fixed wages at too high a level with adverse results

---

[4] H Clegg, *A History of British Trade Unions since 1889*, vol II (Oxford: Clarendon Press, 1985) p 564.

[5] *Ibid* at pp 548–49.

[6] H Clegg, *A History of British Trade Union since 1889*, vol III (Oxford: Clarendon Press, 1994) p 90.

[7] Report on the Working and Effects of the Trade Boards Acts (Cmd 1645).

such as unemployment and uncompetitiveness. Cave found some substance in such allegations but, nonetheless, did not support complete repeal in that it was accepted that trades boards had achieved a number of worthy things. Some of the most vulnerable workers in society had benefited from minimum wage protection and this had also benefited good employers to the extent that wages were taken out of competition. Trade boards were also seen as conducive to better relations between the two sides of industry and to improved organisation on both sides:

> the operation of the system has contributed on the whole to the improvement of Industrial Relations; and this effect is especially marked in the case of the trades to which the Act of 1909 was applied and which have had the longest experience of the working of the system . . . The working of the Trade Board machinery by bringing the two sides together to discuss wages questions 'round a table' has, in most cases, enabled each side to understand something of the other's point of view, and so has contributed to the growth of more satisfactory relations between the two sides and has tended to prevent the occurrence of industrial disputes.[8]

In arriving at proposals for reform Cave's underlying premise was that the true aim of the legislation was to stop 'sweating': 'any further regulation of wages should be left, so far as possible, to the processes of negotiation and collective bargaining.'[9] Perfectly consistently with the foregoing position Cave did not see a wider role for law in industrial relations and, clearly, legal support for collective bargaining was out of the question. Whitley was even invoked to support a more restricted trades board scheme.[10] This conveniently ignored the fact that the 1918 Act was very much in line with the Whitley recommendations. Cave proposed that the grounds upon which a trade board could be set up should be restricted and the formula suggested was that a board should not be established unless

> an unduly low wage prevails in the trade or some branch of it and there is a lack of such organisation among the workers as is required for the effective regulation of wages in the trade.[11]

The whole tenor of discussion suggested that the 1918 Act was an aberration from the true spirit of the trades boards scheme. However, the

[8] *Ibid* at para 46.
[9] *Ibid* at para 54.
[10] *Ibid* at para 64.
[11] *Ibid* at para 56.

proposed amendments would have involved not simply a return to the pre-1918 position but would have made it more difficult to set up a trades board than it had been in 1909. The 1909 Act had allowed for the establishment of a Trades Board if the

> rate of wages prevailing in any branch of the trade is exceptionally low . . . and that the other circumstances of the trade are such as to render the application of this Act to the trade expedient.

Cave also proposed that the scheme of enforcement of awards be revised. At the time he reported an employer who failed to adhere to an award risked enforcement by means of both the civil and the criminal law. Cave believed that such a two-pronged scheme was only appropriate where one was dealing with the minimum 'wage which should be paid to the ordinary worker of the lowest grade of skill engaged in the trade.'[12] Cave accepted that trades boards had to make a higher level of award for groups of workers such as the semi-skilled. However, it was recommended that those awards should not be enforced by criminal sanctions, since the State was only justified in invoking such measures where workers were being paid below the level of subsistence. Instead only civil proceedings would be available. Again the process for determining awards should differ in respect of such workers. Any award

> should be determined by agreement between the two sides of the Board without the vote of the Chairman or appointed members.[13]

This differential approach stemmed from Cave's belief that a Board's primary aim was to

> protect workers by securing to them at least a wage which approximates to the subsistence level in the place in which they live and which the trade can bear . . .[14]

The secondary aim was to use

> the machinery established for that purpose in encouraging the improvement of relations between employers and employed and the development of trade organisations.[15]

[12] Report on the Working and Effects of the Trade Boards Acts (Cmd 1645) at para 57.
[13] *Ibid.*
[14] *Ibid* at para 57.
[15] *Ibid* at para 57.

The Government seems to have been reasonably satisfied by the Cave Committee's deliberations and published a policy statement, in the summer of 1922, on the administration of the trade boards scheme pending further legislation.[16] The general thrust of the statement was that the Government would operate the legislation in line with the Cave Committee report to the extent that the existing framework permitted. For example, a new board would only be set up where the grounds referred to in the report were satisfied. The powers of boards to fix rates could not be restricted without recourse to the legislature but, in a rather oppressive way, the policy statement indicated the Ministry's expectations and took the opportunity to remind the boards of the Ministry's powers of confirmation. It is worthy of note that the hope was expressed that

> the rates other than rates for the general body of workers in the trade would be commonly fixed by the Trade Board by agreement of the two sides.[17]

In 1923 a bill was introduced which by and large sought to implement the Cave Committee report. It did not get beyond its first reading and fell with the election of November, 1923. The incoming Labour administration did not revive the measure; nor did the Conservative government, elected in 1924. However, the new Conservative administration made clear to the Commons that new boards would only be established

> where it has been clearly ascertained by systematic investigation that sweating conditions prevail in any trade and . . . then only after a public inquiry.[18]

In the event, no more trades boards would be set up during the remainder of the 1920s.

After 1924 the prospects of any expansion of the trades boards system looked bleak. Moreover, realistically, they would only be improved by a change of government. One notable achievement, in terms of legal protection of the most vulnerable workers, was the passing of the Agricultural Wages Act 1924.[19] This was required because

> the labourers cannot get a living wage by trade union methods alone. The difficulties of organisation are so great that we cannot get our organisation strong enough to enforce it.[20]

---

[16] Ministry of Labour, Administration of Trades Boards Acts 1909 and 1918, Cmd 1712. This was a re-iteration of the 1909 formula rather than the Cave recommendation.

[17] *Ibid* at p 6.

[18] Annual Report of the Ministry of Labour for 1923 and 1924 (Cmd 2481), pp 171–72.

[19] The Act only applied in England and Wales.

[20] Parl. Deb., 2.6.1924, HC, vol 174, col 914.

So poor were the prospects for collective organisation that it does not appear to have been envisaged that the enactment of the legislation would do a great deal to foster it. The parliamentary debates make little mention of collective bargaining and simply focus on the regulation of wages by statute. The effect that legal regulation might have on trade union organisation and collective bargaining was not discussed. The Act which emerged was almost certainly intended to be purely regulatory in effect. There were obvious similarities with the trades boards system but there were also significant differences. The centre of power was located locally in that Agricultural Wages Committees were to be established for each county who would be under a duty to fix minimum rates of wages. Any award had to be referred to a central Agricultural Wages Board but this referral was purely formal in that the role of the board was simply to make the order to give effect to the award. The Board only had power to make an award on its own terms where the local committee had failed to do so. The rationale for decentralisation was explained in the following way:

> you should settle these matters locally, if you can, because the conditions of agriculture differ so much in different parts of the country that if you attempt to have one general system, or one general minimum wage, it might very well have the effect of being uneconomic in some parts of the country, and of reducing the wages paid at the present time in other parts.[21]

Points of convergence with the trades boards included the possibility of penal sanctions were an award to be breached. The tripartite composition of both the councils and boards also resembled the trades board structure. The Act prescribed the standard by which the councils were to fix wages by stating that

> a committee shall, so far as practicable, secure for able-bodied men such wages as in the opinion of the committee are adequate to promote efficiency and to enable a man in an ordinary case to maintain himself and his family in accordance with such standard of comfort as may be reasonable in relation to the nature of the occupation.[22]

No reference is to be found in the legislation to collectively agreed norms. In the course of parliamentary proceedings an unsuccessful attempt had been made to stipulate an absolute minimum. The legislation allowed for the possibility of officials instituting civil proceedings

---

[21] Parl. Deb., 1.8.1924, HL, vol 59, col 230.
[22] S 2(4).

on behalf of workers. An alternative way of proceeding would have been to hand this role to trade unions.

Provisions of the foregoing type aimed to offer protection to the most vulnerable of employees. Not surprisingly, in the depressed economic circumstances of the 1920s, considerable interest existed in proposals to give legal effect to the 'common rule.' Such proposals had the potential to benefit large numbers of employees in numerous industries. The Industrial Councils Bill was introduced in 1924; it had been drafted by the Association of Joint Industrial Councils. It had two main aims; the first was to promote the formation of JICs. Clause 1 imposed a duty on the Minister of Labour to promote the establishment of an industrial council in respect of every industry for which the establishment of such a council is practicable and expedient. Clause 2 provided for the approval of JICs by the Minister. The Minister could not give approval unless satisfied that the JIC was desired by the industry. In addition, the JIC had to be constituted so that the interests of employers and workers were equally represented on the Council. Where a JIC for an industry had been approved by the Minister it was to be recognised as the official channel of communication in all matters affecting the industry between the Government and the employers and workers in that industry. The second aim of the bill was to apply a common rule provision to JIC agreements. It being felt that such agreements needed the support of legislation, the mover of the bill asserting that

> the lack of this power has caused many of these councils to be disbanded, because they felt that there was no use in going on when they could not use any discipline over their members and had no power to bind them.[23]

Clause 3 entitled an industrial council to submit any written decision for confirmation by ministerial order. It is important to note that the Minister was obliged to make such a confirmation; though this duty was subject to certain provisions as to modification, etc. Any order made could apply to the whole or merely a part of an industry and any evasion of, or non-compliance with, any order made was to be a criminal offence.[24]

The mooted legislation was clearly seen as a support for voluntary collective bargaining. Clause 4 is also of interest. It provided for the establishment of a Central Industrial Board (CIB) composed of an equal number of representatives of employers and workers, one

---

[23] Parl. Deb., 30.5.1924, vol 174, col 765.
[24] Clause 3.

representative from each side to be appointed by each industrial council. The CIB was to have a number of functions including the giving of general advice and assistance to the work of industrial councils. It was also empowered to act as an arbitrator if requested to by both sides of a JIC and to consider appeals against the interpretation of an order issued by a minister. Finally, it was charged with seeking

> the avoidance of conflicting decisions by industrial councils in different industries and the harmonising of the effect of such decisions in the interests of industry throughout Great Britain.

Decisions made by the CIB were also to be the subject of ministerial order and again breach would be a matter for the criminal law. The allocation of this adjudicatory role to representatives drawn from JICs demonstrates a desire to draw on the industrial knowledge and expertise of labour and capital as much as possible. Whilst the aim of the bill was to encourage conditions whereby voluntary collective bargaining might flourish (or at least survive) the legislative structure itself paid tribute to the virtues of industrial self-government.

The bill passed its second reading, on a free vote of the House of Commons, by 236 votes to 16 but the dissolution of Parliament prevented further progress. Support for the bill had been uneven, with those on the left of the Labour party expressing opposition on the basis that it propped up the existing system. Of greater significance was the failure of the Ministry of Labour to provide positive support for the bill. The Minister of State, Margaret Bondfield, explained to Parliament that

> [i]t is held very strongly by the Ministry that the present evidence goes to show that opinion is not yet ripe for the imposition of compulsory powers.[25]

---

[25] Parl. Deb., 30.5.1924, HC, vol 174, col 811. One contemporary commentator, H Clay, in his work *Problems of Industrial Relations*, offered a number of more technical objections to the enactment of a common rule provision:

> [s]harp definition and precise statement are essential in any rule that is to be enforced in a court of law . . . Joint Industrial Council determinations are not likely to satisfy this condition.

For example,

> [t]he terms in which agreements are couched are often very general; which raises no difficulty so long as the carrying out of them depends upon the people who made them, and any misunderstanding or obscurity can be corrected by reference back to the Council.

Though it must be said that this view sits rather uneasily with his belief that similar difficulties did not arise in the case of trade boards, their orders were 'drafted with a view to being enforced in the courts.'

This was despite the fact that the passage of the bill

> would ensure a real uniformity of conditions, and so protect the loyal employers on the Council against the unfair competition of less scrupulous or more hard-pressed firms, that refused to observe the Council's determinations. It would relieve the trade unions of the handicap they labour under in negotiations from the knowledge that they cannot guarantee the observance throughout the industry of the terms for which they stand out.[26]

The Ministry claimed that only 16 JICs had indicated that they wanted compulsion introduced. This would not seem to be particularly relevant in the face of a proposal which would have simply given JIC's the option of giving greater legal import to collective agreements. Bondfield was eager to stress that the Ministry had no objection in principle to this sort of legislation: '[i]t is not that the powers may not be desirable.'[27] However, this strikes a rather hollow note. Indeed Charles has argued that the Ministry persistently viewed requests for this type of legislation as for 'a law compelling the observation of agreements made by all JICs . . .' rather than

> a law permitting compulsion to be applied when the JIC concerned and hence both employers and employed wished to possess such powers.[28]

It is regrettable that the Ministry chose to present an exaggerated and distorted picture of the potential impact of the proposals. It is even more regrettable that such an approach was not a solitary aberration. For instance, the Ministry had previously argued that legislation of this sort would lead to trade unions being sued for breach of collective agreements. However, the enforcement of legislation of this type would lead only to an action of breach of contract between the employer and employee.[29] What explanation can be offered for this ongoing exercise in intellectual dishonesty? The Ministry were clearly reluctant to see such a measure enacted. This stance reflected government policy for most of the 1920s. Collective bargaining was viewed as the most appropriate way to conduct industrial relations but the State was reluctant to support it through any form of legal intervention. An outlook of 'negative' voluntarism prevailed. Collective bargaining might well have made much greater strides during the inter-war period

[26] Clay, above n 25 at p 169.
[27] *Ibid.*
[28] Charles, *The Development of Industrial Relations in Britain* (London: Hutchinson, 1973) at p 206.
[29] Clay, above n 25 at pp 169–170.

had appropriate legal support been forthcoming; sadly the Ministry of Labour were often to feature amongst the guilty parties. It must also be said that trade unions were somewhat ambivalent about the proposals and fears existed that the bill, if enacted, would turn out to be a double-edged sword. For instance, a resolution in support of such legislation had failed at the 1923 annual congress.[30]

<h2 style="text-align:center">THE 1927 ACT</h2>

Shortly after the General Strike ended a Cabinet Committee, under the chairmanship of the Lord Chancellor (Cave), was set up to consider Labour Law reform.[31] The measure which was ultimately enacted was, to say the least, controversial. The terms of the 1927 Act meant that major sympathetic strikes would, thereafter, risk incurring both civil and criminal sanctions. Section 1 of the Act declared any strike to be illegal if it had any object other than or in addition to the furtherance of a trade dispute within the trade or industry in which the strikers were engaged; and it was a strike designed or calculated to coerce the Government either directly or by inflicting hardship on the community. The section was intended to be declaratory of Astbury's judgment in *Reed* and sought to alleviate Government concern that the judgment might be found not to correctly reflect existing law.[32] Clearly in a situation like the General Strike of 1926 section 1 would prohibit other unions coming to the assistance of the one involved in the primary dispute. Anyone organising such a strike would not have immunity from common law liability.[33] This included trade unions who would be unable to fall back upon the protection of section 4 of the 1906 Act. Even more ominously, criminal sanctions applied to anyone inciting a worker to take part in a strike rendered unlawful by virtue of section 1. However, the mere act of striking was not made criminal. This part of the Act also intervened in trade union internal affairs by prohibiting the disciplining of any trade union member for refusing to take part in a strike in breach of section 1.[34]

---

[30] Albeit that one succeeded in 1925.
[31] A Anderson, 'The Labour Laws and the Cabinet Legislative Committee of 1926/7,' (1971) 23 *Bulletin of the Society for the Study of Labour History* 39.
[32] See below at p 215.
[33] S 1(4).
[34] Anderson, above n 31 notes at p 42 that Cave
wanted to vest in the Chief Registrar of Friendly Societies power to sue on behalf of wronged individuals and to claim for the union-leaver a 'surrender value' of accumulated benefits.

The Act did not confine itself to restricting the right to strike in major disputes. The law on picketing was also amended in a manner at odds with trade union interests. Section 3 provided that picketing involving 'intimidation' was unlawful (irrespective of whether it took place in contemplation or furtherance of a trade dispute). The Act stated that to intimidate meant

> to cause in the mind of a person a reasonable apprehension of injury to him . . . or of violence or damage to any person or property.

Injury was also defined widely and included 'injury to a person in respect of his business, occupation, employment or other source of income.' One might argue that section 3 was much more significant than section 1 in that it would impact on day-to-day trade disputes. The section was highly restrictive in that intimidation was not confined to behaviour which induced an expectation of violence. Instead inducing a belief that a person's business or financial interests might be damaged sufficed. What, for example, if a worker had declined to cross a picket line because he feared that, if he did, attempts would be made, after the dispute was settled, to persuade the employer to dismiss him? The scope of the criminal law was also extended in that picketing in breach of section 3 was deemed to be a breach of section 7 of the 1875 Act. Hedges and Winterbottom pointed out that this rendered 'criminal many acts by pickets which hitherto do not seem to have been statutory offences.'[35]

The freedom of association of civil servants was also restricted by the Act. Events during the General Strike prompted the Government to adopt the stance that there was a

> real danger of the entanglement of civil service associations with outside industrial and political bodies in such a way as to place some civil servants in the position of owing a divided allegiance.[36]

Should this danger materialise it would run counter to a principle of 'fundamental importance' that civil servants should owe no allegiance to any authority other than the government of the day. Finally, the Act dealt with the political levy.[37] The 1913 Act had allowed for the possibility of contracting-out. The 1927 Act reversed that stance and

[35] R Hedges and A Winterbottom, *Legal History of Trade Unionism* (London: Longmans, Green and Co., 1930) p 130.
[36] LAB 10/574.
[37] Conservative backbenchers had sought a provision of this sort for sometime. For instance, a private member's bill had been introduced in 1925.

required contracting-in.[38] Such a reversal had been mooted by the Conservatives for some time and it had, in fact, been promised in a 1924 policy document. Prior to the General Strike Baldwin had rejected the idea. However, pressure from employers and from the more aggressively anti-socialist Conservative MPs led to its inclusion. Steel-Maitland (Minister of Labour) was candid in the extreme as to the underlying motive:

> the major part of the outcry against the political levy is not motivated by a burning indignation for the trade unionist who is forced to subscribe to the furtherance of political principles which he abhors. It is based on a desire to hit the socialist party through their pocket and it uses the comparatively small proportion of cases of injustice in respect of the political levy as a smokescreen under which to make the attack.[39]

The legislation was strenuously opposed by the Labour opposition in the Commons; it being claimed that the Bill would cause grave damage to the industrial and political power of the labour movement. The claim may contain a considerable element of exaggeration. What is undoubtedly the case, however, is that the Act could have been much more draconian. An attempt had been made, during the passage of the Bill, to introduce an additional clause which aimed to stipulate a mandatory 'cooling-off' period before strikes could take place in essential services. It was said that this would facilitate conciliation and a 'real investigation into the facts on which the merits of the case depend.'[40] Such a proposal had been aired in the Cabinet Committee; it being envisaged that a cooling-off period would enable a Court of Inquiry to meet. Maitland-Steel opposed this on the basis that it 'would not have the backing of employers, and would be supported by unenforceable penalties.'[41] Comparative experience come to the fore as well, the Minister for Labour arguing that the proposal was based on the Canadian Lemieux Act which he regarded as a failure. The impact of wartime experience was also still potent:

> Governments . . . would not enforce the law because, aware that the right to strike was ultimately determined not by law but by the action of the rank and file, they dared not risk mass non-compliance.[42]

[38] For detailed discussion, see KD Ewing, *Trade Unions, The Labour Party and the Law* (Edinburgh: Edinburgh University Press, 1982) pp 50–63.
[39] Anderson, above n 31, at p 53.
[40] Parl. Deb., 14.6.1927, HC, vol 207, col 844.
[41] Anderson, above n 31, at p 52.
[42] R Lowe, *Adjusting to Democracy* (Oxford: Clarendon Press, 1986) p 109.

Even more ominously the Cabinet Committee had discussed the possibility of repealing, in whole or in part, the Trades Disputes Act 1906. This would have attracted support from some employers; the repeal of section 4 would have been most likely to attract approval. The moderates prevailed in committee and no such proposal was to be found in the Bill. The Attorney-General stating that it was

> too late merely to reverse [it] . . . it has long been regarded even by moderate trade unionists as a charter of protection, and I fear that an attempt to repeal it would be construed as an attack upon trade unions generally and might only result in the return at the next election of a Government pledged to undo it.[43]

The idea of compulsory strike ballots had also been discussed extensively in committee. However, employers were opposed and again Steel-Maitland argued against taking the proposal forward: 'the belief that strikes would be (thus) averted is generally a delusion.'[44] He also added that 'the delay . . . is of little use for the purpose of conciliation,' 'the assumption of a more reasonable rank and file (is wrong),' and that

> there is no evidence to show that any recent strike of importance would have been prevented by the taking of a ballot.[45]

Indeed strike ballots might lead to more strikes in that

> rather than standing up to their extremists, trade union leaders would be encouraged by a ballot to follow a 'a new line of least resistance' and would then find themselves in the position not of leaders but of delegates . . .[46]

The one legislative reform that the Ministry of Labour favoured

> was the restriction of legal immunities to registered trade unions, a move designed to improve long-term industrial relations by enabling the Registrar of Friendly Societies to impose minimum rules of conduct. . . .[47]

Such an interference with trade union autonomy did not appeal to the Cabinet Committee.

---

[43] Anderson, above n 31, at p 48.
[44] Anderson, above n 31, at p 50.
[45] *Ibid.*
[46] Lowe, above n 42, at p 109.
[47] *Ibid* at p 110.

LABOUR LAW IN THE 1920S—AN OVERVIEW

In terms of providing an overview, it is suggested that the deliberations of the Balfour Committee offer a reasonably accurate reflection of the broad thrust of State policy during this period. As we have seen the Committee was content to endorse the merits of collective bargaining. Successful collective bargaining was regarded as being dependent on the

> existence of strong, active and representative organisations on both sides, interested in conducting voluntary negotiations and capable of enforcing the general observance of agreements which depend wholly on moral obligation.[48]

It was regarded as inevitable that law had a role to play but that role was fundamentally an auxiliary one:

> the action of the State has been generally confined, and . . . should continue to be confined, to efforts to promote voluntary agreement between the parties by means of . . . conciliatory machinery.[49]

The provision of trade boards was also endorsed. However, that endorsement was a cautious one as trade boards were viewed as

> only appropriate to those exceptional branches of industry which combine absence or weakness of organisation with relatively low rates of wages, and we should strongly deprecate the encroachment of this type of institution on the field of normal organised industry.[50]

Limited enthusiasm was shown for common rule legislation which was only seen as appropriate where wages were exceptionally low; more extensive legislation of this sort was rejected. It was argued, very unconvincingly, that such legislation might have a detrimental impact on collective bargaining: the difficulty

> is the reaction which the application of compulsion with regard to principles and methods of industrial relations must have on the working of the voluntary machinery for the actual fixing of wages and hours in the industry. It seems to us that the situation thus created would probably end in the absorp-

---

[48] Balfour Committee, above n 1, at p 90.
[49] *Ibid* at p 116. eg the 1896 Act. The Committee (at p 113) also approved of the more informal role of the Ministry of Labour in promoting the establishment of joint machinery.
[50] *Ibid* at p 125.

tion of all of the functions of wage-fixing by the JIC, and the extinction of voluntary methods throughout the industry.[51]

Balfour also doubted whether there would be sufficient support in industry for it. In any event, even if there was,

> we should dread the results on industrial relations of substituting cast-iron legally drafted documents for the present less formal and more elastic agreements and understanding, which are generally loyally observed.[52]

The Balfour Committee reaffirmed the, by now virtually conventional, rejection of compulsory arbitration despite being of the view (somewhat iconoclastically) that the Lemieux Act had worked well[53]—a stance of rejection which reflected the views of both sides of industry. An earlier Ministry of Labour memorandum had set out in detail a justification for this stance:

> It is undesirable because it weakens the responsibility of trade unions (this was shown under [wartime legislation]), it makes industry depend on outside intervention for the settlement of the ordinary human relations of employers and employed, which are the basis of industrial relations, and it runs counter to the deliberate policy of the Government that industry must accept the possibility of self-government. It is ineffective because it cannot stop strikes. It is not possible to imprison one million miners [if they strike} . . .[54]

Moreover, 'it simply makes strikes illegal and ultimately discredits the law.'

In some ways the period 1921–1930 is best viewed as one of both continuity and divergence from the approach adopted in the immediate post-war period. Divergence was manifested by the lack of interest in legislation that would regulate terms and conditions of employment and by the unwillingness to contemplate measures, such as the Trades Boards Act 1918, that would lend actual support to collective bargaining. Of course, at the same time, continuity was demonstrated in state support for collective bargaining through the continued existence (though not expansion) of the trades boards. Again the reforms introduced by the 1919 Act were utilised; for instance, in the period 1921–24 the Industrial Court issued 415 decisions—some of which were of

---

[51] *Ibid* at p 124.
[52] *Ibid* at p 125.
[53] *Ibid* at p 115.
[54] Lab 2/921/7.

significance.[55] Nevertheless, despite the hopes which had accompanied enactment, the Industrial Court failed to contribute to a rationalisation of collective bargaining.[56] Lowe found an

> inability to determine a fixed set of principles on which to base awards and, later, the steep decline in the number of cases submitted to it.[57]

Whilst state intervention in disputes arose, through the operation of the statutory processes of conciliation, the Government in the 1920s tended to be reluctant to go beyond this by indulging in ad hoc intervention in trade disputes. This accorded with the somewhat laissez-faire stance to industrial relations prevalent during this period. Phillips observes that

> Baldwin's administration avoided implicating itself in the settlement of industrial disputes as far as possible, on the general assumption that the state's attempts to act as mediator was usually vitiated by ministerial ignorance and by the undue expectations of public assistance aroused in the adversaries.[58]

LABOUR LAW IN THE 1930S

A number of bills similar to the Industrial Councils Bill, 1924, were introduced in Parliament during the 1930s.[59] None of them became law. One of the more significant was the Rates of Wages Bill, 1931, which had been agreed to by the TUC and employers' representatives. The Bill granted the Minister discretion to make a collective agreement binding in a trade on the joint application of an association(s) of employers and an association(s) of employees. An association of employers could only make an application where its members employed a majority of the workers in the trade. A similar condition applied to trade unions. The 1931 Bill had not become law by the time the Labour government fell and the coming into office of the National

[55] For instance, one award laid down standard rates for railway shopmen in place of the existing widely varying rates. The award took effect in 'practically all the railway systems of Great Britain.' It is also the case that, from the date the 1919 Act came into force to the end of 1924, 13 Courts of Inquiry were appointed.

[56] See ch 6 at p 166.

[57] Lowe, above n 42, at p 101.

[58] GA Phillips, *The General Strike* (London: Weidenfeld and Nicolson, 1976) p 58.

[59] For instance, the Industrial Councils Bill, 1930. And see Charles, above n 28, pp 208–10.

government meant that it never would.[60] A government with an out-look more orientated to the interests of employers proved to be fatal. Many employers being of the view that

> When a firm's profits were declining the correct remedy was to reduce the labour costs; the restoration of profit would stimulate production and thus employment.[61]

The Bill had applied to all agreements between trade unions and employers' associations and not simply to decisions of JICs. On the other hand, it only applied to the elements of such agreements which related to rates of wages.[62] Any order made entitled an employee in the industry (or part thereof) 'to receive from his employer wages at a rate not lower than the rate . . . sanctioned.'[63] Enforcement was to be by way of civil action at the instance of the employee; no criminal sanction was contemplated.[64] It appears that there had been a measure of trade union opposition to earlier bills covering only JIC awards. One reason for this may have been a suspicion that the true motivation behind such proposals was a desire to force JICs into every industry.

The element of TUC and employer agreement might suggest that, but for the change in government, the Rates of Wages Bill would have become law. The position is, however, more complicated. The Ministry of Labour was decidedly unenthusiastic about legislation of this type. For instance, the Minister's attention was drawn to the lack of flexibility the proposed measure possessed compared to collective bargaining: the Bill

> is not sufficiently elastic in its terms to permit of wage adjustments being readily made and . . . the generality of organised employers and workers would [not] wish to be fettered with wage regulations of the kind proposed.[65]

Indeed, somewhat perversely, the Ministry argued in 1932 that organisational difficulties in industry pointed against 'common rule' legislation:

> a time when one of the most noticeable features of industrial development is the persistent weakening of organisation seems to be a most unsuitable

---

[60] Charles, above n 28 at p 209.
[61] R Skidelsky, *Politicans and the Slump* (London: Macmillan, 1967) p 11.
[62] Clause 1(1).
[63] Clause 2(1).
[64] Clause 2.
[65] LAB 2/2012/5.

period in which to confer some measure of compulsory power upon associations of employers and employed covering a majority of persons employed in the trade.[66]

There was also a measure of Ministry of Labour concern that such legislation might in the long term undermine self-regulation.[67]

The Cotton Manufacturing Industry (Temporary Provisions) Act, 1934, was introduced at the request of both sides of the industry, the Minister of Labour remarking, in moving the Bill,

> In this branch of this industry the system of collective agreements is in the process of disintegration and a state of chaos is threatened which could be disastrous to the industry and indeed to the country . . . The question before the industry now is how to secure that the whole principle of collective bargaining does not break down.[68]

The legislation sought to secure adhesion to the 'common rule' which had been lacking in an industry plagued by severe economic problems:

> Individual employers, faced with bankruptcy, in desperation continued to break agreements on production, prices, and wages and neither the employers' association nor the Weavers' Amalgamation was able to bring them to heel. The consequences were serious: a general disillusion with written agreements, organisational chaos (as both employers and workers deserted their respective associations), an intensification of the industry's financial plight (as falling wages and prices failed to increase the volume of production) and rising social unrest.[69]

Under the Act an application could be made to the Minister of Labour seeking an order to give statutory force to a collective agreement 'as to the rate of wages' made between a trade union and an employer's organisation in the cotton manufacturing industry.[70] Should the application be successful a term would be implied into the individual employment contract making payment of the collectively agreed wage mandatory.[71] Moreover, failure to pay such a wage would be a criminal offence.[72] Certain features of the legislation are worthy of note. First, any application had to be made jointly by both sides of industry.

[66] LAB 2/2012/5.
[67] Lowe, above n 42, at p 117.
[68] Parl. Deb., 17.5.1934, HC, vol 289, col 1961.
[69] Lowe, above n 42, at p 117.
[70] S 1(1).
[71] S 3(a).
[72] S 3(b).

Legislation would not be allowed to jeopardise the relationship of the bargaining parties.[73] On the other hand, either side could unilaterally apply for an order to be revoked and the failure to require a joint application at this juncture demonstrates the preference for purely voluntary machinery.[74] Second, there was an express statutory prohibition on any order modifying the collectively agreed terms.[75] The legislation appears to have been regarded as something of a success.[76] For example, a board of inquiry noted that only one prosecution had taken place in respect of a particular order 'but expressed . . . satisfaction that this did not suggest that a "high standard of compliance" had not prevailed' and went on to comment that the industry had 'for the first time for many years enjoyed immunity from the evil effects of wage-cutting and price-cutting.' However, proposals to expand the scope of the legislation to include other branches of the industry did not attract Ministry of Labour support and failed to become law. The Ministry was much more interested in a return to 'pure' collective bargaining. The Act was a classic example of auxiliary legislation. As was stated in the House of Lords:

> the provisions of the Bill have been drawn up with the single aim of strengthening and upholding the principle of voluntary agreements, freely negotiated and loyally observed.

Indeed, the Act was originally to cease operating after three years but was subsequently renewed from year to year until being revoked in 1957.

The passage of the Act might be taken as suggesting that there had been a significant change in government thinking since the failure of the Rates of Wages Bill. However, this was not in fact the case. A number of industries sought legislation along the lines of the 1934 Act.[77] However, the view of the Ministry of Labour was that the Act was 'experimental' and that further legislation of this sort would not be forthcoming until the success of the 1934 Act could be assessed.[78] The Ministry's standard response was illustrated by the reply to a request from the wool industry for an inquiry with a view to setting up a trade

---

[73] S 1(1).
[74] S 4(1).
[75] S 2(2).
[76] Sharp, *Industrial Conciliation and Arbitration in Great Britain* (London: Allen and Unwin, 1950) p 409.
[77] Parl. Deb., HC, 5.3.1936, vol 309, col 1539.
[78] LAB 10/73.

board. The Ministry suggested to the parties that they meet with 'a view to discussing the reinstatement of the voluntary system.'[79] Nevertheless, even if the legislature was not prepared to offer more support, great ingenuity was shown, on occasion, in utilising the legislative support which did exist. The National Union of Tailors were represented on a number of trade boards. They were also engaged in collective bargaining with a number of employers' associations. The union's strategy

> was to negotiate improvements in its agreements with these federations, and then to persuade the trade boards to approve advances in their statutory rates as nearly equivalent as possible to the negotiated wage rates and conditions. The statutory rates would then become binding on the non-federated competitors of the federated firms. Through these means the union secured a series of pay increases for its members in the years 1935–37.[80]

During the inter-war period there emerged numerous 'fair wages' provisions.[81] This reflected Government policy that payment of a fair wage should be a condition of the receipt of state subsidies, subventions or guarantees. The insertion of such provisions into statute was generally uncontroversial. One example was the British Sugar (Subsidy) Act 1925 which provided that the rate of wages, unless determined by a JIC, be not

> less than would be payable if the manufacture were carried on under a contract made between the Minister and the employer containing a fair wage clause which complied with the requirements of any resolution of the House of Commons for the time being in force.

However, the implementation of this policy offered a rather mixed message. On the one hand, a reference to the Fair Wages Resolution might have been thought to suggest an intention to promote adhesion to collectively set norms. On the other, it was highly debatable whether the wording of the resolution was adequate to achieve this aim effectively.[82] Having said that, legislative provision, on occasion, embodied collectively agreed rates as the requisite standard of remuneration

---

[79] LAB 2/2012/5 (IR 683/1935).

[80] Clegg, above n 6, at p 39.

[81] See, for instance, the Housing (Financial Provisions) Act, 1924 and the British Sugar (Subsidy) Act 1925.

[82] See B Bercusson, *Fair Wages Resolutions* (London: Mansell Information Publishing, 1978) ch 9.

much more explicitly than the 1909 Fair Wages Resolution. One instance of this was the Road Haulage Wages Act 1938. More generally, the development of such provisions in the road haulage industry is worthy of attention, the legislature displaying a much greater interest in the terms and conditions of employment in the industry compared to most others during this period.

Section 93 of the Road Traffic Act, 1930, made the holding of a road service licence conditional on an employer observing terms and conditions of employment which would comply with the current fair wages resolution.[83] Ultimately disputes were to be resolved by the Industrial Court. This provision was aimed both at combating unfair competition and the payment of unreasonably low wages. Herbert Morrison observed in the Commons that

> It is fair to the great bulk of employers that they shall not be cut out by employers who impose bad conditions.

The Road and Rail Traffic Act, 1933, extended the scope of the 1930 Act to cover further sections of the industry.[84] Effective enforcement was to be a thorny issue:

> Complaint has been frequently made in evidence that the machinery for enforcement is too complicated and ineffective for the purpose of regulating wages. With this complaint we agree. Owing to the cumbersome machinery for enforcing fair wages and the uncertainty of its operations, only two cases have been brought before the Court; and no licence has ever been withdrawn or suspended solely on account of the rates of wages paid by the licensee.[85]

Bullock comments, in a similar vein, that

> the employers were individualistic in their attitude; competition between them was fierce, and undercutting, the payment of low wages and the systematic evasion of regulations common practice. The men, amongst whom trade-union membership and organisation were poor, connived at this either to retain their jobs, to earn a bribe for keeping their mouths shut . . .[86]

Such concerns led to the establishment of the Baillie Committee in 1936 to review the regulation of wages and conditions of service in the

---

[83] S 93(1). S 19 of the Act limited the time for which drivers could remain continuously on duty.

[84] S 32(2).

[85] Committee on the Regulation of Wages and Conditions of Service in the Road Motor Transport Industry (Goods), (Cmd 5440), para 30.

[86] A Bullock, *The Life and Times of Ernest Bevin*, vol II (London: Heinemann, 1967) at p 545.

industry.[87] Whilst the Committee believed in the efficacy of collective bargaining it maintained that the 'proper organisation of the industry . . . is an antecedent condition of . . . any effective method of regulating wages and working conditions.'[88] Moreover, collective bargaining was seen as

> a potent influence in securing industrial peace and stability and in promoting that close co-operation between employers and employees which is essential for the prosperity of the nation.[89]

Legislation was viewed as a means of encouraging such developments and Baillie recommended strengthening the existing measures in the road haulage sector. The view was taken that, at that stage in the development of industrial relations in the industry, voluntary machinery would not suffice:

> It is essential, however, in the road haulage industry, where a rate of wages is to be made a condition of a licence, whether for the purpose of eliminating unfair competition or for the purpose of ensuring the health of the driver, that a decision when taken should be made operative.[90]

Baillie recommended that a new scheme of boards be set up which would have power to make recommendations on terms and conditions and, in addition, have

> power to establish machinery for the purpose of settling differences between employers and employees whenever or wherever they arise; and to adopt any measure which will promote complete organisation of employers and workpeople either by associations or otherwise.[91]

A recommendation as to wages would be given statutory effect upon confirmation by the appropriate Minister.[92] The statutory machinery was to be withdrawn once self-regulation had developed to the extent that statutory sanctions were no longer necessary.

The Government responded positively and the law was reformed on the basis of the proposals set out in the report of the Baillie Committee. Subsequently the Road Haulage Wages Act, 1938, emerged against a background

---

[87] Committee on the Regulation of Wages, above n 85, at para. 30.
[88] *Ibid* at para 35.
[89] *Ibid* at para 36.
[90] *Ibid* at para 42.
[91] *Ibid* at para 46.
[92] *Ibid* at para 48.

of requests made to the Minister by both sides of the industry to provide effective machinery for determining and enforcing proper rates of wages and conditions of service, and theses provisions are designed to help the industry to assist itself to escape from the chaotic conditions which at present exist in regard to the regulation of wages.[93]

Bevin's enthusiasm for the legislation knew no bounds:

I want to see this Bill on the Statute Book before I go away. I have worked so long to try to get it right that I would not sacrifice it now for anything.[94]

Whilst some progress had been made by voluntary methods those gains

could have been extended only by a bitter and long struggle, and the TGWU leadership was increasingly drawn to a strategy of statutory regulation.[95]

The Act provided for the creation of a trade boards-type scheme for the road haulage industry; both central and area boards were to be established. The central board was comprised of an equal number of worker and employer representatives and also contained a number of independent members. Under the Act a central board had power to submit to the Minister proposals for fixing remuneration (including holiday pay). In framing such proposals the board were obliged to

take into consideration any decision of a joint industrial council, conciliation board, or similar body relating to the remuneration of workers employed on road haulage work.

This provision allowed the board to operate in a manner which would promote adhesion to collectively agreed standards. Proposals of the board became binding once the Minister had made them the subject of a road haulage wages order. Failure to comply with the terms of an order opened up the possibility of both criminal sanctions and civil liabilities. Breach of an order might also lead to revocation or suspension of a licence. The board also had powers to assist in making arrangements for dispute resolution and to promote the voluntary organisation of employers and workers.[96]

The Government's whole-hearted acceptance and implementation of the report is significant. The report sought not only to improve terms and conditions but to foster organisation in the trade and encourage

---

[93] *Ibid* at para 118.

[94] Ernest Bevin to FW Leggett, 28th April 1938.

[95] P Smith, 'The Road Haulage Industry 1918–40: The Process of Unionization, Employers' Control and Statutory Regulation' (1997) *HSIR* (3) 49 at p 72.

[96] S 2(6).

collective bargaining. Part two of the Act, dealing with drivers for private carriers, is worthy of close attention. It sought to address the issue of unfair remuneration but provided that a rate of remuneration paid by an employer would not be deemed to be unfair if it fell within one of a number of specified categories. In particular section 4(3)(b) stated that remuneration was deemed not to be unfair where it was paid in accordance with a collective agreement made between the employer, or any employer's association of which the employer was a member, and a trade union. This allowed the employer to

> protect himself from the charge of unfairness by paying in accordance with the appropriate agreement between a trade union and an employer's association.

The aim of the provision was said to be to further and encourage the making of voluntary agreements. Where the rate of remuneration was not deemed fair under the Act the matter was to be referred to the Industrial Court who came under a statutory obligation to determine a rate. In dealing with these matters the court was obliged to have regard to any collective agreements which regulated the wages of workers engaged in similar work. Any award made was to be in force for a three-year period.[97] Again the Government explanation for the rationale of the scheme is interesting:

> We believe that a very speedy result of this legislation will be a substantial growth of the number of agreements that will be made before any machinery involving penalties will need to be invoked. I cannot imagine an employer, faced with the possibility of being obliged to saddle himself for three years with the obligation to pay certain wages and with all the penalties that attach to nonconformity, preferring to delay making some arrangement.

The structure of part two also demonstrated a concern that its operation might have a regressive impact on existing collective bargaining arrangements. Thus section 4(4) gave priority, in certain circumstances, to jointly agreed disputes procedures over the Act's own enforcement mechanisms. Where such a procedure existed a complaint in respect of unfair remuneration was to be referred to it for settlement and not the Industrial Court. The exception to this was where both parties to the agreement preferred recourse to the Industrial Court. The Government indicated that they were 'anxious to minimise compulsion

---

[97] Provision was made for review.

and to do everything possible to encourage and help voluntary negotiating machinery.'

The 1934 and 1938 Acts might be viewed as heralding a new dawn in terms of state support for collective bargaining and regulation of wages. However, a more accurate portrayal would see those measures as instances of crisis management. This was particularly true of the 1934 Act. Admittedly, it was not only the road transport and cotton manufacturing industries which benefited from state intervention in the 1930s; it is important to note that a number of new trades boards were set up. The spectre of the Cave Committee report was being removed at last. The State was not, however, interested in ensuring a better balance of power in industrial relations. It required the potential collapse of collective bargaining machinery to prompt legislative intervention; or the absence of such machinery. As we have seen, a number of industries would have welcomed legislation along the lines of 1934 Act. Given that the State sought to do no more than it had to it is not surprising that those calls for legislation were unsuccessful, the Ministry of Labour maintaining that the 1934 Act was 'experimental.' Again, in the 1930s, the TUC lobbied hard for revisions to the Fair Wages Resolution. A key concern was to ensure that government contractors should be required to observe national or district agreements irrespective of the extent to which the agreements were, in fact, operative in a particular area. However, the wording of the resolution was not changed until 1946; partly because, as the 1930s drew to a close, the impact on defence expenditure came into play. In any event, the Ministry of Labour displayed little enthusiasm for reform and maintained that the issue could not 'be divorced from the wider question of the compulsory extension of voluntary agreements.'[98] This argument was not particularly strong. The existence of the Fair Wages Resolution demonstrated that the Government accepted that it should behave as a good employer. Indeed it had been accepted, well before the 1930s, that it was legitimate for government to act in this way. Given the increase in the extent of collective bargaining since 1909 the Fair Wages Resolution could not promote adhesion to the standards of good employers without more explicit reference to collective bargaining. The wording of the resolution apart, concern remained over the extent to which government was committed to effective enforcement.

[98] LAB 10/12.

Bercusson points out that in

> the year between April 1934–April 1935, only two firms had been struck off the lists of government contractors for non-observance of the Fair Wages Clause.

The foregoing discussion has concerned wages. However, the continuing failure to legislate for a 48 hour week, as required by the Washington Convention, should not be taken as evidence that there was opposition in principle to legislation of this nature. Thus a number of governments (including the Baldwin administration) during the period were minded to introduce implementing legislation. This was despite the fact that a significant number of UK employers were opposed to such a development. The failure to legislate was, at least in part, due to the perceived difficulty in drafting a bill which would comply with the UK's International obligations but which would also accommodate British working practices. The second Labour government regarded such concerns as genuine:

> It is not practical to propose a Bill which would give full effect to the Washington Convention without arousing very serious opposition not only from employers' organisations, but also from trade unions. This opposition, moreover, would be on points where it would not be in the interests of the workers themselves or industry generally to alter the existing practice.[99]

The pragmatic solution was to bring forward a Bill 'which will be based on British conditions and . . . will contain the substance of the Convention.'[100] Such a pragmatic solution was also far more likely to lead to legislation. As a result, Hours of Industrial Employment Bills were introduced in both the 1929/1930 and 1930/31 sessions of Parliament. The Bills imposed both a daily and weekly limit on the length of the period which could lawfully be worked. Breach of those limits constituted a criminal offence. However, neither Bill received a second reading in the face of pressures on parliamentary time and economic problems (especially in the 1930/31 session).[101]

In 1931 a Select Committee report on shop assistants was published.[102] The report recommended that a 48 hour week should be

---

[99]   R Lowe 'Hours of labour: negotiating industrial legislation in Britain, 1919–39,' (1982) *Economic History Review*, 254 at p 258 quoting from the minutes of the Cabinet Committee which had been set up to draft the legislation.

[100]   *Ibid.*

[101]   *Ibid* Lowe also draws attention, at pp 258–59, to the fact that government enthusiasm may have been diluted by an inter-union dispute between the rail unions and the TGWU.

[102]   Report from the Select Committee on Shop Assistants.

imposed by law.[103] The reasons for selecting that particular figure are also of note. It was the limit sought by all organised bodies of shop assistants. However, it was also

> the limit adopted in the Washington Convention and in the Hours of Employment Bill now before Parliament, as far as industrial workers are concerned . . .

Again it was noted that trade boards would have tended to hold that overtime payments became due in respect of hours worked in excess of 48. The Select Committee also examined the different means of regulating terms and conditions of employment and evinced a preference for regulation through collective bargaining. Accordingly, it was a matter for regret that there was a lack of worker organisation in the distributive trades. This prevented

> any general improvement being effected by agreement and is likely to lead to frequent recourse to Parliament for the settlement of questions which, with close co-operation, might well be settled within the industry.[104]

The committee desired to see

> some machinery set up which would bring employers and employed into closer touch with each other and promote the joint discussion and settlement of questions affecting their mutual interests.[105]

To this end it was recommended that a scheme of local and national advisory boards be set up. Such boards would comprise an equal number of employer and employee representatives.

Bridging the issues of wage and hours regulation was the question of holiday pay. A Holiday with Pay Bill was introduced in 1929 and was supported in principle, by the government, on second reading. However, pressures on the parliamentary timetable and the need for 'full enquiry and consultation' meant that the Bill went no further. The dismal economic circumstances which prevailed towards the latter part of the Labour government's period in office were clearly not conducive to a measure of this sort. In 1936 a Bill was brought forward by Rowson. The TUC was well disposed towards legislation on this issue

---

[103] *Ibid*, paras 187 and 207.
[104] Para 291.
[105] *Ibid.*

because, whilst favouring collective bargaining in general

> there were certain matters which they felt that they would never get if they
> had to rely upon voluntary negotiation for securing them.[106]

The Government responded to Rowson's Bill by setting up a committee of inquiry under Lord Amulree. The committee recommended that employees be entitled to one week's holiday with pay. However, what is perhaps most interesting about the report is the discussion contained therein on the relationship between law and collective bargaining. In sectors where a trades board existed the committee recommended that the powers of the board should be extended so that holidays with pay could be awarded. However, so far as industry in general was concerned, Amulree believed that agreement on paid holiday should be arrived at through collective bargaining. This was partly because legislation on the terms and conditions of employment had the potential to undermine joint negotiation. However, Amulree also viewed paid holiday simply as a dimension of the work-wage bargain. The precise composition of that bargain should, if at all possible, be a matter for the parties. Legislation would

> take away from the employers and workers the freedom of determining for
> themselves the order of priority in such matters.[107]

Accordingly, Amulree recommended that any measure imposing a statutory minimum should not apply across industry on enactment but that there be a transitional period to allow the collective parties to adjust. During that period it was expected that the Ministry of Labour would promote the merits of voluntary agreement on the issue. Amulree was also concerned with the form that legislation applying to all industries might take. He believed that the legislation should delegate as much as possible of the detailed formulation of the obligation, to provide paid holiday, to the collective parties. In the event of a failure to agree arbitration by a mutually agreed person should take place. In the event of an additional failure to agree on the identity of an arbitrator a tribunal nominated by the Minister of Labour would determine the question.

The Holidays with Pay Act 1938 was enacted to implement the report of the Amulree Committee. The Act was primarily concerned with trade boards[108] and gave them power to make awards which

---

[106] LAB 10/53.

[107] Report of the Committee on Holidays with Pay, para 67 (Cmd 5724).

[108] And also the Agricultural Wages Committees and the Road Haulage Central Wages Board.

included paid holidays. It is important to stress that trades boards were not obliged to make such an award. In the same spirit of generosity towards vulnerable employees the maximum award of paid holiday entitlement was not allowed to exceed one week in any 12-month period. Indeed a trades board was empowered to set holiday pay at a different rate to the normal minimum wage.[109] Section 4 of the Act dealt with industries other than those covered by trades boards; where a collective agreement established a scheme providing for the payment of holiday pay the Minister of Labour was empowered to assist in

> the administration of the scheme by attaching officers of the Ministry of Labour to help in the administration . . . and by such other means as he thinks fit.

Entirely absent from the Act was any general requirement (whether immediate or deferred) on employers to provide for paid holidays. The Ministry of Labour had been unenthusiastic about imposing such an obligation, the argument being that it would be better to see if progress by way of voluntary agreement would render legislation unnecessary.

THE 1930S ASSESSED

Any assessment of this period must take account of the fact that Labour were in government for very limited periods of time in the inter-war period. There is evidence to suggest that more labour law measures would have been enacted had matters been different. The first, and particularly short-lived, Labour government had promised to introduce a bill to ratify the Washington convention but had not done so before leaving office.[110] Space in the legislative programme was found to enable the Agricultural Wages Act 1924 to come into being. Moreover, the existing framework for the support of the low paid was preserved by the abandonment of the Trades Boards Bill, which the previous government had introduced to implement the Cave Committee. Admittedly, it was also the case that more might have been done to give support to the Industrial Council's Bill. It is also submitted that it is relevant that some social security law reform occurred. The Unemployment Insurance (No 2) Act 1924 introduced two exceptions to the trades disputes disqualification to give greater protection to

---

[109] S 2(1).
[110] Clegg, above n 4, at p 366.

workers.[111] It is particularly interesting that it was provided that disqualification would not occur where the stoppage is due to an employer acting in a manner so as to contravene the terms or provisions of any agreement existing between a group of employers where the stoppage takes place, or of a national agreement to either of which the employers and employees are contracting parties. The latter provision offered some support to trade union attempts to secure observance of collectively agreed terms.

It would be unfair to have expected a great deal from the first Labour administration who were a minority government and were in office for a very brief period.[112] In addition, one should not expect to find evidence of a detailed legislative programme given that, utterly realistically, they did not expect to be in office for long. The task facing them on arrival in office was daunting with Britain suffering from serious economic and social problems. Account must also be taken of the barriers which invariably have to be overcome by Ministers who have not been in government before. The Prime Minister himself noted in February 1924 that

> officials dominate Ministers. Details are overwhelming & Ministers have no time to work out policy with officials as servants; they are immersed in pressing business with officials as masters.[113]

One immediately thinks of Bondfield's experiences in respect of the Industrial Councils Bill at this juncture. The Prime Minister's general strategy must also be borne in mind. He was firmly of the view that what was crucial to Labour's first spell in government was

> not to defy or even to subvert the established order but to infiltrate it—to prove that they, too, could carry out the King's government if they were given the chance, and in doing so, to consolidate their lead over the Liberal Party.[114]

---

[111] See KD Ewing, 'Collective Agreements, Trade Disputes and Unemployment Benefit—The Employer's Breach Exemption,' (1981) 32 *NILQ* 305.

[112] The King agreed to dissolve Parliament at the beginning of October 1924.

[113] D Marquand, *Ramsay MacDonald* (London: Richard Cohen, 1997) p 306. In her biography (*A Life's Work* (London: Hutchinson, 1949)) Bondfield, parliamentary secretary to the Minister of Labour, notes at p 256 that

> We were a new team, most of us having to learn the rules of the House as well as master the details of Departmental business, with a gigantic mass of papers to read, and . . . no real focusing point for action on any one thing because of the multitude of things to be attempted.

[114] *Ibid* at p 312.

The second Labour government was in office for a mere two years (from June 1929 until August 1931) before being succeeded by the National government. Again it was a minority administration; albeit the Labour party had the greatest number of MPs. The attentions of the Ministry of Labour were dominated by concerns over unemployment benefit. The new Minister of Labour (Bondfield) found that her 'first job upon entering office was to provide sufficient money for unemployment benefit to be paid at all.'[115] A bill on the subject was published in November 1929. More generally, the problem of unemployment occupied the attention of Ministers; more specific labour law reforms were less likely to be high on the agenda. By the beginning of 1930 world economic depression had emerged and with it a heavy increase in the number of the unemployed. Moreover, the Coal Mines Bill

> took up an inordinate amount of parliamentary time and thus threw the whole of the Government's legislative programme out of gear.[116]

Having said all of that, the Industrial Hours Bill represented a practical solution to the long-standing problem of implementation of the Washington Convention. The Rates of Wages Bill was also introduced. If the Government had been in office for anything like a full term both measures might well have become law. Again Bondfield had established an inquiry into conditions in the catering trade with a view to setting up a new trade board. However, she encountered heavy opposition from the employers who resorted to legal action in an attempt to stop a board being created. Bondfield was successful before the Court of Appeal but the employers appealed to the Lords. At the end of the day, the Government withdrew the appeal.[117] The sweating problem in catering was a serious one though Bondfield may well have been over ambitious in trying to resolve it through the trade board scheme. However, the fact that she was willing to try suggests that, had Labour held office for longer, more reforms (legislative or otherwise) which favoured workers may well have taken place. The brevity of the period of office apart, the restrictions imposed by minority government cannot be left out of account; these were amply demonstrated by the difficulties encountered in amending the 1927 Act. The Liberals made clear that they would block this measure unless electoral reform occurred.

[115] M Bondfield, above n 113, p 281.
[116] Skidelsky, above n 61, p 158.
[117] Report of the Ministry of Labour for 1932 (Cmd 4281), p 85.

The Government were forced to agree to bring forward a bill providing for the alternative vote. As we have seen section 1 of the Act had sought to be declaratory of Astbury's judgment in Reed. Clause 1 of the Bill to amend the 1927 Act offered a cautious response to this. It provided that industrial action with a primary object other than that of furthering purposes connected with trade objects was illegal. The caution displayed is in part explained by the realities of minority government. However, it was also an indication of the importance the MacDonald government placed on constitutional propriety. The Bill passed its second reading but, nevertheless, the Government abandoned it after the Liberals and Conservatives combined to amend clause 1 in an unacceptable manner.

JUDICIAL ATTITUDES

The period between the wars was said by Kahn-Freund to be one in which voluntarism extended to the courts.[118] It is not altogether easy to assess the validity of this view on account of the limited amount of case law during this period. For instance, the strength of the protection afforded by the trade dispute immunities was rarely tested during the inter-war period. The 1919 case of *Valentine v Hyde* indicated that, were that to occur, problems might arise.[119] The dispute arose over the fact that the plaintiff refused to join the relevant trade union. It became clear that the employer would dismiss if the plaintiff maintained this position. It might have been thought obvious that this was a dispute between workmen and workmen connected with the employment of any person and accordingly a trade dispute within the meaning of the legislation. However, Astbury J insisted that 'some limitation must be placed on the expression "connected with the employment or non-employment of any person" ' and went on to impose a requirement of directness and concluded that there was no trade dispute in existence. Moreover, even if a trade dispute had been in existence, immunity would still have been forfeited—apparently on the basis that the action was coercive. It must be said that coercion is integral to the taking of industrial action; to find against a trade union on this basis is, in effect, to condemn the validity of industrial action in general. Astbury J dis-

---

[118] 'Labour Law' in M Ginsberg (ed) *Law and Opinion in England in the 20th Century* (London: Stevens, 1959) pp 242–43.
[119] [1919] 2 Ch 129.

regarded the fact that the 1906 Act established which acts of this nature were legitimate and which were not. A similar dispute arose in *Hodges v Webb* but on this occasion a trade dispute was held to exist and doubt was cast over the reasoning in the case of *Valentine*.[120] The stance taken over 'coercion' in *Valentine* was questioned and Peterson J pointed out that there are 'few strikes or lock-outs in which either employers or workmen or both could not say that they were coerced.'[121] More significantly, the reasoning in *Valentine* was struck down by the Court of Appeal in *White v Riley*:

> It is quite possible that the extension of this legislation, which was originally passed for the benefit of workmen in their disputes with their employers, to disputes between workmen and workmen, has produced results which many workmen in some trade unions did not anticipate, but it does not seem to me that there is any reason for not giving to the subsection its natural meaning.[122]

A further difficulty in assessing judicial attitudes to industrial action at this time is presented by the case of *National Sailors' & Firemen's Union v Reed*; the decision has been much discussed and might be taken as evidence of judicial hostility at this time.[123] An injunction was sought by a trade union to restrain branch officials from calling a strike without the authority of the union executive. The injunction was granted on two grounds. First, that the general strike was contrary to law: the

> so-called general strike called by the TUC is illegal, and persons inciting or taking part in it are not protected by the Trade Disputes Act, 1906.[124]

Second, that the defendants were acting contrary to the rules of their own union. It is the first ground which has provoked controversy. It is not clear what weight should be placed on the judgment. After all, the defendants were not represented and the judgment was delivered extempore. Academic opinion since then has predominantly been of the view that the general strike was lawful in that it occurred in furtherance of the dispute between the miners and the mine owners. It may be noted that Astbury J, who decided the case of *Valentine*, also

---

[120] [1920] 2 Ch 70.
[121] *Ibid* at p 86.
[122] [1921] 1 Ch 1 at p 20.
[123] [1926] 1 Ch 536. See AL Goodhart, *Essays in Jurisprudence and the Common Law* (Cambridge: CUP, 1931) pp 226 et seq.
[124] *Ibid* at p 539.

gave the judgment in *Reed*. It is difficult to know what weight to place on *Reed*.

The two most famous labour law cases in the post First World War period are probably *Reynolds v Shipping Federation*[125] and *Crofter Hand Woven Harris Tweed Co Ltd v Veitch*.[126] In *Reynolds* an agreement had been arrived at between the National Union and the Shipping Federation that seamen were to be employed exclusively by the former. An action of conspiracy was raised by a seaman belonging to another union who had been excluded from employment by virtue of the closed shop arrangement. It was held that liability for conspiracy did not arise given that the aim of the conspiracy was to 'advance the business interests of employers and employed alike by securing or maintaining [the] advantages of collective bargaining.'[127] In *Crofter*, liability for the tort of simple conspiracy did not arise because

> the predominant object of the respondents in getting the embargo imposed was to benefit their trade-union members by preventing under-cutting and unregulated competition, and so helping to secure the economic stability of the island industry. The result they aimed at achieving was to create a better basis for collective bargaining, and thus directly to improve wage prospects. A combination with such an object is not unlawful, because the object is the legitimate promotion of the interests of the combiners.[128]

These decisions demonstrate that the courts adopted a much more accommodating attitude to the interests of labour than in the period 1890 to 1914. They may be bracketed along with *White v Riley* and *Hodges v Webb*. Kahn-Freund went further and claimed that the *Crofter* case showed 'the acceptance by the courts of the principle of non-intervention in industrial disputes.'[129] Whilst it may be accepted that both cases clearly showed judicial understanding of collective interests how far a judicial policy of non-intervention existed is problematic. Certainly, *Reynolds* and *Crofter* represented a recognition of trade union interests by the courts and reversed the inequity of divergence of approach in *Mogul Steamship v Quinn*. In *Reynolds* the aim of the conspiracy was to preserve the interests of the union by maintaining the closed shop and thereby uphold a prop to collective

125 [1924] 1 Ch 28.
126 [1942] AC 435. Proceedings having originated in 1938.
127 *Reynolds*, above n 125, at p 39.
128 *Crofter*, above n 126, at p 447, per Viscount Simon.
129 Kahn-Freund, above n 118, at p 242.

bargaining. The court acknowledged that employers might also benefit from the existence of the closed shop:

> Here, the employers, instead of being forced against their wills into employing union men only, have recognised that advantages may arise from adopting such a course of action voluntarily, and have accordingly made an agreement with the trade union to that effect.[130]

About the same time that *Reynolds* was decided *Brimelow v Casson* suggested that the defence of justification to the delict of inducing breach of contract might evolve in such a way as to benefit trade unions.[131] Given the subsequent lack of development of a defence of justification the case has been marginalised and portrayed as being about sexual immorality. However, the judgment also suggests that the payment of an insufficient wage was, *per se*, viewed as unsatisfactory.

On the whole, labour law cases between the wars showed a willingness to acknowledge trade union interests. *Reed* can, it is submitted, be fairly regarded as an aberration. The evidence pointing to judicial acceptance of non-intervention is less clear-cut. Certainly the Court of Appeal adopted a purposive interpretation to the golden formula in *White v Riley*. On the other hand, would the courts have refused to enforce a collective agreement? Three pre-war cases had appeared to assume that collective agreements were legally enforceable.[132] After the war the case of *Bradford Dyers' Association Ltd v National Union of Textile Workers* is relevant.[133] There the defendant unions had expressly agreed in submitting to a consent judgment that the collective agreement involved was binding and enforceable. Again Kahn-Freund stated in 1943 that conflicts as to rights were 'legal questions which— but for s.4 of the Trade Union Act, 1871—could be taken before a Court of Law.'[134] Is there any reason to assume that a court in the interwar period would have viewed matters differently? Admittedly, an obiter statement by Lord Russell of Killowen in delivering the advice of the Privy Council in *Young v Canadian Northern Railway* is of

[130] *Reynolds*, above n 125 at p 40.
[131] [1924] Ch 202.
[132] *Read v Friendly Society of Stonemasons* [1902] 2 KB 702, *Smithies v National Association of Operative Plasterers* [1909] 1 KB 310, *East London Bakers' Union v Goldstein* The Times, 9.6.1904, KW Wedderburn, *Cases and Materials on Labour Law* (Cambridge: CUP, 1967) p 272.
[133] The Times, July 24, 1926 and discussed by Selwyn, 'Collective Agreements and the Law' (1969) 32 *MLR* 377 at p 381.
[134] O Kahn-Freund, 'Collective Agreements under War Legislation (1942–43)' *MLR* at p 138.

relevance. On one reading he seems to assume that a collective agreement could not be enforced by legal remedies. However, what reason
in law would have existed to support such a stance? In the absence of
Kahn-Freund's later writings a court in the inter-war period would
have been unlikely to have had resort to the concept of intention to
enter legal relations. Instead they would have probably taken the view
that

> unless the agreement is of a domestic or social nature it would appear that
> the parties may only ensure that the terms of their contract are not legally
> binding upon them by expressly providing for this in their contract.[135]

CONCLUSIONS

The inter-war period saw continued consolidation of the process of
collective bargaining as the primary means of regulation in industry.
The value of collective bargaining was commended in numerous quarters. By their willingness to establish, and maintain, collective bargaining machinery both sides of industry endorsed the process through
their actions. More explicit praise was readily found. For instance, the
Baillie Committee referred to the 'instinctive preference in this country'
for voluntary collective bargaining.[136] The Minister of Labour (Brown)
in the 1935 Government remarked to the Commons in 1938 that

> The value of our voluntary collective bargaining system cannot be over-
> estimated. The development of individual freedom in this country has gone
> side by side with industrial freedom, and it is becoming increasingly
> recognised that our voluntary collective system is one of the most potent
> instruments for the stability of our national life.

At the same time, it must be acknowledged that the policy of establishment of JICs had a limited impact and not all survived. It is significant
though that those that did confirmed the long-standing trend of steady
growth of collective bargaining in the UK:

> The fifty or sixty Joint Industrial Councils that survive represent a big exten-
> sion of organised and systematic negotiation into territory formerly gov-
> erned by intermittent and haphazard meetings. They have effected a
> considerable standardisation of terms of employment and codification of

---

[135] JH Gayler, *Industrial Law* (London: English Universities Press, 1955) p 173. See
also *Rose and Frank Co v Crompton Bros* [1923] KB 261.
[136] Baillie, above n 85, at para 100.

agreements and customs, and so fixed, as it were, a habit of collective bargaining, which the war had encouraged, just before the post-war depression came to discourage it.[137]

During this period the part played by legal regulation did not increase to any significant extent. The nature of the provisions contained in the 1927 Act meant that they would not impact in a major way on day-to-day industrial relations. It is important to emphasise that the lack of expansion of the extent of legal regulation was not because the use of law was seen as inappropriate. Moreover, account must be taken of the fact that state intervention may take a variety of forms; including Government's role as employer. We find, for instance, that the Government adopted the principles of the Whitley report for both the civil service and industrial establishments of the Government. In general, however, a fundamental reason why more labour law measures were not enacted was, not because resort to legal regulation was viewed as inappropriate in principle but because, for most of this period, Government was not particularly well disposed to the interests of trade unions and workers. Use of law to adjust the balance of power between the two sides of industry would have had limited appeal. In general, Government was unlikely to supplement collective bargaining by statutory regulation unless the poverty of voluntary arrangements absolutely compelled them to do so. A situation where there was a reluctance to resort to the use of legislation struck a chord with a significant number of employers. However, others would have welcomed legislative intervention on topics such as the 'common rule' which would have enabled them to begin or continue to collectively bargain. A number of employers would have being willing to move to joint regulation

> if they could have the assurance that their competitors would not be able to undercut them by evading the agreement.[138]

Government reluctance to legislate was reinforced by the Ministry of Labour who believed in a policy of 'home rule for industry.' Such an attachment to voluntarism had both a positive and negative dimension. It was undoubtedly the case that the officials of the Ministry saw much that was commendable in a policy of self-regulation and were genuinely committed to its pursuit. Certainly, lessons about the limits of the law had been acquired:

[137] Clay, above n 25, at p 176.
[138] Clegg, above n 6, at p 92.

As the network of regulation becomes more complex, a larger part of the general social rules, under which industry is carried on, must be devised for industry by the people engaged in industry themselves. Some of them involve technical considerations which no one outside industry is competent to judge, others (such as the fixing of wage-rates) turn on considerations of expediency, which Parliament and the public departments are ill-adapted to assess.[139]

Nevertheless, caution over resort to law may have been taken rather too far:

General laws . . . were rejected on the grounds that they ignored the needs of particular industries; but simultaneously sectional improvements were rejected on general economic grounds . . . or on the pretext that they might establish unwelcome precedents.[140]

Such a stance contained inherent problems given the chronic imbalance of power in industrial relations at this time. Having said that, the Ministry played a very active and effective role in combating suggestions for legal measures which would positively favour employers. For instance, the Ministry opposed suggestions made in the early 1920s that strike ballots be made compulsory. The Ministry was sceptical as to whether the results would be much different; discontent would also arise as a result of interference with trade union internal machinery. Moreover, there would be a weakening of the responsibility of trade union leaders. There were also some indications during the 1930s of the emergence of a more supportive stance towards collective bargaining. The Ministry of Labour, for example, made it clear to employers in the road haulage industry that unless voluntary machinery was improved legislation might result:

if voluntary machinery could be set up for the purpose of fixing a reasonable set of conditions on which the Industrial Court could administer the fair wage provisions in the 1933 Act, it might be a means of avoiding more drastic statutory control of the industry.[141]

A good illustration of the minimalist way in which the law was used to support the voluntary process is provided by the fate of proposals for statutory recognition in the aviation industry. Section 37 of the British Overseas Airways Act 1939 provided that in determining the wages and

---

[139] Clay, above n 25, at p 147.
[140] Lowe, above n 42, at p 125.
[141] Lab 2/2049/1 quoted in P Smith, above n 95, at p 69.

conditions of employment of persons employed by the corporation, the corporation shall take into account representations made to them by any body or organisation the membership of which comprises a substantial proportion of the class or classes of employees concerned. There had been an attempt during the passage of the bill to make trade union recognition compulsory. The Ministry of Labour were very much opposed to this.[142] There was a concern that such a measure might provoke inter-union competition. There may also have been disquiet as to what enforcement of a recognition obligation might involve. For instance, if an employer refused to comply would a mechanism be required whereby terms and conditions might be imposed. However, the primary concern was that a precedent would be set which would be invoked with vigour by the union movement. The Ministry were able to present their stance, in a positive light, as one consistent with self-regulation: 'collective bodies should remain voluntary and . . . their recognition also should be a matter for voluntary action.'

---

[142] Lab 10/100.

8

The Impact of the Second World War

INTRODUCTION

T HE INDUSTRIAL RELATIONS issues confronting Government at the beginning of the Second World War were broadly similar to those which had pertained in 1914. Once again it was anticipated that wage control would prove to be a thorny issue to tackle; concern also existed that continuity of production might be hampered by industrial action. There were also fears that productivity might be adversely affected unless movement of labour was controlled and dilution achieved. The legislative framework established by Government, in fact, bore a good deal of resemblance to that which had been in place between 1914–1918. This, however, should not be allowed to conceal the fact that industrial relations policy was driven by a very different vision.

WARTIME CONTROLS

Movement of Labour

At the outset of war Government was, potentially, concerned that, on the one hand, workers should not leave employment where it was not in the public interest for them to do so and, on the other hand, that workers might be required to move to work of a more pressing nature. Initial government intervention took the form of the Control of Employment Act 1939 which was a somewhat limited measure. This was partly because the Ministry of Labour, consistent with its pre-war policy, thought it best if industry was left to resolve manpower difficulties on its own. More significantly, the Chamberlain government did not believe that it could enact a more radical measure in the absence of TUC support. In broad terms the 1939 Act gave the Government powers to stop the poaching of labour. Section 1(1) empowered the

Minister of Labour and National Service to issue an order forbidding employers specified in the order from advertising for employees without the consent of the Minister. The same section also empowered the Minister to issue an order preventing an employer from hiring staff without the consent of the Minister. Before any such order could be issued it had to be referred to a joint committee consisting of trade union and employer representatives. The Minister's powers to prevent an employer from hiring an employee were constrained; consent could not be refused unless the employer was satisfied that an opportunity of suitable alternative employment was available to the employee. The employee also had a right of appeal. Where an appeal was successful the employee was entitled to compensation 'in respect of any loss occasioned to him by reason of the refusal against which the appeal was brought.' Breach of an order could result in the employer being fined; no penalty was placed on the employee. Moreover, it was expressly provided that an employment contract formed in contravention of an order was not unlawful on that ground alone.

Matters were to change very significantly in 1940 with the emergence of the Undertakings (Restrictions on Engagement) Order which restricted employers in certain industries (building, civil and general engineering) from hiring workers. Such employers had first to notify a vacancy to the local office of the Minister of Labour. They were then only permitted to fill that vacancy by hiring a worker submitted to them by the local office. The order also imposed a corresponding obligation on employees. A worker seeking employment in such an industry had to register at the local office of the Ministry of Labour and might only obtain employment by means of being submitted to an employer. The regulation aimed to prevent disruption of production in key industries through the movement of workers. It also aimed to combat inflation by preventing employers from poaching labour by offering higher wages. Further provisions of the order also sought to prevent workers moving away from agriculture and coal-mining. Employers were forbidden from hiring any worker whose normal occupation was mining except for work in that industry. An identical provision applied to agriculture.

The foregoing provision was very much aimed at restricting movement but Government envisaged that it would, on occasion, be necessary to require workers to move to other sorts of employment. As a result the government added regulation 58A to the Defence (General) Regulations 1939 by order in council in 1940. The order gave the

Minister extraordinarily wide powers, the Minister being empowered
to direct any person to perform such services in the UK as were specified in the order. The services required were to be performed upon the
terms and conditions of service directed by the Minister. However, it
was provided that the Minister had to have regard to the terms and
conditions of employment set out in any relevant collective agreement
or JIC award. In the absence of the foregoing regard was to be had to
'practice prevailing among good employers in that trade in the district.'
Initially, limited use was made of this power; in the first year that the
regulation was in force less than 3,000 orders to individuals were
issued.[1] Workers did not have a statutory right of appeal against such
an order though one was normally granted by way of administrative
practice.[2] Nevertheless, the fact that an order might be made may well
have helped 'persuade' a far larger number of workers to move into key
war industries.[3] The official history also took the view that

> if directions had been issued more freely and with less regard for welfare
> conditions, the result might well have been a growing dissatisfaction among
> the transferred workers with no compensating increase of productive
> output.[4]

In his commanding biography of Bevin Bullock was also to conclude
that

> thirty years' experience of persuading working men to combine convinced
> Bevin that to start brandishing compulsory powers and ordering people
> about as soon as the new Government got into power would do harm to the
> new-found national unity out of all proportion to the amount of extra work
> it would produce.[5]

Certainly, government intervention could be highly effective even
where an order was not issued. For instance, recruitment and retention
of building workers in remote areas was problematic. In one particular
case, involving building work on the island of Orkney, the Ministry
took the view that enhanced terms and conditions of employment
might well improve matters. The co-operation of the relevant employers was secured. As a result

[1] A Bullock, *The Life and Times of Ernest Bevin*, vol II (London: Heinemann, 1967) at p 16.
[2] Report of the Ministry of Labour and National Service for the years 1939–1945 (Cmd 7225), p 41.
[3] *Ibid.*
[4] HMD Parker, *Manpower* (London, 1957) at p 117.
[5] Bullock, above n 1 at p 18.

turnover declined from 90% to 10% and for some months to come it was possible to find and keep the necessary labour on the sites without the use of directions.[6]

As the war progressed more and more workers were compelled to move by virtue of a direction being issued. Whilst the total number of orders issued by the end of 1941 was only 15,000, by the end of the war this had increased to over one million. Nevertheless, the official history took the view that 'the number of directions actually issued . . . was in relation to the vast redeployment of manpower surprisingly small.'[7] It may be the case that the use of sanctions offered valuable support to the voluntary system: sanctions provided 'a guarantee that those who tried to evade their duty would not be allowed to get away with it.'[8] Whilst the Government may well have preferred not to issue directions, they were prepared, on occasion, to take a hard line where directions which had been issued were ignored. For instance, a number of directions requiring workers to work in the mines were flouted. Some 500 workers were prosecuted for non-compliance, 143 of whom were imprisoned. The minister took the view that

> when a man after serving 2 periods of imprisonment or one 3 months' sentence again refused to comply with a direction, he should not again be prosecuted but, if medically fit, he should be called up to the forces and if found unfit, should be sent to appropriate civil employment.[9]

A further tool in the Government's possession was registration requirements. It became apparent early in the war that the Government did not know enough about the composition of the workforce to enable efficient manpower planning to take place. A variety of regulations were issued requiring workers to register. An early example was the Industrial Registration Order 1940 which required employees engaged in certain skilled occupations to register at the local office of the Ministry of Labour and provide prescribed particulars.

---

[6] Parker, above n 4 at p 127.
[7] Parker, above n 4 at p 224.
[8] Bullock, above n 1 at p 142.
[9] Parker, above n 4 at p 255.

Terms and Conditions of Employment

In the First World War the State found itself intervening to an increasing extent in the regulation of wages.[10] However, limited consideration was given to appraising the fairness of terms and conditions of employment in the round. The coalition government, where Bevin's influence on industrial relations matters was huge, took a very different view. It became evident that employment relations policy was that the quid pro quo for the imposition of restrictions on workers was that they be properly rewarded. Given this aim the content of the work-wage bargain had to be viewed as a totality. Such a stance was both justifiable as a matter of principle and because, pragmatically, the way in which workers were treated by their employer had great potential importance in terms of achieving workforce stability. Workforce stability would in turn further the war effort. Such considerations form the background to the passing of the Essential Work Orders (EWO).

An EWO could be made in respect of an undertaking where the work carried on appeared to the Minister to be essential for the defence of the realm or the efficient prosecution of the war or to be essential to the life of the community. As a matter of practice, before the Minister considered applying the terms of an order to undertakings within any particular industry, a process of prior consultation with both sides of industry was undergone. The primary object of an EWO

> was to prevent unnecessary turnover of labour and thereby to increase production and secure economy in the use of labour.[11]

The orders restricted the freedom of movement of workers in a way that would have been unthinkable in peacetime. However, given that workers could be compelled to move employment by virtue of the defence regulations, and be restrained from moving by an EWO, it was crucial that the element of compulsion was matched by fair terms and conditions of employment. As a consequence, before the provisions of the EWO could be applied to an undertaking, the Minister had to be satisfied that: (a) the terms and conditions of employment in the undertaking were not less favourable than the recognised terms and conditions provided for by Order 1305[12] (b) satisfactory provision for the

---

[10] See p 142 above.
[11] Ministry of Labour, above n 2 at p 48.
[12] See below 'Wage Control'.

welfare of persons employed in the undertaking exists or is being made, (c) where in his opinion provision should be made in the undertaking for the training of workers adequate provision exists or is being made for such training. One reason why the requirement as to terms and conditions was important was that, in the absence of recognised terms and conditions, the Minister would insist on payment of a reasonable rate of wages. In such cases the opportunity was also taken to encourage collective bargaining.

Where an EWO applied to an undertaking the freedom of both sides to terminate the employment relationship was restricted very considerably. The employer carrying on the undertaking was not allowed to terminate the employment relationship (except in the case of serious misconduct) unless he had obtained the permission of a national service officer. Similarly an employee could not leave in the absence of such permission. Moreover, even where permission was forthcoming both sides had to give at least one week's notice. Appeals against refusal of permission and dismissal for serious misconduct could be made to Local Appeal Boards who had a tri-partite composition. The Boards had powers to make recommendations to the national service officer who had full power to review the earlier decision. Indeed the national service officer could require the re-instatement of an employee who had been dismissed for serious misconduct where, in the view of the Board, dismissal was not justified. Whilst an employee's freedom of movement was restricted there were corresponding benefits conferred by the EWOs. Employees working in an undertaking governed by the EWO were entitled to a guaranteed wage. For a significant number of employees this offered a very welcome improvement on the pre-war position. Entitlement to the guaranteed wage was conditional on the worker being capable of, and available for, work. Moreover, a statutory flexibility clause was also imposed; the guaranteed wage was conditional on the employee being willing

> to perform any services outside his usual occupation which in the circumstances he can reasonably be expected to perform when work is not available in his usual occupation.

In wartime matters of discipline become somewhat problematic—particularly in areas where a shortage of labour exists. The sanction of dismissal may hold little threat when a worker can easily get a job elsewhere. In any event, under an Essential Work Order the employer's prerogative over termination of the employment contract was heavily constrained. However, under an order an employer might report a worker to a National Service Officer where the worker was absent from work without reasonable cause or was persistently late. Ultimately, the officer was entitled to give directions under regulation 58A

> to that person to perform his work, and any such directions may contain provisions as to the method or manner of work and the times at which and during which that person shall present himself for and remain at work.[13]

Breach of such an order had the potential to result in prosecution and prosecutions did, in fact, take place. Nevertheless, prosecution did not take place on a large scale for fear of 'resentment and discontent among the body of workpeople' being caused.[14] In May 1942 Bevin reported to the Commons that

> Proceedings taken represent one worker per 10,000 covered by the order since they have been operated. Imprisonment has been imposed in one per 50,000.[15]

He went on to indicate that he would find it more than preferable 'If the magistracy of the country use the system of binding over and the man or woman concerned obeys.' However, given the prevailing belief in the merits of joint regulation, the EWO provided that where there was a joint works committee

> appropriate to deal with absenteeism or lateness, the matter was first to be referred to that committee before prosecution could take place.

The Ministry of Labour took the view that such matters were more likely to be dealt with effectively internally.[16] However, it became apparent that one difficulty in the way of joint committees dealing with discipline was worker unwillingness to serve on a body with this function. By December 1941 the principal EWO had been applied to some 27,000 undertakings across 55 industries. This affected some 4.5 million workers.[17] To this total one should add over a million other workers whose employment was regulated by industry specific

---

[13] Subsequently, the EWO was amended so as to allow a worker to be suspended without pay for up to three days.

[14] P Inman, *Labour in the Munitions Industries* (London, 1957) at p 284.

[15] Parl. Deb., HC, 21.5.42, vol 380, col 425.

[16] Ministry of Labour, above n 2, at p 122.

[17] Parker, above n 4, at p 139.

essential work orders. By the end of the war 8.75 million workers were covered by the various orders.[18]

A key feature informing the content of the EWOs was a sense of mutuality of obligation. The one-sided nature of the World War One leaving certificates and the resulting discontentment may have been influential here.[19] However, it seems likely that what was even more significant was Bevin's acute sense of where collective bargaining had fallen short in terms of arriving at acceptable terms and conditions. Whatever the motivation, the notion of mutuality of obligation became something of a recurring theme in wartime legislation. For instance, in relation to the docks, which had been plagued by industrial relations problems flowing from casual employment, a statutory scheme was introduced. This provided dockers with employment on a weekly basis and, crucially, with a guaranteed wage. Through his approach to EWOs etc Bullock sought to overcome

> the legacy of an industrial outlook which treated workpeople as so many hands, indifferent to their well-being or to any obligation beyond paying them the lowest wages possible.[20]

A further point of divergence between the approaches taken in the two wars was that, in the second, there was not a clear dichotomy between war and post-war measures. The elements of the EWOs which benefited workers, such as the guaranteed wage, were seen as setting the standard for post-war industrial relations:

> Do not rely upon the Government only to maintain it. Why not weave it into your collective agreements at the earliest opportunity? We are not anxious to have the duty of enforcing it by law. Do not turn the rising generation too much to the law and not enough to you.[21]

In the case of the docks the wartime framework was to form the basis for the post-war scheme.

Just as in the first world war dilution was a major concern for government and, once again, it proved much easier to achieve agreement at national level than implementation on the ground.[22] In promoting

---

[18] Ministry of Labour, above n 2, at p 49.

[19] See above at p 128.

[20] Ministry of Labour, above n 2, at p 45.

[21] Bullock, above n 1, at p 274.

[22] It was the case that the Restoration of Pre War Trade Practices Act 1942 obliged employers to restore trade practices abandoned during the war period. The obligation was subject to criminal penalties.

dilution the Government relied heavily on persuading and cajoling the two sides of industry. The potential benefits of, and means of securing, dilution were publicised in various ways. For instance, from June 1941 a free monthly magazine—'Engineering Bulletin'—was published. It dealt with

> such subjects as the breaking-down of skilled processes, up-grading, training, and the employment of women on skilled and semi-skilled operations.[23]

Again, as in the First World War, government officials worked with individual employers on improving productivity through dilution. Considerable patience was often shown. For example, in 1942, directions were issued to fitters in South Wales which were ignored: 'The AEU objected that it had not been given sufficient opportunity to discipline its members and it was decided not to prosecute.'[24] By the end of the war the aim of the directions had still to be achieved.

Wage Control

The Conditions of Employment and National Arbitration Order (SR & O 1940/1305)

The experience of wages control in the First World War provided much food for thought for the Ministry of Labour in the years immediately prior to the Second World War. The somewhat pious conclusion drawn from past experience was that the most effective way of reducing the number of strikes over wages was not through statutory prohibition of industrial action but by means of fair and impartial dispute resolution.[25] In any event, the Ministry hoped that, if at all possible, wage regulation should be left to collective bargaining. It was also hoped that a measure of control might be exerted over the ability of employers to raise wages:

> It would be better to leave it to the supply departments to exercise a control over the movement of wages through the powers they possessed to regulate the terms of their contracts. The most effective way of preventing an employer from raising wages above the normal scale was to make it clear to him that he did so at his own cost.[26]

---

[23] Ministry of Labour, above n 2, at p 80.
[24] Bullock, above n 1 at p 62.
[25] Parker, above n 4 at p 45.
[26] *Ibid* at p 47.

When war did actually break out limited control was indeed taken over wages. This was, to some extent, because of the difficulties in securing trade union co-operation in the absence of control over price rises and profits. Certainly, for as long as the Chamberlain government remained in office it was unlikely that a relationship of trust and co-operation would develop with the trade union movement. Clearly the advent of the coalition government changed matters. However, Bevin's tenure at the Ministry of Labour meant that, for decidedly different reasons, regulation by law was unlikely. Bevin was a whole-hearted exponent of the process of collective bargaining and believed that it should continue to function normally, in so far as was possible, in wartime. Indeed the industrial relations stability that exponents portrayed as a key virtue of joint regulation might be expected to be found to be an even greater virtue in wartime.

Between 1914 and 1918 the Government had found itself taking on board responsibility for the setting of the actual rates of wages to an ever-increasing extent. In stark contrast, between 1940 and 1945, the legislature did not go down this road at all. Instead wage regulation was left, primarily, to the normal collective bargaining machinery: 'every day innumerable questions including general wage changes are settled by negotiations without outside intervention.'[27] However, while it was one thing for collective bargaining to carry on as normal resort to industrial action (and consequent disruption to production) was another matter. Radical measures, on a par with those taken in World War 1, were enacted. Workers were prohibited from striking, and employers from declaring a lock-out, by Order 1305. The one exception to this was where 21 days had elapsed since a dispute had been referred to the Minister and the matter had not been referred for settlement in accordance with the statutory provisions. Contravention was punishable by fine or imprisonment. Moreover, compulsory arbitration was provided for. However, it is important to note that this process would not come into play unless, where a trade dispute existed, it had been referred by either side to the Minister. Neither side was under any obligation to make such a reference. However, if voluntary negotiation had proved unsuccessful resort to industrial action was not permissible and compulsory arbitration would then become the only lawful alternative to continuing negotiations. In devising a scheme providing for compulsory arbitration the Government were anxious not to

<hr>

[27] LAB 10/654.

undermine voluntary machinery. Thus we find that, following a reference to the Minister, where adequate voluntary machinery existed for settlement of the dispute, the Minister was obliged to refer the dispute to that machinery. Where such machinery did not exist the Minister was obliged to promote a settlement of the dispute and had a discretion to refer the matter for settlement to the National Arbitration Tribunal (NAT). A dispute might also be referred to the NAT after it had been referred to voluntary machinery and there had either been a failure to reach agreement or undue delay in arriving at one. In any event, referral to the NAT would normally take place within 21 days. Any award made by the NAT was binding on employees and employers, the terms of the award being implied into the employment contract.[28] The NAT was comprised of a chair and two other members, one being a worker representative and the other an employer representative. During the war some 2,200 cases were referred to the Minister; roughly half of which were withdrawn or settled by the parties themselves.[29] Of the disputes that went to arbitration about one-sixth went to the Industrial Court or a single arbitrator; the rest went to the NAT.[30] The figure for references to the Minister seems distinctly low and it appears likely that the spectre of compulsory arbitration acted as a spur to voluntary negotiation.

From the perspective of the labour movement the trauma of the introduction of compulsory arbitration was mitigated by the inclusion of a common rule provision in Order 1305. The provision applied where, in any trade or industry in any district, there were in force terms and conditions of employment which had been settled by bargaining between the collective parties. However, by way of qualification, the collective parties had to be organisations of employers and trade union representatives respectively of substantial proportions of the employers and workers engaged in that trade and industry. Where the provision applied all employers in that trade or industry in that district had to observe the recognised terms and conditions or such terms and conditions as were not less favourable than the recognised terms and conditions. The obligation was enforced by means of the criminal rather than civil law. A failure by an employer to observe the obligation was to be reported to the Minister, as were questions as to the

[28] It was also the case that an agreement made by the parties, following a reference by the Minister, was binding.
[29] Parker, above n 4, at p 456.
[30] *Ibid.*

nature, scope or effect of the recognised terms and conditions. Interestingly enough any such question could only be reported to the Minister by any organisation of employers or any trade union which habitually took part in the settlement of wages and working conditions in the trade or industry concerned. Once a question had been reported the Minister had a variety of powers—including referring the matter to the NAT for settlement. Where the issue was referred to the NAT any award made became an implied term of the employment contract.

When it came to the enforcement of the prohibition on industrial action, the Government viewed recourse to penal sanctions as a matter of last resort:

> The policy of the department has been to continue to deal with disputes involving stoppages of work on the basis of co-operation with the organisations in the industry and not on the basis of using its powers under the Order for penal purposes.[31]

Moreover, prosecution has

> to a large extent been limited to cases where the strikers have ignored trade union discipline and deliberately and knowingly denied themselves the remedy of constitutional methods, or where the objects have been deliberately mischievous.[32]

The department took the view that the provisions had a deterrent effect and 'strengthened the hand of responsible leaders.' It was noted that a very large number of stoppages had still taken place but

> most of these have been of short duration, which means that the workpeople concerned have been prepared to accept constitutional methods for the settlement of their grievances as soon as their responsible leaders come on to the scene or they have assured themselves that attention is being given to their complaints.[33]

As in World War I the limitations of a statutory scheme which prohibited strikes, and was accompanied by penal sanctions, soon became apparent. Such limitations came to the fore in the course of a dispute which arose at the Betteshanger colliery in Kent. Arbitration had taken place but the employees rejected the award and went on strike in breach of Order 1305. The Government sought to prosecute some 1,000 miners (though potentially 4,000 were at risk of prosecution).

[31] Lab 10/ 654
[32] *Ibid.*
[33] *Ibid.*

This gave rise to significant practical problem in processing the prosecutions:

> Charges against 1,000 persons could only be handled satisfactorily if the men pleaded guilty. If each man pleaded 'not guilty' the proceedings might last for months. The Union was asked if they would instruct their members to plead guilty, and accept a decision on a few test cases. The Union obligingly did so.

As a result 3 union officials were imprisoned. In addition, 'thirty-five men were fined £3 or one month's imprisonment, and nearly one thousand were fined £1, or fourteen days.' However, the sentencing process had no impact on the strike. As a result

> negotiations were re-opened and five days after the hearing an agreement was signed, in prison, between the colliery management and the Kent Miners' Union. Apart from some face-saving words, it gave the men what they wanted. Then the Secretary for Mines took a deputation to the Home Secretary asking for the immediate release of the three local officials. The men would not start work until their leaders were free. After eleven days in prison they were released. The mine reopened and in the first week the normal output of coal was nearly trebled.[34]

The government's problems did not end there as virtually every miner who had been fined refused to pay. The penalty of imprisonment was not a realistic option. Moreover,

> The company also wanted to avoid further trouble. They asked if they could pay the fines on behalf of the men; the cost to them would be so much less profits tax! They were told on no account to do this. The Court was advised not to enforce the unpaid fines.[35]

The conclusion drawn by many was encapsulated in the following passage from a letter to the Times in 1945:

> Imprisonment for non-payment of fines for illegal wartime striking, however juridically logical and theoretically justifiable, was under modern conditions (ie those of 1916) industrially ineffective and nationally undesirable- that in practice it operated to impair respect for the rule of law. You cannot imprison the whole of a large body of strikers. Alternatively, to pick out a selected few and make examples of them only elevates them into popular martyrs and brings in the always effective industrial rallying cry of 'victimization.'[36]

[34] Royal Commission on Trade Unions and Employers' Associations (Cmnd 3623), appendix 6, para 6.
[35] *Ibid* at para 8.
[36] Bullock, above n 1 at p 268.

The lesson learnt by the official history was a somewhat cynical one:

> Where large numbers decided to take the law into their own hands, they
> could be fairly confident that no punitive measures could be effectively taken
> against them. On the other hand, where the number of strikers was rela-
> tively small and prompt action was taken, an appearance in Court had at
> times salutary corrective consequences.[37]

After the Betteshanger dispute no worker was imprisoned for breach of
order 1305,[38] though there was a regrettable lack of consistency in sentencing practice:

> some magistrates were ready to adjourn a case to give an opportunity for a
> settlement of the dispute and for the return of the men to work, others
> imposed fines that at times seemed out of proportion to the gravity of the
> offences.[39]

It would be easy to conclude that the experience at Betteshanger con-
firms both World War I experience, and longer standing concern, that
penal sanctions would not deter industrial action.[40] Moreover, one
might take the view that, in a collective dispute, the use of criminal
sanctions has the potential to intensify the conflict and render dispute
resolution more difficult. However, the overall verdict on the use of
penal sanctions between 1940 and 1945 was much more mixed. For
instance, prosecutions over failure to obey directions to work did not
produce the sort of backlash seen at Betteshanger and may well have
led to greater adherence to that element of the wartime framework. As
a result, one could not say that wartime experience conclusively
demonstrated that penal sanctions had no role to play in labour law.

---

[37]   Parker, above n 4 at p 469.
[38]   *Ibid* at p 468. Despite this reg 1AA was introduced in 1944. It provided that no person shall declare, instigate or incite any other person to take part in, or shall otherwise
act in furtherance of, any strike among persons engaged in the performance of essential
services or any lockout of persons engaged.' HA Clegg, *A History of British Trade
Unions Since 1889*, vol III (Oxford: Clarendon Press, 1994) at p 257 quotes Croucher to
the effect that Bevin

> chose to promulgate a new regulation because it was apparent that what was needed
> was a political pronouncement of the government's intention to come down hard on
> industrial militancy in general.

> Ministry of Labour records are not inconsistent with this: 'The regulation should
> strengthen the hands of trade unions in dealing with irresponsible elements.' (LAB
> 10/457).

[39]   Parker, above n 4 at p 468.
[40]   See above at p 125.

Consultation

If one strand of industrial relations policy was to ensure that workers were rewarded by way of fair terms and conditions, then another important strand was that labour should be genuinely involved in matters which impacted on the lives of working people. This manifested itself in a number of ways. Indeed we find that, as would be the case for many years to follow, extensive use was made of joint consultation with both sides of industry. Most notable of all was the Joint Consultative Committee set up to advice the Minister of Labour. It had a membership of seven employer representatives and seven from the TUC. The establishment of the committee was not an exercise in tokenism and it met on a regular basis. Such steps can be seen as the introduction of

> a tripartite pattern of consultation and co-operation between Government, employers and unions as a way of dealing with industrial and economic problems.[41]

Movement towards corporatism was very much underway.

Employee involvement in decisions affecting their working lives may also come about by means of trade union participation in collective bargaining. Government policy was very much to favour that process. As a result, the role of joint regulation over wages and other terms of employment was largely undiminished; in the settlement of trade disputes collective bargaining, not compulsory arbitration, was the norm. Moreover, in trying to bring about dilution, much was left to the two sides of industry. The role of Government was often more to inform and persuade. A number of important collective agreements dealt with the subject of dilution.[42] Again, in the munitions industry, joint committees were established to formulate dilution schemes which might then be applied to individual undertakings.[43] One interesting contrast with the First World War is thrown up by the experience of trying to achieve dilution in the sheet metal industry. A government committee had recommended greater use of female workers. However, negotiations between the employers and unions broke down over wage rates. Unlike World War I there was no resort to statutory control of wage

---

[41] Bullock, above n 1 at p 97.

[42] In 1940 various dilution agreements were entered into between the Engineering Employers' Federation and a number of trade unions (see Inman, above n 14, p 57).

[43] Parker, above n 4 at p 221.

rates despite the fact that 'the position about dilution in the sheet metal shops remained unsatisfactory to the end of the war.'[44]

Government belief in the virtues of self-regulation is borne out by the example of the iron, steel and chemical industries where decision-making, in a key area, was devolved to the industry. In those industries the intention was that those already employed therein were to be retained but that some movement of labour would be required. The management of that process was delegated to the two sides of industry:

> to carry out this scheme local committees of employers and workers, . . . were set up under the chair of the Ministry of Labour, and they were given the responsibility of arranging for transfers of workers from one undertaking to another within the industry.[45]

INDUSTRIAL RELATIONS BEYOND THE HOSTILITIES

The Government's desire to carry the labour movement with them had been graphically illustrated by the appointment of Bevin to the post of Minister of Labour in the coalition. This had a number of significant consequences. Not least of which, in contrast to World War I, was the greater degree of convergence between industrial policy in normal and emergency conditions. As Bevin himself put it

> I am not one of those who do not separate pre-war, war and post-war, as if they were three separate states of existence. One is an intensification of another; what you do in one has a great effect on the other.[46]

As we have seen the bulk of dispute resolution during the war was left to collective bargaining. However, Bevin was very strongly of the view that the Ministry of Labour should give that process much greater support, both during and after the war, than had tended to occur between the wars. It was no longer enough for Government merely to commend the virtues of joint regulation; actual support was required. This stance was adopted very much with an eye to post-war industrial relations. Nevertheless, government support for collective bargaining was, in fact, evident throughout the war. Moreover, the enactment, during the war, of measures such as the Wages Councils Act 1945 indicated that trade unions could expect auxiliary legislation to be forthcoming,

---

[44] Inman, above n 14 at p 62.
[45] Parker, above n 4 at p 222.
[46] Parl. Deb., 9.2.43, HC, vol 386, col 1201.

when required, in the post-war period. 'Positive voluntarism' could be anticipated; there would be no return to the laissez-faire stance of the inter-war period. The provisions in the 1945 Act concerning failing voluntary machinery offer a clear demonstration of this.[47] This was partly because joint regulation by means of collective bargaining was regarded as valuable in itself. It was also because a recognition had emerged that the actual terms and conditions of employment of workers had to be satisfactory.

Wartime and Beyond

It is very much to Bevin's credit that, in the midst of dealing with the exigencies thrown up by the war, much was done that would endure beyond it. In 1940–41 a number of new JICs were set up at the instigation of the Minister.[48] Indeed 46 were to be established between 1940 and 1945.[49] Bevin took an expansive view of their function (and of the proper scope of collective bargaining):

> he took every opportunity to urge the newly founded councils to extend their interests to other questions besides wages and hours, and to discuss such matters as the future prospects of their industries, training, redundancy, post-war reorganisation and anything else which might affect the lives of those who worked in them.[50]

More significantly, the Catering Wages Act was passed in 1943.[51] In 1944, with a view to the post-war period, Bevin contemplated bringing in three measures to support voluntary collective bargaining. First, that statutory wages boards be substituted for JICs where the latter were failing. Second, that trade boards should have their powers extended in line with the provisions of the Road Haulage Act 1938. Third, that collective agreements become legally enforceable, throughout a trade or industry, on the joint application of the collective parties. Interestingly enough both sides of industry expressed some concern:

> They feared that the growth of State control over wages might jeopardise voluntary machinery, and the TUC were at first apprehensive lest a

---

[47] See below at p 244.
[48] Parker, above n 4, at p 438.
[49] Bullock, above n 1 at p 93.
[50] Bullock, above n 1 at p 94.
[51] See below at p 241.

wide extension of state wages enforcement might retard the growth of
unions.[52]

Bevin did not share these fears. He believed that

> by far the greatest part of industrial employment will continue to be
> regulated by voluntary collective bargaining and state measures would be
> confined to necessary safeguards against possible deficiencies in the
> voluntary system.[53]

However, it was vital that the State should intervene where collective
bargaining did not regulate—to ensure the adequacy of workers' terms
and conditions. All the proposals mooted by Bevin became law with
the exception of the third. The latter had, however, been developed in
some detail by the Ministry. It was envisaged that it would result in the
provisions in a collective agreement dealing with terms and conditions
of employment becoming binding on all employers in a trade or industry. In the event of breach by the employer the employee would be able
to sue on the basis of an implied term in the employment contract. The
measure would also be policed by penal sanctions. Before the terms of
a collective agreement were extended in this way a number of conditions would have to be satisfied. First, the parties to the collective
agreement would have to be organisations of employers and trade
union representatives of substantial proportions of employers and
workers in the trade or industry covered by the agreement. Second,
there had to be a joint application by the collective parties. Third, a
Board of Inquiry had to be established to investigate and report.
Fourth, public notice of the proposals had to take place and objections
had to be considered. The provisions on interpretation of any order
made are of note. In essence such questions were to be left to the industry itself. It was provided that questions of interpretation be left to the
arbitration machinery of the industry; in the absence of such machinery the Industrial Court should adjudicate. Should such a question
arise in the course of traditional court proceedings (civil or criminal)
then those proceedings should be adjourned to allow for a decision by
the appropriate body.

Ultimately, Bevin abandoned the aim of enacting such a common
rule provision. He took the view that the legal and administrative difficulties involved were considerable.[54] Interestingly enough, in view of

---

[52] Parker, above n 4 at 440.
[53] Lab 10/276.
[54] LAB 10/655.

earlier TUC ambivalence about legislation of this type, Citrine argued that to fail to legislate would be to discourage the voluntary system.[55] The difficulties that Bevin had in mind included the question of proving that the parties to the agreement represented substantial proportions of employers and workers in the trade or industry. There was also concern about the difficulty of defining the scope of any order and of avoiding overlap between agreements.

The Catering Wages Act

In 1943 Bevin brought forward a bill to regulate wages in the catering industry. It is important to stress that it could not be portrayed as an emergency wartime measure. It was also the case that the production of the bill was a major enterprise:

> Catering was left as the largest industry in the country in which wages, hours and conditions of work were uncontrolled by collective agreement or statutory regulation.[56]

This was an enterprise which had been embarked upon unsuccessfully by the second Labour government.[57] The challenges involved in producing legislation of this nature for an industry as large and diverse as catering were considerable. However, they were not dissimilar to those which had been involved in road haulage and in that respect Bevin was at a marked advantage. In his earlier role as trade union leader he had taken

> a particular personal interest in the road-haulage industry. He had begun his trade-union career by organising the Bristol carters and road haulage remained, with the docks and mining, one of the industries in which he played a unique role extending far beyond the organisation of the trade-union side.[58]

The Bill had some immediate aims; if working conditions in the industry were not improved workers would leave the industry and that would be detrimental to the war effort. The Bill also sought to regulate the industry in both war and peace and, as a consequence, also contained more standard aims, one of which was to ensure that workers

---

[55] *Ibid.*
[56] Bullock, above n 1 at p 220.
[57] See above at p 213.
[58] Bullock, above n 1 at p 544, and see above at p 205.

attained more satisfactory treatment over remuneration. In addition, the Bill was based upon the belief that trade board type legislation fostered organisation in an industry and helped voluntary machinery to evolve. The promoters of the Bill regarded it as a means

> to develop joint machinery by which a foundation can be put in the trade, where collective bargaining does not exist and is not at present a practical possibility.[59]

In the scheme established by the Act a new tripartite body—the Catering Wages Commission—had a pivotal role. A core function was to make such enquiries as were thought fit, or directed by the Minister, into the existing methods of regulating the remuneration and conditions of employment of catering workers. The Commission was also empowered to make recommendations on such matters (as well as on health and welfare issues) to any government department. In providing for enquiry into existing machinery the Government acknowledged both the diversity of practice within the industry and the policy of promoting and respecting industrial self-government. The Act explicitly accepted that on enquiry the Commission might establish that satisfactory mechanisms of joint regulation existed in parts of the sector. It also envisaged that the existing machinery might be less than wholly adequate but, nevertheless, susceptible of improvement so that it would, in time, regulate effectively remuneration and conditions of employment. In the latter case the Commission was entitled to make suggestions for improvement; the Minister in turn was obliged 'to take such steps as appear to him to be expedient and practicable to secure the improvements in question.' In considering the adequacy of existing machinery the Commission was obliged to consider

> not only what matters are capable of being dealt with by that machinery but also to what extent those matters are covered by the agreements or awards arrived at or given thereunder and to what extent the practice is in accordance with those agreements or awards.

The foregoing requirement gives a clear indication of Bevin's approach to state interference in industrial relations. It did not suffice to pay lip service to the merits of collective bargaining; actual support on occasion was required. Moreover, state intervention might be appropriate where voluntary machinery functioned but was ineffective in terms of

---

[59] Parl. Deb., 9.2.43, HC, vol 386, col 1271.

the substantive outcomes achieved or in securing adhesion to collectively agreed norms.

Where voluntary machinery did not exist, or was inadequate and not susceptible to improvement, the Commission might recommend the establishment of a wages board. The Minister was entitled to establish such a board upon receipt of such recommendation. Provision also existed for the abolition of a board. It was contemplated that this would be used where voluntary machinery had developed to a satisfactory extent; the acid test being whether agreements made were actually adhered to.[60] Wages boards had power to make proposals as to the remuneration to be paid, rest periods, holiday entitlement and holiday pay. Such a recommendation became binding on the industry once the Minister had made a Wages Regulation Order.[61] The terms of the order were implied into the employment contract; breach of an order might also result in penal sanctions. Wages boards also had power to consider any matter affecting the remuneration, conditions of employment, health or welfare of all or any of the workers in relation to whom the board operates or affecting the general improvement and development of that part of the industry in relation to which the board operates and were entitled to submit a report thereon. This broad remit reflected the importance given to the aim of promoting industrial self-government; properly conducted voluntary collective bargaining should take on board all these matters.

Wages Councils

Towards the end of the war the existing trade boards scheme was replaced by the Wages Councils Act 1945. There was a reason for the change of name: the Act not only widened

> trade boards legislation but is a declaration by Parliament that the conception of what was known as a sweated industry is past.[62]

Whilst a more robust scheme was required wholescale state regulation of wages was not an option since it was not a practical proposition:

---

[60] Parl. Deb., 9.2.43, HC, vol 386, col 1207.
[61] By virtue of s 8(4) the Minister's discretion was confined to acceptance of the recommendation or referral back to the board for re-consideration.
[62] Parl. Deb., 16.1.45, HC, vol 407, col 69.

I cannot believe that Parliament could ever satisfactorily adjust the actual wages to be paid to the people in respective industries, in view of the change in conditions that continually takes place in the industries. Therefore the legislature took a middle course. It adopted the principle of legal enforcement, together with the creation of autonomous boards to say what the wages which were to be enforced should be.[63]

The Minister was empowered to set up a wages council where he was of the view that no adequate machinery existed for the effective regulation of the remuneration of the workers concerned and that, having regard to the remuneration existing amongst those workers, or at least some of them, it is expedient that such a council should be established. It should be noted that the criteria remained the same as in 1918. However, it would not be reasonable to conclude from this that nothing had changed. There was, in fact, every reason to suppose that, by virtue of the intended manner of administration, the wages council provisions would play a greater role than during the inter-war period. Bevin believed that it was the entitlement of every worker to have his basic conditions fixed either by collective bargaining or by state regulation.

The Act also innovated by dealing with the situation where effective collective bargaining had existed in an industry but either had failed or was likely to. Bevin was determined that legislative assistance be offered here. Thus the Act made provision for the situation where the existing machinery for the settlement of remuneration and conditions of employment was likely to cease or be inadequate for that purpose. In such circumstances a number of bodies, such as JICs, could apply to the Minister to establish a wages council.[64] Upon receipt of such an application the Minister had a discretion to refer the matter to a commission of inquiry. He also had a discretion to authorise an inquiry of his own volition. A report of a commission of inquiry could lead to the establishment of a wages council. At least two motives existed here. First, the establishment of a wages council might help stabilise organisation in an industry and, in time, lead to voluntary machinery functioning effectively again. Second, a wages council might be required to ensure that reasonable terms of employment existed. Bayliss states that

---

[63] Parl. Deb., 16.1.45, HC, vol 407, col 71.

[64] An application could also be made by any organisation of workers and any organisation of employers which claim to be organisations that habitually take part in the settlement of remuneration and conditions of employment for the workers concerned.

the establishment of a wages council where voluntary collective bargaining was failing

> would ensure the continuation of negotiations between employers and trade unions, and through the legal enforcement of its minimum wage and conditions would prevent the deterioration of standards through competition to lower wages costs. When the depression was over, and the bargaining power of the two sides became more equal, they would apply for the abolition of the council and return to voluntary collective bargaining.[65]

As with the 1943 Act, in considering whether any machinery was or was likely to remain adequate for regulating the remuneration and conditions of employment of any workers, the commission were to consider not only what matters were capable of being dealt with by that machinery, but also to what extent those matters were covered by the agreements or awards arrived at thereunder, and to what extent the practice was, or was likely to be, in accordance with those agreements or awards. The Minister also had power to abolish, or vary the field of operation of, a wages council. Moreover, an application for the abolition of a wages council might be made to the Minister jointly, by organisations of workers and organisations of employers, which represented respectively substantial proportions of the workers and employers with respect to whom that council operates. Such an application could be made on the basis that those organisations jointly provided machinery which was, and was likely to remain, adequate for the effective regulation of remuneration and conditions of employment.

The powers of wages councils were similar those conferred by the Catering Wages Act in that they could recommend to the Minister the remuneration payable, holiday entitlement and holiday pay.[66] A wages council would have power to set a guaranteed weekly wage. The terms of the wages order were implied into the employment contract. As well as civil proceedings defaulting employers might also face criminal proceedings. The passage of the Act meant that the

> wages and conditions of work of fifteen million men and women, the overwhelming majority of the working population, would come under the protection of negotiated agreements or statutory regulations.[67]

---

[65] FJ Bayliss, *British Wages Councils* (Oxford: Blackwell, 1962) p 56.
[66] The one difference was that there was no power to make any recommendation as to rest periods.
[67] Bullock, above n 1 at p 354.

CONCLUSIONS

It is certainly the case that there were significant resemblances between the legislative frameworks in the two world wars. Take the position in respect of alteration of terms and conditions. In both wars the Government established a process of arbitration, by virtue of which the awards were binding, which the parties were not compelled to use. Indirect pressure to arbitrate did exist in that the parties' capacity to resort to industrial action, in the event of disagreement, was heavily restricted. However, in both wars, provided the two sides were willing to compromise, collective bargaining could carry on as normal. This position was qualified in the First World War in that the Government took control of wages in controlled establishments from the outset and, as the war progressed, became more and more drawn into the process of fixing wages. This did not happen in the second war where matters were much more left to collective bargaining. Not only did collective bargaining retain a greater role, it also gained legislative support from the enactment of a common rule provision. In the First World War such a provision had not emerged until 1917. Collective bargaining was also promoted in a variety of other ways; such as by the establishment of a number of new JICs and the enactment of the Catering Wages Act. Bevin viewed the process of collective bargaining as particularly important in wartime. How was the UK to match German organisation and production? Bevin believed that

> the right way was to stick to the basic principle of democracy, government by consent, and rely on the willingness of people in an emergency to make greater sacrifices willingly than they could be dragooned into making by compulsion.[68]

In the industrial relations context 'government by consent' meant collective bargaining.

It also became apparent, during this period, that it was not enough to simply endorse collective bargaining; government had to be concerned with the outcomes of the bargaining process. It no longer sufficed that the worst features of the employment market be ameliorated; as the experience of the Essential Work Order had demonstrated it was important to consider whether the terms of the work-wage bargain

---

[68] Bullock, above n 1, at p 44.

were equitable. In the parliamentary debates on the Wages Council Act Bevin made clear that the existence of the councils was needed in order that the level of remuneration was reasonable.[69] Moreover, employers should not compete 'on the basis standard of wages.'[70]

[69] Parl. Deb., 16.1.45, HC, vol 407, col 69.
[70] Parl. Deb., 16.1.45, HC, vol 407, col 70.

9

Concluding Remarks

IN ASSESSING THE period from 1867 to 1945 one might say that the most striking feature is the continuous acceptance, by the State, of the role of collective bargaining. This is apparent from the publication of the Royal Commission report of 1869 onwards. Thus the minority found that where collectively agreed terms exist,

> no questions appear to arise but those of interpretation and we find the employers on perfectly amicable footing with the union, and both parties often co-operating with each other.[1]

In a similar vein, the premise of the report of 1894 was that the route to industrial peace lay through collective bargaining:

> where a skilled trade is well organised, good relations tend to prevail and countless minor quarrels are obviated or nipped in the bud.[2]

By the time that we reach the 1930s there is even said to be an 'instinctive preference' in the UK for voluntary collective bargaining. From the mid to late nineteenth century onwards employers too were increasingly likely to regard joint regulation as the way forward. It is striking that, in the aftermath of *Taff Vale*, employers did not attempt to push back the role of joint regulation and trade unions. Again, during the inter-war period, a similar picture can be painted. However, the primacy of the role accorded to collective bargaining should not be taken as indicating that law was viewed as an inappropriate means of regulating industrial relations; during the period under review it was not thought to be wrong to resort to law. No one would have subscribed to the view that

> there exists something like an inverse correlation between the practical significance of legal sanctions, and the degree to which industrial relations have reached a state of maturity.[3]

---

[1] Royal Commission on Trade Unions (Cd 4123, 1869) p xlix.
[2] Fifth (and final) Report of the Royal Commission on Labour, (Cd 7421, 1982), para 90.
[3] Kahn-Freund, 'Legal Framework', in Flanders and Clegg (eds), *The System of Industrial Relations in Great Britain* (Oxford: Blackwell, 1954) p 43.

It is certainly the case that regulating industrial relations through the institution of collective bargaining presented considerable attractions—not least of which was that it avoided the need for intervention by government:

> As the network of regulation becomes more complex, a larger part of the general social rules, under which industry is carried on, must be devised for industry by the people engaged in industry themselves. Some of them involve technical considerations which no one outside industry is competent to judge, others (such as the fixing of wage-rates) turn on considerations of expediency, which Parliament and the public departments are ill-adapted to assess.[4]

Government would, however, have found it very difficult to avoid intervention had collective bargaining not been regarded as successful. However, the views of the Royal Commission of 1894 were that

> where a skilled trade is well organised, good relations tend to prevail and countless minor quarrels are obviated or nipped in the bud.[5]

This stance soon gained the status of orthodoxy. The focus moved to the sorts of problems which can arise in the absence of adequate organisation. The glowing endorsement of collective bargaining by the Donovan Commission in the 1960s would have come as no surprise to the various official bodies who considered industrial relations between 1867 and 1945.

The undoubted merits of collective bargaining notwithstanding, if law was, in fact, an appropriate means of regulating industrial relations why did it not gain a greater role? The answer to this question may be found by examining the functions performed by labour law. Laws of this sort may exist for the benefit of both sides of industry; common rule legislation offers an obvious example here. However, in so far as labour law exists to regulate, and offer a counter-weight to, the inherent imbalance in employment relations then employers may be less than receptive to legal regulation. In the latter situation the composition of government becomes paramount in determining the probable nature of any legislative reforms. Much has always been made of the uneasy relationship between the trade union movement and the judiciary. However, the political persuasion of government is also of great importance. It is crucial to appreciate that the period under

---

[4] H Clay, *Problems of Industrial Relations* (London, 1929) p 147.
[5] Royal Commission on Labour, above n 2, para 90.

review includes only two Labour governments; both of very short duration. There are signs that had they held office for longer, more in the way of labour law measures would have been enacted.[6] Given that they did not do so, it is not surprising that more could often have been done to, for instance, support or promote collective bargaining. Similarly it is not surprising that the existence of inadequate terms and conditions of employment often went unchallenged by the State. The absence of law

> may mean that in sectors of the economy where trade union organisation is weak social standards lag behind those enforced in other countries in which more emphasis lies on legislation and less on collective bargaining.[7]

Of course, in appropriate circumstances, the absence of law may be regarded as a virtue. Kahn-Freund believed that reliance on legislation may be 'especially on the side of the unions, frequently a sign of weakness, certainly not a sign of strength.'[8] Certainly, a position whereby trades unions are overly dependant on legislation will be an unhealthy one. However, I believe that it is also true that the absence of law may be a sign of weakness and that this was true for much of the period under review. There may well be occasions where the inability of the labour movement to procure legislative support is damaging to unions and/or individual workers. The lot of workers prior to World War I would almost certainly have been much improved by legislation regulating hours of work and wages. It is also hard to believe that, for instance, during the inter-war period, trade unions would not have benefited from the support that common rule legislation would have given to collective bargaining. Had more supportive legislation been introduced trade union bargaining power might well have become stronger; unions might also have found it easier to recruit. In the inter-war period the failure of government to intervene to a greater extent was to favour the interests of employers. Government was, on the whole, not disposed to assist the labour movement. The policy tended to be one of 'negative voluntarism':

> The state retreated in terms of its role as institution builder, with the result that the parties were left largely to their own devices, albeit in some

---

[6] See above at p 211.
[7] Kahn-Freund, 'Labour Law', in M Ginsberg (ed) *Law and Opinion in England in the 20th Century* (1959) p 222.
[8] Kahn-Freund, above n 5, p 44.

cases within a framework which had been created with the help of the State.[9]

Again, during the 1930s, a number of industries would have welcomed legislation along the lines of the Cotton Manufacturing Industry Act 1934. They were to be disappointed. Against such a back-drop, it is probable that the only form of legislation that would have been endorsed unequivocally by Government throughout the inter-war period was legislation dealing with voluntary conciliation etc:

> the action of the State has been generally confined, and . . . should continue to be confined, to efforts to promote voluntary agreement between the parties by means of . . . conciliatory machinery.[10]

Collective laissez-faire may allow

> free play to the collective forces in society, and to limit the intervention of the law to those marginal areas in which the disparity of forces in society . . . is so great as to prevent the successful operation of collective bargaining.[11]

However, it is very much a value judgment as to when collective bargaining is operating satisfactorily and when state intervention is justified. Indeed the whole notion of satisfactory collective bargaining sits uneasily with the existence of huge disparities in power and wealth in society. Collective bargaining may be regarded as operating successfully if it continues to regulate but the outcomes it produces, in terms of substantive terms and conditions, may nevertheless be utterly unsatisfactory from the perspective of the workers involved.

It is also the case that trade unions, in their view of the merits of legal regulation, adopted a more pragmatic approach than has sometimes been allowed for. Flanders has noted that

> the balance of the mix of voluntary and legal action which trade unions have favoured has changed over the years and has differed from union to union, but the tradition of voluntarism in this country has never excluded a positive attitude towards some kinds of labour law.[12]

It is also worth recalling that the objects of the TUC included, between 1924 and 1945 (and beyond), both a maximum on working hours and

---

[9] KD Ewing, 'The State and Industrial Relations: "Collective Laissez-Faire" Revisited' (1998) *HSIR* 1 at p 24.

[10] Final Report of the Committee on Industry and Trade (Cmd 3282) p 90.

[11] Kahn-Freund, above n 7, p 224.

[12] A Flanders (1974) *BJIR* 352 at p 353.

minimum wage set by law.[13] A further instance of the pragmatism displayed by the union movement is the fact that they were quite content
that even a matter concerning remuneration, such as holiday pay,
should be the subject of legislation. If collective bargaining was failing
to produce acceptable results it was only sensible to look elsewhere.
Kahn-Freund observed, with reference to the absence of a statutory
right of recognition, that

> Does not the unwillingness of the unions to invoke the help of the law at a
> point at which, as is well known, the American unions found it to be of the
> greatest assistance, demonstrate how much the aversion against State inter-
> vention in industrial relations, how much in particular union preference for
> industrial rather than political or legislative action, dominates the impact of
> public opinion on the development of labour law in our time?[14]

However, the unwillingness of the unions to seek such legislation may
well have been related to the extremely low chances of Parliament
responding favourably. After all, if Parliament, during the inter-war
period could not be persuaded to grant common rule legislation to support existing collective bargaining machinery, it was even less likely to
introduce a right of recognition. When such legislation was sought, in
the aviation industry, it was denied. Intriguingly, the Ministry of
Labour were opposed to such an enactment, in an individual industry,
primarily because they were concerned that a precedent might be
set. Between 1867 and 1945 it was often the case that government
would have been unconcerned about the balance of power favouring
employers.

In any event, the foregoing notwithstanding, there were periods
when it seemed likely that law would play a greater role. Prior to the
outbreak of World War I the UK seemed to be moving towards a position where law would regulate industrial relations to a greater extent.
At that point in time state intervention in society was increasing
dramatically; an expansion of social legislation featured prominently.
New labour law measures were part of this process; enactments dealt
with core issues such as hours and wages. It was also significant that
industrial action might act as the legislative catalyst. Trade unions and
their members did not appear to have the slightest problem with the
'method of legal enactment.' They did object strongly to inadequate
terms and conditions of employment. If the First World War had not

[13] *Ibid* at p 358.
[14] Kahn-Freund, above n 7, p 229.

broken out it is not unreasonable to suggest that there would have been a steady increase in the extent of legal regulation of employment conditions. The passing of the Coal Mines Regulation Act 1908 had demonstrated that Parliament might be persuaded, by industrial action or the threat thereof, to intervene, in the face of employer intransigence, and improve core aspects of terms and conditions. As trade union membership continued to grow during this period other unions may well have harboured hopes that, in time, they too would become sufficiently strong so as to be able to compel government in this way. Again greater legal regulation of labour relations was very much 'on the cards' as part of post-war reconstruction. One manifestation of this was the initial enthusiasm, on the part of government, for the recommendations of the NIC.[15] There a number of reasons why more by way of legal regulation did not emerge in the immediate post-war period.[16] Undoubtedly, one factor was that unions did not push harder, perhaps by the threat of industrial action, for government intervention. Had they done so, during a period when government was greatly concerned about the impact that industrial action might have on social stability, they might well have been successful. Once the decline in the economy set in such prospects rapidly evaporated.

In assessing the extent to which law has permeated industrial relations in the UK it may be that the distinction between auxiliary and regulatory legislation is not entirely helpful. One should perhaps make the further distinction between 'pure' auxiliary legislation such as the Industrial Courts Act 1919[17] and 'dual purpose' legislation which aims not only to support collective bargaining but also to regulate employment conditions. Trade boards would clearly fell into the latter category; as would measures such as the Industrial Councils Bill 1924. The 1918 Act was founded on the premise that trade boards were to be 'a temporary expedient facilitating organisation within the industry, so that, in the course of time, the workers or the employers will not have need of the statutory regulations.' However, there may be a danger in placing too much of an emphasis on this auxiliary function and, in the process, overlooking the on-going regulatory function. Moreover, the predominant purpose of a measure, in practice, may diverge from the legislative intention. Thus, whilst the establishment of a trade board may foster collective bargaining in a particular industry, an even

---

[15] See above at p 158.
[16] See above at ch. 6.
[17] See above at p 166.

greater factor may well be the general economic conditions. A period of economic depression may not be conducive to an expansion of organisation and collective bargaining. During such a period the regulatory function of the legislation may predominate once more. Thus even after the 1918 Act went on to the statute book

> the chief requirement in practice remained the need to protect the weakest workers against sweating—the object of the 1909 Act.[18]

There has perhaps been something of a tendency in the UK to regard wartime labour laws as standing apart from the mainstream. I would like to suggest that this may be a mistake. Lessons learnt in wartime can have a lasting influence on the system. The best known example of the long-term effect of wartime legislation is, almost certainly, the Betteshanger colliery dispute (partly because of the publicity given to it by Donovan):

> The experience of Compulsory Arbitration during the war has shown that it is not a successful method of avoiding strikes, and in normal times it would undoubtedly prove even less successful.'

However, it had already been accepted for a considerable time that compulsory arbitration was unlikely to be a practical option in peacetime industrial relations. For instance, during Government deliberations on the content of the 1927 legislation, proposals for a mandatory cooling-off period were rejected:

> Government . . . would not enforce the law because, aware that the right to strike was ultimately determined not by law but by the action of the rank and file, they dared not risk mass non-compliance.[19]

In some ways, Betteshanger simply served to confirm what had long been suspected and indeed confirmed during World War I. At the same time, however, wartime experience can give rise to fresh understanding as to the merits of legal regulation. Wartime regulation of wages between 1914 and 1918 demonstrated to Government that their involvement in this area could easily be an ever-increasing one:

> To establish statutory bodies for collective bargaining, like the Trades Boards . . ., to make the determinations of such Boards and of voluntary joint bodies mandatory on whole trades, to assist collective bargaining by providing facilities for conciliation and arbitration, are all in line with this

---

[18] FJ Bayliss, *British Wages Councils* (Oxford: Blackwell, 1962) p 15.
[19] R Lowe, *Adjusting to Democracy* (Oxford: Clarendon Press, 1986) p 109.

policy, and great extension of such activity is possible . . . But with the actual fixing of rates in normal times . . . no Government that has studied the experience of the Ministry of Munitions and can by any means avert that necessity, will be inclined to meddle.[20]

Thereafter, it was going to be likely that there would be a desire to avoid enacting measures which involved an arm of Government in determining actual rates of wages. On the other hand, there was nothing to suggest that measures such as ones promoting adherence to the 'common rule,' or trade boards legislation, would be less likely to be favoured in the future. Other lessons were there to be learnt but the opportunity was not always taken. The administration of the First World War legislation had interesting implications for the rule of law given that an element of that principle is 'the conviction that the administration of law is impartial, objective, even-handed and essentially non-political.'[21] In 1915 the Government had found a way out of a troublesome situation by persuading the unions to pay the fines involved of imprisoned workers and, hence, securing the release of the men.[22] Formally the law was upheld but only as a result of executive interference in the administration of justice. The sequence of events in the First World War bears significant similarities to events occurring during the life of the Industrial Relations Act:

> the reaction to the Act also affected the way the courts enforced the law. They conveniently discovered that there was an Official Solicitor who could act for some of those who refused to seek to put a case before them. The NIRC freed unrepentant contemnors when their continued imprisonment threatened to cause industrial chaos. It accepted money from an unnamed third party in payment of a union's damages and costs.[23]

One might suggest that the drafters of the Industrial Relations Act would have benefited from paying greater attention to what past UK experience suggested were the potential complications of introducing penal sanctions into industrial relations.

---

[20] OHMM, vol. 5, pt 1, p 143.
[21] B Weekes et al, *Industrial Relations and the Limits of the Law* (Oxford: Blackwell, 1975) p 231.
[22] See above at p 126.
[23] Weekes et al, above n 19, p 229.

Index

Agricultural Wages Act 1924, 187–9

Baillie Committee, 203–4
Balfour Committee, 183, 196–7
Boot and shoe trade, 61–2
British Sugar Subsidy Act 1925, 202

Catering Wages Act, 241–3
Cave Committee, 184–7
Coal Mines (Minimum Wage) Act 1912,
    69–70
Coal Mines Regulation Act 1908,
    72–4
Collective agreements (legal
    enforcement):
    Industrial Council of 1913, 76–7
    Royal Commission of 1869, 8–9
    Royal Commission of 1894, 41, 43
    Royal Commission of 1905, 99
    Trade Union Act 1871, 12–13
    Whitley, 154
Collective bargaining:
    attitude of Board of Trade, 85–6
    Baillie Committee, 204
    Balfour Committee, 183, 196–7
    Catering Wages Act, 242–3
    Industrial Council Report of 1913,
        74–7
    Road Haulage Wages Act 1938, 206
    Royal Commission of 1869, 6
    Royal Commission of 1894, 39–43
    Taff Vale, 63
    Wages Council Act 1945, 243–5
Compulsory arbitration, 47, 81–2:
    Balfour Committee, 197
    Lemieux Act, 77–80
    Munitions of War Act 1915, 121–3
    railways dispute (1907), 65
    Royal Commission of 1894, 44
    South Wales mines dispute, 125
    Whitley, 153–4
    World War Two, 232–6
Conciliation Act 1896, 44–5
Conspiracy and Protection of Property
    Act 1875, 21–4

Cotton Manufacturing Industry Act 1934,
    200–1
Criminal Law Amendment Act 1871,
    13–14
    judicial reaction to, 15–17
    statutory reform, 21–3

Economic torts:
    Allen v Flood, 31
    Quinn v Leathem, 32–4
Emergency Powers Act 1920, 169–71

Fair Wages Resolution (1891), 50–1
Fair Wages Committee (1907), 70
Fair Wages Resolution (1909), 71–2
    proposed reforms (1930s), 207–8

Government intervention in trade dis-
    putes, 64–5

Harrison (Frederick), 3, 14–15, 88
Holidays, 209–11:
    Holidays With Pay Act 1938, 210–11
Hours of Work, 57–8:
    Coal Mines Act 1872, 57
    Coal Mines Regulation Act 1908,
        72–4
    Hours of Industrial Employment Bills,
        208
    ILO, 160
    Mines (Eight Hours) Bill 1892, 50
    Ministry of Labour, 165
    National Industrial Conference,
        159
    Railway Regulation Act 1893, 55–6
    Royal Commission of 1894, 46–7
    Select Committee on Shop Assistants,
        208–9
    TUC policy, 47

ILO, 160
Industrial Councils Bill 1924, 189–92
Industrial Council Report (1913),
    74–7
Industrial Courts Act 1919, 166–8

Joint Industrial Councils, 151–4, 239
Judicial attitudes:
  between the wars, 214–18
  legislation of 1871, 15–17
  legislation of 1906, 106–9, 114–15

Labour Exchanges Act 1909, 82–3

Minimum wage, 72:
  Agricultural Wages Act 1924, 187–9
  Australia and New Zealand, 67
  Catering Wages Act, 241–3
  Coal Mines (Minimum Wage) Act
    1912, 69–70
  Cotton Manufacturing Industry Act
    1934, 200–1
  Industrial Councils Bill 1924, 189–92
  Ministry of Labour, 163–4
  National Industrial Conference, 159
  Rates of Wages Bill, 198–200
  Road Haulage Wages Act 1938, 204–7
  Royal Commission of 1894, 48
  Trade Boards Act 1909, 65–9
  Wages Council Act 1945, 243–5
Ministry of Labour, 162–5, 190–2,
    198–202

National Industrial Conference,
    158–60
Nationalisation, 171–80:
  mining, 172–7
  railways, 177–80

Osborne v ASRS , 109–13

Picketing:
  Combination Act 1825, 6
  Connor v Kent, 28
  Conspiracy and Protection of Property
    Act 1875, 23
  Criminal Law Amendment Act 1871,
    15–17
  Farmer v Wilson, 29
  Lyon v Wilkins, 28
  Trade Disputes and Trade Unions Act
    1927, 193

Rates of Wages Bill 1931, 198–200
Railway Regulation Act 1893, 55–6
Recognition (British Overseas Airways
    Act 1939), 220–1
Restoration of Pre-War Practices Act
    1919, 150

Right to strike:
  compulsory strike ballots, 195
  options after Taff Vale, 89–93
  rights or immunities, 115–17
  Royal Commission of 1905, 88,
    95–100
  Trade Union Act 1871, 14–15
  trade union response to Taff Vale,
    100–1
Road Traffic Act 1930, 203
Road and Rail Traffic Act 1933, 203
Road Haulage Wages Act 1938, 204–7
Royal Commission of 1869, 1–10
Royal Commission of 1875, 19–20
Royal Commission of 1894, 38–49
Royal Commission of 1905, 88, 95–100

Taff Vale v ASRS, 87:
  background, 35
  CA, 36–7
  first instance, 36
  HL, 37–8
  trade union response, 100–1
Trade Boards Act 1909, 65–9
Trade Boards Act 1918:
  Cave Committee, 184–7
  enactment, 155–6
  lack of expansion, 161–3, 165
  Whitley report, 154
Trade Disputes Act 1906, 64, 88:
  earlier bills, 93
  emergence of s.4, 100–5
  Government proposals, 101–6
  judicial reaction to Act, 106–9,
    114–15
  rights or immunities, 115–17
  royal Commission of 1905, 88,
    95–100
  trade union perspective, 100–1
  view of Conservative Government,
    94–5
Trade Disputes and Trade Unions Act
    1927, 192–5, 213–4
Trade Union Act 1871, 10–13
Trade Union Act 1913, 113–14, 193–4

Unemployment Insurance (No 2) Act
    1924, 211–12

Wages Council Act 1945, 243–5
Wages (Temporary Regulation)
    Act 1918
Whitley Committee, 151–6

Workmen's Compensation Act 1897, 51–5
World War One:
  compulsory arbitration, 121–7
  dilution, 134–42
  industrial action, 148
  mobility of labour, 127–33
  Munitions of War Act 1915, 120
  South Wales mining dispute, 125
  Treasury Agreement, 120
  unrest on the Clyde, 125–6

wage control, 133–4, 142–6
World War Two:
  compulsory arbitration, 232–6
  consultation, 237–8
  essential work orders, 227- 31
  mobility of labour, 223–6
  reconstruction, 238–45
  right to strike, 232–6
  terms and conditions, 227–31
  wage control, 231–6